STRUGGLING WITH "IOWA'S PRIDE"

LABOR RELATIONS, UNIONISM, AND POLITICS IN THE RURAL MIDWEST SINCE 1877

WILSON J. WARREN

STRUGGLING WITH "IOWA'S PRIDE"

LABOR RELATIONS, UNIONISM, AND POLITICS IN THE RURAL MIDWEST SINCE 1877

UNIVERSITY OF IOWA PRESS Ψ Iowa City

University of Iowa Press, Iowa City 52242

Copyright © 2000 by the University of Iowa Press

Printed in the United States of America

http://www.uiowa.edu/~uipress

Significant portions of this book were adapted from a series of articles
by the author in the *Annals of Iowa*. The State Historical Society of
Iowa has graciously given permission for their adaptation in this book.

The publication of this book was generously supported by the
University of Iowa Foundation.

Printed on acid-free paper

Library of Congress
Cataloging-in-Publication Data
Warren, Wilson J.
    Struggling with "Iowa's pride": labor relations, unionism, and
politics in the rural midwest since 1877 / by Wilson J. Warren.
        p.   cm.
    Includes bibliographical references and index.
    ISBN 0-87745-712-3, ISBN 0-87745-713-1 (pbk.)
    1. United Packinghouse Workers of America—History.
2. Packing-house workers—Labor unions—Iowa— Ottumwa—
History.   3. John Morrell and Company—Employees—History.
4. Iowa—Politics and government.   5. Democratic Party (Iowa)—
History.   I. Title.

HD6515.P152 U559   2000
331.88'1649'00977793—dc21   99-058067

00   01   02   03   04   C   5   4   3   2   1
00   01   02   03   04   P   5   4   3   2   1

FRONTISPIECE
John Morrell and Company and packing community, 1943.
Courtesy Ottumwa Public Library.

Cover photograph from the collection of Michael W. Lemberger.

For

Bob Warren, Richard Geiger,

and the late Wayne DeJohn,

my favorite history teachers

CONTENTS

ACKNOWLEDGMENTS

This project has been a labor of love of mine for nearly two decades. In the process of researching and writing, I have incurred many debts over the years. I began interviewing former Morrell employees in 1981. Although many of these people are now deceased, I would like to recognize the help I received from Gilbert Baker, Art and Virgil Bankson, Leo Barnett, Paul Bissell, Jim Collins, Dorothy Daeges, Loren Dooley, George Gail, Albert "Whitey" Lewis, Charles Logan, Bob Long, Jack Moses, Bill and Earl Paxson, Harold Poncy, Ralph Ransom, Lawrence Reedquist, Donald Schaub, and Olin Vittetoe. Dan Varner provided me with valuable perspectives on Hormel's history in Ottumwa. Without a doubt, I would not have been inspired to pursue continued research on Ottumwa's meatpacking and labor history if I had not been fortunate enough to have listened to these men and women share their stories. The passion these people felt for their workplace struggles resonated with me then, and my memories of these conversations serve as a constant reminder to me that fairness and justice matter as much in our work as in any other aspect of our lives. In addition, I am sincerely grateful to Mark Smith, president of the Iowa Federation of Labor, AFL-CIO, who gave me permission to read interviews in the Iowa Labor History Oral Project at the State Historical Society of Iowa in Iowa City before they were made available to the general public.

I became interested in history at an early age because my father, Bob Warren, a longtime Western Civilization teacher at Ottumwa High School, told so many exciting stories about past events. I was also fortunate to have him as my eleventh-grade history teacher. As an undergraduate, I studied history with two wonderful professors. Richard Geiger and the late Wayne DeJohn inspired me to pursue history as a career. Wayne also read my very first history of Morrell, and gave me incisive and constructive comments. Richard and Wayne remain my models of inspirational teaching.

Early in my graduate studies, I was fortunate to work with several scholars who encouraged my research on Morrell-Ottumwa, and helped me to refine my insights. Ellis Hawley, Shelton Stromquist, Merle Davis, and Greg Zieren read my early essays and provided much useful criticism. Later in my graduate education, Richard Oestreicher, Maurine Greenwald, Sam Hays, Mark McColloch, Ted Muller, and Rubie Watson helped me place my Iowa research in a larger context of American working-class history. Since completing graduate school, I am grateful for the criticisms of my work provided by Roger Horowitz, Bill Pratt, Steven Rosswurm, John Schacht, Ralph Scharnau, and Bob Zieger.

Over the past two decades, I have been a frequent user of the resources provided by the State Historical Society of Iowa in Iowa City. I appreciate the assistance provided by the society's many fine staff people, especially Mary Bennett, who have helped me use their collections over the years. I also thank the librarians at the University of Iowa Special Collections Department, the State Historical Society of Wisconsin, and the Ottumwa Public Library for their assistance in locating meatpacking records. Kris Mueller at Valley City State University helped me obtain manuscript census records through interlibrary loan. Bob McCown, manuscript librarian at the University of Iowa Special Collections Department, guided my mining of the John Morrell and Company collection.

Marv Bergman, editor of the *Annals of Iowa*, where much of this book first took shape, has been a consistent supporter and constructive critic of my efforts. Because of his thoughtful and diligent criticism, I credit Marv with much of the improvement I have made in my writing over the years. Bruce Fehn read the entire manuscript and provided very useful comments based on his own extensive understanding of packinghouse workers and unionism. Holly Carver, director of the University of Iowa Press, has been an enthusiastic supporter of this project.

I gratefully acknowledge the financial assistance I have received over the years for work on various aspects of this history. While working on my dissertation, where some of this book's research was completed, the University of Pittsburgh aided my research effort with an Andrew Mellon Predoctoral Fellowship. Later, the State Historical Society of Iowa and Iowa Historical Foundation awarded me an Iowa Sesquicentennial Research grant that helped me complete the research on Morrell's early years. Most recently, Indiana State University provided me with assistance to complete my research on Iowa's political transformation with a University Research Committee grant.

I am very fortunate to have many supportive friends and family members. Curt Miner, Chuck Chalberg, Ralph Leck, Tim Cary, and Paul Riggs have listened to me talk about this project over the years and added their own scholarly insights. My mother, Joyce Kramer, always encouraged my studies and supported my interests. She and Patricia Warren, my stepmother, helped to keep me current on Ottumwa's socioeconomic climate by sending me newspaper clippings and information from school district records. I benefited from hearing stories about Morrell from my stepfather, Bill Kramer, who worked as a salesman for the company during the 1950s. My mother- and father-in-law, John and Joanna Blyth, have also cheerfully talked to me about my meatpacking and labor interests.

To my wife, Jane Blyth Warren, and children, John, James, and Katherine, I owe my greatest debts. Jane has listened to me talk about Morrell and Ottumwa for as long as we have known each other. She and my children have also lovingly tolerated all the time that I spent on this project. Without their love and support, I would not have completed the book.

PREFACE

I first became interested in labor relations and unionism at Ottumwa's John Morrell and Company meatpacking plant nearly twenty years ago. A native of Ottumwa, I decided to do my senior history research paper at St. Ambrose College on the history of the plant. Although I grew up in a middle-class household where affairs at the Morrell plant were seldom a subject of conversation, I became increasingly interested in the social class divisions I had first noticed among my classmates in junior high and high school. I had also been intrigued in high school by a couple of lines in our school song: "North-side, south-side, and all around the town, we'll all join in together to root for OHS." I remember wondering why anyone would have thought this facet of the town's structure — north and south sides of the city created by the Des Moines River's passage — worthy of inclusion. At about the same time I became aware that the south side of Ottumwa had become populated primarily after World War II by Morrell employees and their families who, experiencing marginally greater affluence, moved away from the plant's immediate environs in the east end of the city on the north bank of the river. Most middle-class residents, especially the managerial and professional "elites" of Ottumwa, lived on the north side. Apparently, the song's author, like many Ottumwans, was aware of the class divisions that pervaded this small, industrial city.

In choosing to research Ottumwa's industrial history more than fifteen years ago, I was also motivated by the statewide perception I felt about my hometown as one of Iowa's most disreputable urban places. I often recalled that my uncle would refer to Ottumwa as the "armpit" of Iowa. This was funny since he lived in Centerville, an even smaller town in south-central Iowa, economically stagnant since the death of the state's coal industry in the 1930s, and certainly not a place too many would have thought snobbish enough to look down on someplace else in Iowa. People joked about a restaurant in the state capital of Des Moines, located about eighty miles northwest of Ottumwa on the Des Moines River, that proudly displayed a sign in its men's room that said, "Flush twice, Ottumwa needs the water." After I moved away from Iowa, most people who asked me about my hometown, if they had heard of Ottumwa at all, only knew it as the Appalachian-like home of Radar O'Reilly on TV's *M*A*S*H*. TV and film actor Tom Arnold, one of Ottumwa's more recent famous sons, has brought further notoriety to the city by frequently making it the butt of his redneck humor. Ottumwa's city fathers encouraged further snickering about the town during the economically depressed mid-1980s when they deemed it the "video game capital of the world."

Why did the city have its less than flattering reputation? I guessed that it might have something to do with other expressions I had heard while growing up there. The distinctive stench emanating from the east end of town was deemed "the smell of money." Occasionally, older residents would refer to the city as "Little Chicago." Ottumwa, home to John Morrell and Company's largest meatpacking plant, a fair-sized John Deere manufacturing plant, and several other manufacturing facilities earlier in this century especially, was one of Iowa's preeminent industrial cities. My early research efforts convinced me that Ottumwa was not a laughable place, but an intriguing one, especially in terms of its industrial history centered on the Morrell plant. In later years, as I expanded on my earlier research and writing efforts, I discovered that Ottumwa's packing workers had participated in many of the great industrial developments and upheavals of the twentieth century. Although perhaps not typical of America's industrial or labor relations history, Ottumwa's packing workers' history is central to understanding several facets of Iowa's and the Midwest's larger industrial and labor history, including the CIO's impact in Iowa's industrial and political history. It is also a history that dramatically illustrates the rise and fall of industrial labor and unionism in this century.

Much of this book builds on essays published in the *Annals of Iowa* over the past several years. Chapter 2 is based on "Evangelical Paternalism and Divided Workers: The Nonunion Era at John Morrell and Company in Ottumwa, 1877–1917," 56 (Fall 1997), 321–48. Chapter 3 expands on "The Welfare Capitalism of John Morrell, 1922–1937," 47 (Fall 1984): 485–512. Chapters 4, 5, and 6 include material from "The Heyday of the CIO in Iowa: Ottumwa's Meatpacking Workers, 1937–1954," 51 (Spring 1992): 363–89. Most of Chapter 5 and parts of Chapter 7 build on "When 'Ottumwa Went to the Dogs': The Erosion of Morrell-Ottumwa's Militant Unionism, 1954–1973," 54 (Summer 1995): 217–43. Chapter 6 also includes parts of "The 'Peoples' Century' in Iowa: Coalition-building among Farm and Labor Organizations, 1945–1950," 49 (Summer 1988): 371–93.

STRUGGLING WITH "IOWA'S PRIDE"

LABOR RELATIONS, UNIONISM, AND POLITICS IN THE RURAL MIDWEST SINCE 1877

1

COMPANY TOWN, PACKING COMMUNITY, LABOR RELATIONS, AND POLITICS

Much of the United States is now littered with dead or dying industrial cities and towns. Many think of Pennsylvania or Massachusetts as the location of such places. Yet the Midwest is home to more than its share of urban, industrial relics. Many of the less visible midwestern deindustrialized locales are relatively rural, small cities. A prominent example is Ottumwa, Iowa, home to John Morrell and Company's flagship meatpacking plant from 1877 to 1973. Known between 1880 and 1910 by its trademark label, "Iowa's Pride," Morrell was the nation's fifth-largest meatpacking company for much of the twentieth century.[1] Ottumwa was, and still remains, a predominantly blue-collar community in which relations with one dominant employer influenced all dimensions of community life. Labor relations at the Morrell packing plant through 1973, and two other packing companies' plants since 1973, have permeated the city's development. To understand Ottumwa's history, like many other blue-collar towns in the United States, one must understand the history of its workers and their relations with their dominant employer. To date, more than twenty years after the Morrell plant's closing, this deep relationship reverberates still.

What possible larger significance is there in studying labor relations in an admittedly obscure and relatively small industrial city in a state that few Americans know much about? On several levels, Ottumwa is not "typical." For instance, Ottumwa was largely bypassed by the waves of eastern and southern Europeans who re-created the composition of the working class of most large northeastern and midwestern cities in the early twentieth century. Yet just how representative are studies of workers in those sorts of cities? Lizabeth Cohen, for instance, argues that Chicago's working-class history between World War I and II was the "one national story" for that period. This assertion does not hold up under scrutiny. Although Chicago may have shared a broadly comparable economic, social demographic, and union heritage with other cities in the urban Northeast and Midwest, even among these cities Chicago stands out as atypical. Gary Gerstle, John Cumbler, and Tamara K. Hareven and Randolph Langenbach have produced exemplary studies of laborers in specific communities over long periods of time, but it would be difficult to argue that their findings explain the behavior of all American workers. An investigation of any one city cannot fully capture the complexity of the American working class. Consequently, this study does not pretend to convey insight into the general development of American workers from the late nineteenth to the late twentieth centuries in the fashion that a typical case study might argue.[2]

Instead, this history of Ottumwa's meatpacking workers provides insights into the development of several forms of labor relations, including evangelical Christian paternalism, welfare capitalism, and unionism that were distinctive to one community, but that were also experiences that intersect with those of other workers in many other rural midwestern industrial communities. The advantage of this study is that it examines the evolution of workers' behavior in one community over more than a full century, a degree of continuity not typically found in working-class histories. As is true of other case studies, this intensive focus on one community illuminates the dynamics of the particular personalities and ideas involved in creating the various forms of labor relations that emerged over the century of Morrell-Ottumwa's existence. It also remains sensitive to and intersects with other studies that have attempted to synthesize general themes on workers' experiences. Beyond providing illumination of themes that developed generally during the same era in other places, this history provides specific details about the role of Morrell-Ottumwa's labor relations and unionism in the labor and political history of Iowa and the Midwest. Historians have only recently begun to chart Iowa's participation in the major industrial and labor developments of the past century, especially the Congress of Industrial Organizations (CIO) era. Ottumwa was at the center of the transformation wrought by the CIO and the Democratic party in Iowa. Moreover, even the most recent histories of meatpacking unionism in the twentieth century have not fully illuminated the significance of workers' efforts in Ottumwa and similar packing communities in the rural Midwest to the larger national union movement.[3]

To a degree not found in large, more diversified industrial cities like Chicago, meatpacking dominated Iowa's relatively small manufacturing cities, such as Sioux City, Cedar Rapids, Waterloo, Fort Dodge, Mason City, and Ottumwa, for most of the twentieth century. Most obvious about Ottumwa's history from the last quarter of the nineteenth century through three-quarters of the twentieth was the importance of John Morrell and Company as the city's economic lifeblood. Ottumwa's population grew from close to 9,000 in 1880 to 18,000 in 1900 to close to 40,000 during World War II before declining by almost half to date. Before 1900, the city's economy was built on one large employer, Morrell, and many small manufacturing employers. Several small coal mines, the Hardscog Manufacturing Company, maker of coal-mining equipment, the Joseph Dain (later John Deere) farm equipment works, several small cigar manufacturers, and the Chicago, Burlington and Quincy, Chicago, Milwaukee and St. Paul, and Chicago, Rock Island, and Pacific Railroad Companies all employed blue-collar workers in Ottumwa before the turn of the twentieth century. Still, Morrell, with roughly 1,000 employees when it operated at peak capacity, provided 40 percent of the city's manufacturing jobs in 1900. Increasingly after 1900, the smaller employers declined or disappeared. Indeed, especially between the turn of the twentieth century and the midcentury point, Ottumwa became increasingly reliant on Morrell for blue-collar employment. By 1950, Morrell's 3,500 production employees constituted 63 percent of Ottumwa's manufacturing workers, and no other company except for Deere, which primarily manufactured hay-making equipment, employed more than 500 workers. Before massive layoffs began in 1971, presaging the plant's closing two years later, Morrell still employed approximately 30 percent of the city's manufacturing workers. In this sense Ottumwa was one of Iowa's and the Midwest's preeminent company towns.[4]

Meatpacking's central importance in Ottumwa's economic development in the twentieth century defines not only that city, but several other rural manufacturing communities in the Midwest. This development stemmed from one of the two main marketing patterns that emerged in the midwestern meatpacking industry between the end of the Civil War and the first third of the twentieth century. The first, the terminal marketing pattern, did not involve cities in Iowa except for Sioux City. It evolved after 1865 as entrepreneurs with large capital resources increasingly located their packing plants in relatively large cities with terminal marketing facilities, also called stockyards. Here, animals were shipped by rail and later by truck to be sold for slaughter or for resale as feeder animals to farmers. The terminal marketing centers in Chicago, Kansas City, Omaha, Indianapolis, Milwaukee, South St. Paul, and Wichita remained important overall in the meatpacking industry through the mid–twentieth century, but crucially, in each of these cities, the relative importance of meatpacking as a proportion of all manufacturing employment declined between 1900 and 1950. Only in the somewhat smaller terminal marketing cities of St. Joseph, Missouri, Sioux City, and East St. Louis did meatpacking employment increase relative to other manufacturing employment between 1900 and 1950.[5]

The second marketing pattern in midwestern meatpacking developed in the "direct-buying" centers in the rural Midwest. It initially involved less capital-intensive meatpacking operations located in smaller and more rural cities where animals could be purchased directly from nearby farmers. Established with greater frequency after 1890, such packing centers depended on farmers driving herds of animals, and later animals driven by truck, to them for direct sale. Unlike the terminal marketing centers in which beef production was especially important, the direct-buying centers typically focused on pork production. This species divergence was important in terms of the labor relations experiences of workers in the two types of packing communities. Beef packing required a more skilled, and therefore a more typically unionized (and union-minded), workforce than pork packing. Ottumwa and Cedar Rapids were the earliest direct-buying packing centers in Iowa. Austin, Minnesota, was another direct-buying packing center that emerged before the turn of the twentieth century. After World War I, Waterloo, Mason City, and Fort Dodge in Iowa as well as Topeka, Kansas, Madison, Wisconsin, Albert Lea, Minnesota, and Sioux Falls, South Dakota, became important direct-buying packing centers. By 1950, meatpacking workers constituted no less than one-third and as much as 93 percent (in the case of Austin) of all manufacturing employees in each of these cities. Although the midwestern terminal market packers still outproduced the direct-buying centers by the end of World War II by a ratio of approximately 60 to 40 percent of all cattle and hogs, the direct-buying centers had made serious inroads into the terminal market packers' earlier dominance of the industry. This trend would accelerate after World War II, especially with the emergence of companies like IBP, which tended to locate their plants in even smaller, more isolated rural communities in the Midwest.[6]

Social demographic patterns also distinguished the terminal market from the direct-buying cities in the midwestern segment of the packing industry. The variations in these patterns contributed to the differences in union and political experiences that stemmed from the underlying cultural variations among workers who lived in the two main types of packing cities. In the terminal packing cities in the late nineteenth century, Irish, Germans, and Bohemians typically dominated the ranks of the skilled butchers. These workers also provided the backbone of the Amalgamated Meat Cutters and Butcher Workmen (AMCBW-AFL), the most important union in the packing industry at the turn of the century. When the Dillingham Commission issued its report on immigrants in meatpacking in 1909, they estimated that Anglo Americans and African Americans made up 18 percent of the employees in Chicago's packinghouses. Bohemians made up another 18 percent, followed by the Irish with 16 percent, Poles with 15 percent, Germans with 15 percent, Lithuanians with 10 percent, and Greeks and Slovaks with another 8 percent between them. By the end of World War I, however, most of Chicago's 40,000 packing workers were new immigrants and African Americans. Although not as pronounced quite as early as Chicago, similar patterns of successive migration would create comparable workforce structures in the terminal market cities of Kansas City, Omaha, Milwaukee, and East St. Louis. South St. Paul, St. Joseph, and Sioux City also had relatively large proportions of new immigrants and nonwhites working in their packing plants before World War II.[7]

By comparison, new immigrants and nonwhites, especially African Americans, were not significant contributors to the workforces in the direct-buying packing centers. A mix of older, northern and western European stock workers, primarily of English, Irish, German, and Scandinavian extraction, whose ancestors had settled in the Midwest or migrated there from upland southern areas of the United States during the nineteenth century, typically constituted the workforces in these communities. With the exception of Cedar Rapids and Austin, in 1935 new immigrants made up less than 10 percent of the packing workers in each of the direct-buying packing communities. And in all cases, nonwhites made up less than 10 percent, and usually no more than 5 percent, of these towns' packing workers. In contrast, in each of the terminal marketing cities except for Sioux City and South St. Paul, nonwhites constituted anywhere from nearly 20 to 40 percent of the packing workers in 1935.[8]

These social demographic patterns significantly influenced the range of union involvement among workers in the different types of midwestern communities. In the first two decades of the twentieth century, the Amalgamated Meat Cutters and Butcher Workmen's organizing efforts focused overwhelmingly on workers in the terminal market packing centers. They failed largely because of the incomplete recruitment of the latecomers to those plants, especially black workers.[9] When union efforts resurfaced in force in these communities again during the 1930s, labor organizers, especially in the CIO, confronted social and cultural divisions, now primarily between whites and blacks, that had to be bridged before unionism could take root. These efforts peaked during the late 1940s to the mid-1950s when the civil rights programs of the CIO's United Packinghouse Workers of America (UPWA) emerged as the most important concern of workers in the terminal market packing communities.[10]

Because the direct-buying packing centers' importance in the industry had increased significantly by the 1930s, labor organizers both emerged in and gravitated to these newer packing communities. However, amelioration of ethnic and racial conflict was generally not the most important union or broader political concern among workers in these communities. Instead, workers concentrated on union and political efforts to stem conflict with rural employees and, more important, gain greater control and power in their communities. Specifically, because of meatpacking's dominance in the local economies of the direct-buying centers, workers often were more focused on carving out a greater degree of control over their lives from that exerted by the local packing elites, such as the Hormel family in Austin.[11]

Meatpacking workers in Ottumwa were centrally concerned with wresting greater control at work and in the larger community from the local power elite in this Morrell-dominated town. The Foster family's guiding hand defined Ottumwa's status as a company town. John Morrell and Company was founded in England in 1827. John Morrell's nephew, Thomas Dove Foster, established the Morrell packing plant in Ottumwa, and was the plant manager as well as president of the American branch of the company from 1877 until his death in 1915. After a brief interlude, T. D. Foster's three sons, Thomas Henry, George Morrell, and John Morrell Foster, presided over the company and the Ottumwa plant from 1921 to 1952. A fourth son, William Henry Thomas Foster, was the manager of the Morrell plant in Sioux Falls, South Dakota, from 1913 to 1939. The Foster family and their mostly English-born cohort of managerial associates dominated Ottumwa's business community for nearly a century. The Fosters and their fellow managers made their homes in Ottumwa, especially in an area known as the Bluff, to the northwest and overlooking the packing neighborhood that developed in the immediate environs of the plant on the city's east side. The paternal relationship T. D. Foster tried to cultivate with his workers in the late nineteenth century turned increasingly sour with his sons. This harsher climate in turn formed part of the basis of the packing community's militant unionism during the 1930s.

Key to this study's conception of labor relations is the interconnection between Ottumwa's status as a company town and the development of what is described as a packing community or packing neighborhood in the plant's immediate environs. The John Morrell and Company plant became the focal point for a vibrant community of meatpacking and other blue-collar workers from the late 1870s through the 1960s. By the latter date, the company's "urban renewal" efforts and working families' post–World War II flight primarily to Ottumwa's south side across the Des Moines River eroded the neighborhood surrounding the plant. Situated immediately west (primarily along South Iowa Avenue), north (along East Main Street), and somewhat to the east of the plant, in what was Ottumwa's Ward (later, Precinct) One, the packing neighborhood was home to two-thirds of Morrell-Ottumwa's workers in 1880, about 45 percent in 1900, nearly 60 percent in 1915, and 40 percent in 1935 before tailing off rapidly in the 1950s to just 15 percent in 1965.

Chapters 2 and 3 chart two distinct yet related stages of the packing community's development in Ottumwa defined by relative submissiveness on workers' parts. Workers' nonunion status until the New Deal era stemmed from both external and internal conditions. From the late 1800s through World War I, Morrell, especially Thomas Dove Foster, engaged in an active program of evangelical Christian paternalism to keep workers from pursuing union affiliation. During this period, divisions among workers as well as the employment irregularities of the pork-packing industry also prevented workers from successfully creating a stable union movement. Although Morrell's welfare capitalist efforts in the 1920s and early 1930s also forestalled any union-building efforts, this period saw the emergence of several conditions that would prove crucial for later unionism. In particular, Morrell workers, increasingly more unified along social demographic lines and occupational experiences, expressed greater resentment against the plant's "foreign" managers, a perception sparked by the English origins and snobbiness of the Foster family and their cohorts. Workers also despised the drive system of management still used in the plant.

Chapter 4 explains the emergence of a much more unified and assertive packing community during the 1930s. After a half-century of employer dominance, Ottumwa's meatpacking workers successfully formed a powerful CIO union. Sparked by several factors that attracted workers in the rural Midwest like those in Ottumwa as well as other workers throughout the United States, the CIO was the first truly widespread and successful, though certainly not the first, effort to provide union representation for the masses of unskilled and semiskilled industrial workers. Workers across the United States embraced the CIO for a variety of reasons. Anger with the effects of the Great Depression, acceptance of radical alternatives, charismatic leadership, and faith in the New Deal's legislative and administrative initiatives all contributed to the CIO's success.[12]

As had been true of workers' earlier nonunion status, the conditions for unionism at Morrell in Ottumwa were likewise both external and internal. Federal government support for unionism and its creation of the legal machinery that allowed it were major external components that contributed to successful unionization in Ottumwa and elsewhere in the United States. Yet the mass production or industrial unionism, especially within the CIO, that was flourishing even before the Supreme Court had stamped its approval on the National Labor Relations Act (and Board) in March 1937 was an even more powerful external precondition for Ottumwa workers' success. Although many historians have explored the rise of the CIO, most studies have examined workers in settings not unlike those found in the terminal market meatpacking centers, that is, workforces made up mostly of new immigrant-stock whites and African Americans in large manufacturing cities. The existing literature on the rise of the CIO in meatpacking also stresses such workers, particularly since Chicago was the center of the industry in the 1930s. Yet, as Walter Galenson's study of the CIO's challenge to the AFL showed forty years ago and Roger Horowitz's recent study elaborates, two of the most important movements for industrial unionism that would eventually feed into the CIO emerged in two direct-buying centers, Austin and Cedar Rapids. The Independent Union of All Workers (IUAW), based in Austin, and the Midwest Union of All Packing House Workers (MUAPHW), established in Cedar Rapids, were both active during the mid-1930s and organizing workers in other midwestern direct-buying packing centers.[13]

In Ottumwa as well as many other direct-buying packing centers in the rural Midwest, the emergence of a cohesive packing community with a broadly homogeneous social demographic identity and a shared set of grievances against the company was the necessary internal development for sustained union efforts. Furthermore, and crucially, *sustained* militance centrally defined Ottumwa workers' CIO unionism. That is, the generation of workers who dominated Ottumwa workers' packinghouse union movement from the mid-1930s to the early 1950s consistently and unhesitatingly used spontaneous job actions, or the threat thereof, to signal their collective desire to exercise greater control over plant affairs. Strikes were Ottumwa workers' most powerful job actions. In particular, even after 1943, when a CIO international union exercised central control over unions in the packing industry, Ottumwa's CIO local used unannounced and unsanctioned, or wildcat, strikes against Morrell. Whereas episodic worker militance was widespread across industrial America during the 1930s, sustained militance, especially through the 1940s and into the 1950s, was not. As historian Robert Zieger maintains, "militancy, solidarity, and class consciousness were not universal among industrial workers [e]ven in the relatively favorable climate of the mid- to late 1930s." Even though arguably more intense than elsewhere, studying the sustained militance of Morrell-Ottumwa's union movement provides insights into a central facet of the direct-buying packing communities in the rural Midwest. As historian Rick Halpern has described this portion of the CIO packing union movement, packing union workers in the "outlying locals in Iowa, Nebraska, and

Minnesota[,]" whose communities were "small, predominately agricultural . . . and which supported only a single packing plant[,]" were "fiercely independent, [and] represented an extreme antibureaucratic tendency within the PWOC [the Packinghouse Workers Organizing Committee of the CIO]."[14]

Whereas Chapter 4 examines the character of this sustained militance, Chapter 5 and parts of Chapter 7 analyze the conditions that undermined it. The internal unity of Ottumwa's meatpacking workers that sparked militant unionism in the 1930s was by its nature exclusive. Simply stated, white men created and dominated Ottumwa's meatpacking unionism during its militant heyday. Like many industrial workers in the rural Midwest, these white men of British, German, and Scandinavian extraction were overwhelmingly born and bred in the immediate region of Iowa, Illinois, and Missouri. A farm to factory exodus over several decades before the 1930s then created the relative social demographic homogeneity that characterized Ottumwa's as well as many other rural industrial workforces. After World War II, new influxes of farmers and other rural (and formerly rural) residents were especially destructive to the Ottumwa packing community's exclusive identity. They brought concerns with them that clashed with the objectives of the generation of workers who had fashioned the militant union. In particular, Ottumwa's white male militants, like many other white men across the rural, industrial Midwest, were not receptive to the civil rights challenges of blacks or, as was especially true in Ottumwa's case, women in the post–World War II years. In this sense, militant unionism in Ottumwa should not be equated with the goals of modern, pluralist American liberalism. As historians have increasingly demonstrated, other white CIO communities and workers were much like Ottumwa's packing community in this regard. Because of its exclusivity and inability to adapt to demands brought on by demographic and other changes, the local's sustained militance eroded and eventually withered.[15]

The local's character and goals also changed after the early 1950s because militant unionism had been primarily focused on a single workplace goal, control over the pace of work. Although they were not strictly syndicalists, since workplace control was not their only goal, Morrell-Ottumwa's militants were committed first and foremost to protecting their informal control over job loads created in a favorable workplace environment of the late 1930s to mid-1940s. When Morrell-Ottumwa's managers took the offensive against the local's control over job loads following World War II, specifically through the creation of an industrial engineering department, the militants fought them at every available opportunity. Yet the militants' goals increasingly alienated new workers who entered the plant during and after the war. Cooperation with managerial goals was more important to the newer workers, and their more cooperative view of unionism replaced the militants' agenda during the 1950s.

Although the key to Morrell-Ottumwa's militant unionism was an informal, noncontractual control over job loads, the militants were also committed to industrial democracy, as was true of CIO union activists and members not only in the rural Midwest but all across industrial America during the New Deal era. Like others, Ottumwa's unionists wanted "fair and orderly procedures to govern the daily lives of workers" on the factory floor. In this sense, workers wanted to end the informality that had governed previous industrial relations with Morrell and replace it with formalized procedures. Favoritism of various sorts had long pervaded the era of evangelical paternalism and even the welfare capitalist period at the plant. Militants wanted written agreements that spelled out workers' and managers' respective obligations.[16]

Significantly, struggles for power in the Morrell-Ottumwa plant extended far beyond the factory. Chapter 6 examines how Ottumwa workers' union efforts developed into larger political efforts, eventually helping to reconstruct Iowa's political system. Militant unionism among Morrell-Ottumwa workers started a process of political transformation that spread from Ottumwa and a few other industrial cities to Iowa's state-level politics. Because of workers and their unions' efforts, by the mid- to late 1950s Iowans had cast off their long-standing Republican party allegiances, rooted in the late nineteenth century, and created a two-party political system. As was true in many northern states during the New Deal era, Iowa's workers and industrial unions were at the forefront of this more powerful Democratic party. Yet this study sheds a different light on the class politics that emerged during the New Deal era. Although a variation on the class politics as masterfully described by historian Richard Oestreicher, Iowa's class politics did not emerge from an urban, second-generation immigrant base.[17]

Rural, white industrial workers in Ottumwa and many other midwestern cities increasingly voted for Democratic candidates beginning in the 1930s. Ottumwa's militant union leaders themselves became involved in city and state politics between the late 1930s and mid-1950s. At the state level, Ottumwa's militants significantly shaped the politics of the state CIO council. Nevertheless, it was not the militants who would achieve the most political success at the local or state level. New union leaders emerged who rejected some of the militants' goals. Because a greater sense of cooperation informed their political agenda, instead of viewing politics as a means to punish those with whom they disagreed, as the militants typically emphasized, the new union leaders worked with similarly minded union and Democratic leaders around the state to achieve political goals that transcended issues of power and control in the Morrell plant. Through their central involvement in the merged AFL-CIO Iowa Federation of Labor, the new generation of union leaders who replaced the militants would help Iowa's Democratic party achieve significant success and gains for working people across the state. Indeed, these new leaders were instrumental in working with other union leaders around the state in making the state's Democratic party a vehicle that not only promoted labor goals but also liberal reforms that appealed to middle-class voters as well. This study connects Ottumwa's union struggles to the larger process of Iowa's post–World War II political transition, a development that has not been examined thoroughly.[18]

Chapter 7 probes the impact of unionism on Morrell's decision to close the Ottumwa plant in 1973. The internal divisions that rent the packing workers' local union from the 1950s on played into the hands of managers who saw the plant as obsolete and not worth saving. Although two other meatpacking companies have filled Morrell's void somewhat since 1973, Ottumwa's workers, lacking any comparable sort of packing community base and caught in the dissolution of their powerful international union, have been manipulated fairly easily and left mostly adrift. The closing chapter of Ottumwa's packing workers' story is not a pleasant one, but it is illustrative of the problems that face American workers in a deindustrialized, and more importantly, deunionized nation.

Ultimately, this history of Ottumwa's packing workers attempts to illuminate the human concerns and conflicts at the core of a great struggle over working people's quests for respect and power. Their struggle is no less important because it occurred in an obscure location. This is a story of working people searching for power, control, and meaning in their lives, issues at the root of all true human interest stories.

2

EVANGELICAL PATERNALISM AND DIVIDED WORKERS: THE NONUNION ERA, 1877–1917

From the mid-1930s to 1973, the John Morrell and Company meatpacking plant in Ottumwa, Iowa, was a union stronghold. A hotbed of the CIO's United Packinghouse Workers of America (UPWA), Ottumwa was a community in which militant unionism revolutionized workplace relations at the Morrell plant, the city's dominant blue-collar employer, and transformed community life and politics. Ironically, this aggressive union tradition emerged out of an older nonunion heritage that did not presage workers' later commitments. Until the World War I era, unionism was absent at Morrell-Ottumwa except for a brief span from 1901 to 1904.

This virtual lack of unionism among turn-of-the-century Morrell-Ottumwa workers seems puzzling given developments in Ottumwa and elsewhere during this period. The Knights of Labor, America's first widespread industrial union movement, gained support throughout the Midwest during the 1880s. Local assemblies also proliferated in Iowa, including several assemblies, primarily consisting of coal miners, founded in the south-central part of the state between the late 1870s to 1890s. Ottumwa's Knights of Labor Local Assembly No. 7126, in existence from 1886 to 1893, enrolled 300 mostly coal-mining members in 1888. In the same year, Ottumwa members of the railroad brotherhoods were discharged in the great rail strike. Although the depression of the 1890s "obliterated the midwestern remnants of the [already declining] Knights of Labor," Morrell's workers certainly knew of various union movements.[1]

Several factors explain the lack of packinghouse unionism at Ottumwa during this era. Some were peculiar to the Morrell plant. Perhaps the most important consideration was the role of Thomas Dove Foster. Plant manager and company president from the plant's founding in 1877 until his death in 1915, Foster presided over his employees with a paternalist hand. His efforts discouraged the unionization of Morrell-Ottumwa's workers. Several other developments, shared with other packing plants during the same period, reinforced nonunionism. Workers were divided between those who worked year-round and those who did not; the bulk of the plant's workers during the pre–World War I years were seasonal. Furthermore, differences in skill and ethnicity fragmented workers. The ineffectiveness of the Amalgamated Meat Cutters and Butcher Workmen of North America (AMCBW) in recruiting workers who did not work in meatpacking plants in large midwestern cities also contributed to the plant's nonunion standing.

The Plant's Nonunion Foundations

Buried in a side column in the middle of the November 13, 1877, issue of the *Ottumwa Daily Courier* was a brief announcement: "The pork house commenced operations, this afternoon." Obscurity thus characterized the start of Ottumwa's economic mainstay for the next century and one of the most prominent meatpacking plants in the Midwest. The company was founded in Bradford, England, in 1827, by a wool comber turned entrepreneur named George Morrell. His son, John, for whom the company was named, became president in 1842. After establishing a meatpacking plant in Castlecomer, Ireland, the company moved its headquarters to Liverpool in 1860. Morrell opened its first North American packing plant in London, Ontario, in 1868. A packing plant was opened in Chicago in 1871, and three years later moved the headquarters of its American branch there from New York City.[2]

In 1874, Morrell officials decided to find a new location for their hog-slaughtering operations and company headquarters. By that time Iowa had already been a major corn-hog producer for three decades. Because meatpacking in the Civil War and Reconstruction eras was strictly seasonal — without mechanical refrigeration pork could only safely be packed once freezing temperatures generated lake or river ice in late fall — the state's first packinghouses were located in towns along the Mississippi and Des Moines Rivers. Ottumwa had been Iowa's major interior packing center since the 1860s. As was true in most midwestern packing centers then, merchant-wholesalers dominated the city's meatpacking industry. According to historian Margaret Walsh, merchant-wholesalers were involved in selling a variety of agricultural com-modities, but they would set aside part of their warehouse space during the winter months to accommodate meatpacking operations. The Jack D. Ladd and Mitchell plant, run by the so-named merchant-wholesalers, reached its peak production in 1862–1863, but then struggled in the postwar years. When Thomas Dove Foster, John Morrell's nephew, was sent out from Chicago to look for a new plant location, he found the Ladd facility defunct but suitable for initial production. Ottumwa's location on major railroad lines, the ice-cutting potential of the Des Moines River, and the city's location in what would soon be the top hog-producing state in the United States — Iowa sur-passed Illinois and Ohio by 1880 — clinched Foster's decision to recommend the city for Morrell's new pork-packing plant, one specializing in packing and not part of a broader wholesale-merchant operation.[3]

Ottumwa was just over three decades old when Morrell launched its pack-ing business there in November 1877. Since being founded by six developers of the Appanoose Rapids Company, the town had reached a population of nearly 9,000. Situated in Iowa's coal country and already an important railroad nexus, Ottumwa was also a market center in southeast Iowa. Although the city had its share of business leaders, including George Ballingall, another capital-ist who began as a merchant-wholesale packer in the Civil War era, Thomas Dove Foster quickly assumed top billing among the city's business elite.[4]

Born on November 25, 1847, Foster was the grandson of George Morrell and the son of George's daughter, Mary, and William Foster, a longtime busi-ness associate of George's. "T. D.," as he was usually referred to, spent much of his adolescence in Castlecomer, Ireland, where he learned the pork-packing business as both a laborer and hog buyer. A valued employee before his twen-tieth birthday, T. D. was made manager and chief representative of Morrell's American branch in 1871. According to company lore, Foster's strict Presby-terian background and training in the family business singled him out in John Morrell's eyes.[5]

Many old Morrell hands accompanied Foster to Ottumwa when the pack-ing plant opened. Among them was a small group of hog butchers and T. D. Foster's cousin, Richard N. Morrell, an office manager from the Chicago plant. The hog butchers included Alex Crosby, Fred Bullock, Robert Williams, John Cassiday, John Van Hewesling, and Peter Liddy. Bullock, who had worked at Morrell's London, Ontario, plant and would later become the Ottumwa plant superintendent, was born in England. Williams was born in Wales, Cassiday in Ireland, and Van Hewesling in Germany. Starting a trend that continued through much of the nonunion era, Morrell relied on foreigners, especially English, for its skilled and managerial positions. Although foreigners also dominated the "butcher aristocracy" in other midwestern meatpacking plants, they were often Germans and Irish, as they were in Chicago.[6]

Through at least 1880 Morrell used both the old Ladd plant building and a new building, constructed on the east edge of the city in 1878. During the winter peak of slaughtering in 1880, Morrell employed some 265 men. The core, year-round workforce appears to have been just less than half that figure. Thirty percent of the workforce in 1880 was foreign-born, compared to 15 percent of Ottumwa's total population. Sixty-five percent of the workers lived in Ward One, where the plant was also situated, compared to 30 percent of the city's total population. Many Morrell workers boarded in company-owned housing located in the Hayne's Addition of Ward One, a neighborhood just west of the plant. Most notable about the workers was the division in nativity between the core of foreign-born, mostly English, skilled men and the predominantly native-born unskilled workforce.[7]

Morrell rapidly expanded and modernized its Ottumwa plant in the 1880s and 1890s. Although total employment figures are misleading since meatpacking in this era relied heavily on seasonal labor, the plant employed about 500 people at peak production in 1889 and upward of 750 during the early 1890s. Morrell's managers modernized pork processing operations by introducing steam-powered continuous chain and overhead rail movement of disassembled animal parts. Aiding the modernization of the plant was the discovery of deep underground reservoirs of water in 1887. Artesian wells were immediately dug to tap this free and pure water source.[8]

It was just such modernization and mechanization in meatpacking that had first sparked workers in Chicago and Kansas City to pursue unionization; skilled knife men wanted to protect their trade from incursions by lesser skilled people. The Knights of Labor organized in both cities, especially among cattle butchers. Although the Knights often organized unskilled workers, in meatpacking they formed assemblies in both cities consisting primarily of cattle butchers. This strategy left the Knights vulnerable, because unskilled workers could learn knife work quickly and then be used to replace skilled workers during strikes. Indeed, packers were able to smash a strike in Chicago in 1886 by replacing skilled workers with unskilled strikebreakers.[9]

During the 1880s and 1890s, Ottumwa's packing workers did not attempt to unionize partly because the Morrell plant lacked a core of skilled workers opposed to management's modernization plans. Pork packing did not require as much skill as beef packing, so workers were not as threatened by mechanization. Because of the predominance of pork packing in the state as a whole between 1881 and 1887, there was only one strike during that period in all the food preparation trades in Iowa. Still, the Knights of Labor was able to organize several assemblies in other industries in Ottumwa between 1881 and 1884: one for black coal miners, one for women cigar makers, and three others for mixed constituencies, two of which were primarily coal miners. Moreover, in the 1880s, Ottumwa's coal miners, printers and publishing compositers, cigar makers, and railroad engineers and firemen all went out on strike at various times.[10]

Instead of pursuing union affiliation, Morrell's most highly skilled workers — those also most likely to want and be able to organize effectively — maintained close company ties. The original hog butchers, handpicked company men with long ties to Morrell and T. D. Foster, typically moved up quickly into supervisory roles. For example, Fred Bullock, one of the hog butchers who arrived with Foster in the 1870s, became a foreman in the 1890s and plant superintendent by 1900. Like 13 percent of the other butchers and supervisory personnel, Bullock was also English-born and Protestant, traits important to Foster. In contrast, English Protestants made up only 5 percent of the unskilled ranks. When a mutual benefit association was founded in 1893 to provide disability payments to sick or injured workers, it appealed to the upper echelon of skilled packinghouse workers, not to those who were seasonally employed or to the unskilled majority of workers who could not afford the regular voluntary payroll deductions that funded the benefits. All three founders and early officers of the Packing House Mutual Benefit Association were hog butchers, one was also born in England, and one was Presbyterian. Of the eighty "enthusiastic" charter members, nearly all were butchers or other skilled workers.[11]

Thomas Dove Foster's Evangelical Paternalism

The Packing House Mutual Benefit Association was just one of the means Thomas Dove Foster used to cultivate paternalistic labor relations in Ottumwa from the 1880s until his death in 1915. Like many industrialists of the Gilded Age, Foster wanted to promote a cooperative relationship between workers and management. He saw himself as a friend to his employees and prided himself on how all of his workers recognized him by his red hair.[12] Given Foster's role as a prominent member of Ottumwa's elite, the relatively small size of the Morrell plant for much of this period, and his reformist and welfarist concerns, Foster's paternalism resembles the "familiar style" of paternalism that Philip Scranton has identified in nineteenth-century American textile mill towns. Mill owners there occupied a patriarchal role: they knew their workers by name, "pressed their souls toward church or chapel," and attempted to preserve "customary social forms." Although workers were treated as children, they could benefit from the welfare features of the system "so long as neither party betrayed the other by departing from the script."[13]

An admirer and follower of Dwight Moody, a leading evangelist at that time, Foster formulated programs that expressed his strong evangelical commitments. Employees hoping to move into managerial positions often joined either the East End Presbyterian Church, Foster's church built largely with his financial support and located in the packing neighborhood until 1903, the First Presbyterian Church near the central business district, or one of the city's five Methodist churches. In 1895 about a third of Morrell's butchers and skilled or supervisory employees were Presbyterians or Methodists.[14]

More than simply rewarding employees who were similarly motivated, Foster's evangelical Christian paternalism pervaded the plant's labor relations from the 1880s until World War I, reflecting his interests in his employees' "moral and spiritual welfare." Foster, like other paternalistic employers of the period, wanted to "recast the worker in a middle-class mold: uplifting him, bettering him, and making his family life more wholesome." Foster's paternalism was largely shaped by his leadership in the Young Men's Christian Association (YMCA) in Ottumwa and by the dominant concerns of that organization in the late nineteenth century. Started in London in 1844 and transplanted to the United States in 1851, the YMCA espoused a nondenominational evangelical Protestant mission centered on a fourfold program of spiritual, social, mental, and physical development of young men. Dwight Moody began his career in Chicago's YMCA movement. During the late nineteenth century, businessmen compelled by a sense of social responsibility dominated the movement, and local branches typically depended on businesses for financial support. The YMCA's most successful formal relationship with industry was its associations with railroads, though even among railroad workers the YMCA typically only gained strong support in the aftermath of strikes.[15]

In Ottumwa T. D. Foster represented the business community's interest in the YMCA. In 1892 he donated $5,000 for the construction of the city's first YMCA building, situated not coincidentally in the packinghouse district. For the next two decades, Foster diligently pursued what he saw as the YMCA's true work: the spiritual conversion of young men, especially those employed at his plant. Ottumwa's YMCA, as part of a growing trend among YMCAs nationwide, sponsored a variety of athletic leagues, industrial training classes, religious instruction, and factory shop hygiene talks. These activities allegedly built character, as historian Clifford Putney put it, by "monitoring the habits of young men for the purpose of keeping them home-tied and heaven-bound." As president of the YMCA in Ottumwa in 1896, Foster noted the rapid increase in the number of people using the Y's recreational and bathing facilities, but he expressed disappointment in the drop-off in conversions and Bible class attendance from the previous year. He called for "impressed earnestness and effort" toward achieving the YMCA's primary goal: spiritual conversions to his evangelical brand of Christianity. Moreover, beginning in the 1890s, Foster also sponsored Sunday services conducted by the East End Presbyterian Church's pastor in a tent outside the packing plant during warm weather and in the plant cafeteria during cold weather.[16]

The annual company picnic, Foster's first paternalistic program for Morrell workers, though not formally associated with the YMCA, nevertheless suggests how the undergirding philosophy of that organization informed Foster's evangelism. Started in 1886, company picnics, for Foster, fulfilled a charitable social role that was fundamental to his paternalist outlook. Held that first year at the fairgrounds in the nearby town of Agency, the picnic featured food and entertainment for workers and their families provided by the company. In addition, Morrell paid each worker's regular wages for that day, a policy he would continue through his death in 1915. Six hundred men, women, and children attended the first picnic. The *Agency Tribune* reported that T. D. Foster "was the ring leader of the affair and was busy the entire day looking after the comfort and pleasure of the employes [*sic*]."[17]

The contrast between Foster's public paternal remarks and his private concerns regarding his involvement with Ottumwa and the Morrell plant is striking and suggests the coercion lurking in his evangelism. In his 1897 speech at the annual Morrell picnic, after being introduced as a man who "takes the highest interest in the welfare of his men," Foster pontificated, "The life of a good man is like a stone wall; the stones represent the work and the mortar the days of recreation. A wall without mortar is a poor wall, and a pile of mortar without stones is of no account at all. Tis so with life, we must have work and lots of it, but in between times we must have days of recreation, like this occasion." Yet in 1893, when contemplating a move to Memphis, Foster showed disgust for Ottumwans' failure to recognize all that he had done for them. Establishing a new plant in Memphis, he suggested, would help the company in Ottumwa, "as Ottumwa people have a kind of idea that we are coming and that it is Ottumwa that is doing it and not John Morrell and Company and we shall never stand where we should in their eyes until they see we can do as well or better somewhere else. The people of these interior points are growing insulting." Although Foster resented Ottumwans' failure to appreciate his good works, a disastrous fire in that same year forced him to reconsider relocating. Instead he rebuilt and actually expanded the Ottumwa plant, where he continued to reward employees who participated in YMCA activities and evangelical Protestantism.[18]

The Erosion of Evangelical Paternalism

The number of Morrell employees who were able to benefit from T. D. Foster's evangelical Christian paternalism declined after the turn of the century. The plant's growth and divisions among workers rendered Foster's paternalism less successful. By 1900, when meatpacking was Iowa's leading industry in total product value, second in total capital invested, and fourth in total manufacturing employment, Ottumwa had passed Cedar Rapids as the state's leading packing center, although Sioux City would soon begin to outpace Ottumwa. The plant also clearly dominated Ottumwa's industrial sector by then: 40 percent of all manufacturing workers in the city worked there. Although the core workforce numbered between 500 and 600, during heavy hog runs the number employed jumped to as many as 1,300. During the week of July 13–20, 1901, for instance, 20,600 hogs were killed. Yet just three weeks later, only 4,489 hogs were slaughtered. A large, floating workforce was needed to cope with these fluctuations in demand for hogs. Workers with butchering skills used downtimes in Ottumwa to ply their trades in other midwestern meatpacking towns. In 1901 the *Ottumwa Daily Democrat* noted that Andrew Streeby, recently employed in a St. Joseph packinghouse, was back at Morrell's kill and cut. According to the paper, Streeby was "another 'prodigal'" like other "truants" who had recently returned from St. Joseph.[19]

As the plant expanded following the fire in 1893, the most basic division among Morrell employees at the turn of the century was in terms of day-to-day employment. Detailed wage data from an 1899 employee time book reveals further divisions. For the week ending February 25, 658 employees earned from $28.75 per week ($4.80 per day — employees worked six days per week) by Frederick Bullock and William H. O'Malley, an Irish Catholic hog butcher turned foreman, and $23.00 per week ($3.83 per day) by Alexander R. Brown, a Scottish-born Presbyterian hog butcher turned foreman, down to 50 cents per day by twenty-six workers. More specifically, aside from the three highly paid supervisors, the remaining 655 employees earned between 50 cents and $3.75 per day. Twelve (2 percent) earned between $3.00 and $3.75, 88 (13 percent) made between $2.00 and $2.99, 336 (51 percent) made between $1.00 and $1.99, and 219 (33 percent) made less than $1.00 per day. Of the twelve highly-paid workers, seven of the nine who had indicated a religious affiliation in the 1895 census were Presbyterians, Methodists, Baptists, or "Christian"; four were foreign-born (Dutch, Swedish, and British); and all were either foremen, butchers, or skilled members of the hog-kill department.[20]

In many respects, the data on the general workforce in 1900 reinforces trends that were already noticeable in 1880. Women continued to be notably absent from the Morrell workforce; no women were employed at the plant until 1905, when they assumed positions as labelers and sausage makers. Nearly one-half of Morrell's workers continued to live in Ward One, where the boundaries had changed somewhat but not extensively since 1880; another one-quarter lived in Ward Two, north of and adjacent to Ward One. In the same year, a third of Ottumwa's total population lived in those two wards, with the city now divided into seven total wards. Unlike in 1880, about 10 percent of Morrell workers (and 12 percent of the city's total population) now lived in Ward Five, located southwest of the plant across the Des Moines River. Although the number of first- and second-generation workers at the plant had declined from two-thirds to two-fifths between 1880 and 1900, the plant's workers were still more often of foreign extraction than was true of the city as a whole (30 percent). Among first- and second-generation foreigners at the plant, 38 percent were Irish, 24 percent were Swedes, 16 percent were Germans, and 11 percent were English, with most of the foreigners, especially the English, disproportionately represented in the plant's supervisory ranks. Twelve (80 percent) of the fifteen foremen identified in the manuscript census were first- or second-generation foreigners compared to 49 percent of the butchers and 36 percent of the laborers. In addition, of the 337 Morrell employees designated in the 1895 Iowa census, 61 (18 percent) were Presbyterians compared to just 5 percent of Wapello County's population as a whole in 1915. This hints perhaps at Foster's influence, especially among the highly skilled and managerial workers or those who aspired to these ranks.[21]

One of the most striking changes in the Morrell workforce between 1880 and 1900 was in its racial composition. In 1880, there were no blacks employed at the plant. In 1900, 13 percent of the workers were classified in the census as blacks or mulattos, compared to just 3 percent of Ottumwa's total population. Between the 1880s and World War I, coal companies, situated primarily in the south-central part of the state, were among the largest employers of African Americans living in Iowa. Ottumwa was located near Buxton, one of the largest black coal-mining communities during this period, with 2,700 blacks among its 5,000 residents in 1905. Indeed, some of Ottumwa's black workers appear to have moved back and forth between Ottumwa and Buxton, working in the mines during the summer and the packing plant in the fall and winter.[22]

Perhaps the most interesting facet of Buxton's history was the apparently amiable relationship between blacks and whites. Although blacks' residences in Ottumwa were dispersed throughout the city, they, unlike blacks in Buxton, were nevertheless subject to discrimination. As John Hudson notes, native-born descendants of upland southerners, unlike Yankee descendants, were not known for their strong sympathies for blacks. A vague yet ominous reference in the *Ottumwa Daily Democrat* in 1901 noted that "Deputy Sheriff George Slavin has been busy serving notices on the colored population at the packing plant." The *Morning Democrat* of April 1, 1903, reported that a race riot had broken out the day before on South College Street near the packing plant and involved several hundred people and the city police.[23]

The skill, religious, ethnic, and racial divisions among workers made the prospect of unionizing a substantial part of Morrell's workforce a daunting task. Beginning in 1897, a new union representing both retail and packing-house butchers, the Amalgamated Meat Cutters and Butcher Workmen of North America (AMCBW), part of the decade-old American Federation of Labor (AFL), was formed in Cincinnati. The Amalgamated grew very slowly until Michael Donnelly, a South Omaha sheep butcher, was elected president in December 1898. Donnelly was successful in gaining recruits, and set his sights on the biggest potential union prize in the United States: Chicago's stockyard and packinghouse district. Although the butchers initially left the unskilled to fend for themselves, Donnelly pushed the butchers to approach the unskilled since division of labor had eroded much of the butchering trades' special status. The Amalgamated locals did not become full-fledged industrial unions. By 1903, they had, however, formed a Packing Trades Council that allowed joint action. Unionization in Chicago found support from the full gamut of ethnic groups represented in the packinghouses, and coincided with a larger union movement that swept industrial Chicago during these years. Packinghouse workers fought for more regular employment and retention during slack times as well as higher wage levels. They used "control" strikes, and were helped by the generally prosperous economic times of the 1900–1904 period that made packers willing to bargain with union departmental committees. By summer 1904, however, packers were no longer willing to tolerate the informal bargaining with union committees that had gone on since 1902, and an industrywide strike ensued in July. Although the union membership was highly disciplined initially, packers were able to import strike-breakers, undermining workers' collective efforts. The Amalgamated halted the strike on September 5.[24]

The AMCBW organized meatpacking workers in many places outside Chicago. Yet its most successful midwestern organizing efforts were in Omaha, East St. Louis, Kansas City, St. Joseph, and Sioux City. Chicago had 29 meat-packing locals, Omaha and East St. Louis had 12 each, Kansas City had 10, St. Joseph had 6, and Sioux City had 2, for a total of 71 (47 percent) of the 150 meatpacking locals organized along departmental lines in January 1904. Outside Sioux City, there were only three other meatpacking locals established in Iowa.[25] Chicago's predominance among the meatpacking locals was not accidental for Donnelly and the AMCBW. For them, Chicago was the key to successful unionization throughout the industry. Since most of the major packers' largest plants were in Chicago, this strategy was logical. Whereas James Barrett's history of the Chicago unionizing effort in 1900–1904 stresses the permeation of unionism among skilled and unskilled workers of all ethnic backgrounds, David Brody's earlier depiction of the period may be more telling in regard to the real focus of the union efforts, creation of uniform wage scales among cattle butchers. Although diminished in skill and prestige, cattle butchering still was considered the highest art in meatpacking. In Ottumwa, there was little cattle butchering until 1909, when a new beef house was constructed.[26]

Unlike many cities in Iowa that experienced considerable union membership growth between 1900 and 1904, Ottumwa saw the number of unions increase from twenty-three to thirty-six but actually lost total members, declining from 1,510 in 1900 to 1,341 in 1904. The Amalgamated reached Ottumwa in 1901, when Morton Walker was elected chair of AMCBW Local No. 144, a local that included both retail butchers and meatpacking workers, though the leadership of the local was dominated by Morrell workers. At its inception, it seems Ottumwa's union, like those in Chicago, attracted workers from the skilled and unskilled ranks of Morrell employees. Walker, a thirty-four-year-old native of Iowa with American-born parents, was a member of the hog-killing gang at Morrell, and was paid the relatively high wage of $3 per day in 1899, suggesting that he was a butcher. Charley McDavid, a member of the lard refinery department, a part of the industry not known for skilled workers, was the secretary of Local No. 144 in 1901. Iowa labor statistics for 1901 state that the local enlisted 600 members, meaning that about one-half of the entire workforce would have joined. The following year, however, the state labor statistics report just thirty members for Local No. 144, and for 1903–1904 membership is listed at only nine. In the absence of any event that would have caused such a drastic falloff in membership, it is likely that the figure for 1901 is simply wrong. The paltry number of members, likely just butchers, involved in Local No. 144 in 1904 largely explains the emphatic statement by Daniel Gallagher, local secretary and a butcher himself, regarding Ottumwa's reaction to the Amalgamated's July strike: "There is no possibility of a strike being called in Ottumwa under the present circumstances. . . . We haven't even discussed the matter in our council. It is a matter that does not concern us in the least at the present time. You may say for me as secretary of the council that there will not, under the present circumstances, be a strike participated in by the members of the council in this city." With only a handful of members in Local No. 144, including some who may have been retail butchers, it is no wonder that Gallagher felt this way. Indeed, as the strike raged in Chicago, 4,000 Morrell workers and their families took four trains to Keokuk for the annual company picnic, organized by the Packing House Mutual Aid Association, previously called the Benefit Association.[27]

Several factors accounted for Ottumwa workers' quiescence during the 1900–1904 period, some of which may have been similar to those that impeded union efforts in other midwestern packing centers. Divisions among workers in terms of employment, skill, ethnicity, and religion, bolstered by the attraction of Foster's evangelical paternalism to key components of the workforce and the failure of the Amalgamated to diligently pursue unionization outside Chicago and a few other major midwestern packing centers, contributed to Ottumwa workers' lack of unionism. Between 1904 and World War I, moreover, several of these factors continued to undercut any new union developments. The AMCBW itself withered nationwide after the strike, Foster's Christian paternalism persisted, and workers continued to be divided in various ways.

Following the Amalgamated's defeat in 1904, its membership among packinghouse workers collapsed virtually everywhere, especially in the Midwest. The deep recession of 1908–1909 finished off most of the packinghouse locals that survived the strike; because of spotty employment opportunities they simply could not retain dues-paying members. The economic slump and a growing open-shop movement after 1903 likewise gutted many union constituencies across the state of Iowa. In 1903 total state membership peaked at 48,734. By 1909, it dropped below the 1900 level with just 25,000 members. Between 1907 and 1912, the largest meatpacking companies, especially Swift, Armour, and Morris, contributed to the erosion of union membership among skilled butchers, especially when they began offering financial benefits, like stock purchasing plans and pensions. Ottumwa's paltry band of AMCBW members marched in the city's Labor Day parade in September 1904, but there is no indication that the Amalgamated, if it continued to limp along, marched in any other Labor Day parade in Ottumwa through the World War I years. Between 1907 and 1909, in fact, the number of trade unions in the city declined from twenty-seven to fourteen and total membership dropped from 1,109 to 702. By 1911, there were only nine unions with 503 members left in the city.[28]

In this climate of declining union membership, T. D. Foster continued his evangelical Christian paternalism. As before, he stressed religious activities, company picnics, and YMCA work as evidence of his benevolence and as examples for workers to follow. In 1902, Foster's East End Presbyterian Church hired William Henry Hormel, brother of George A. Hormel, president of the Austin, Minnesota, meatpacking company, as its new pastor. For the next decade the Reverend Hormel plied his trade not only at the church but among the packinghouse workers at the plant. In conjunction with the Labor Day celebration in 1906, for instance, the Reverend Hormel gave two sermons, "The Wisdom and Power of God for the Solution of Our Problems" and "Loyalty to the Kingdom of Christ, the Only Solution to All of Our Problems," the titles of which both strongly suggested the antiunion potential of such Christianizing.[29]

Foster used the annual company picnics, which continued to attract several thousand workers and their families through the World War I years, as opportunities to expound his evangelical paternalism. The Packing House Mutual Aid Association, led by Morrell employees closely tied to Foster, selected the sites and activities for the picnics. Speaking before approximately 4,000 people in Ottumwa's Caldwell Park in 1907, Foster explained the function of the picnics.

> The object of these annual outings are [sic] to give the employees a day of recreation, an opportunity to meet each other socially, and grow acquainted, establishing a friendly brotherly basis between them. Also these annual picnics give the employer and employed a much desired opportunity of growing acquainted with each other and establishing a better understanding thereby, bringing them closer together. It is the aim always of the employers to make this one day set aside each year for the men who are employed by John Morrell and Co., as pleasant as is within their power. So on this day the wages of each employe [sic] is paid him or her just the same as though the holiday had not been granted. Where there is friendship and open dealing between employe [sic] and employed, there is no excuse or necessity for labor unions. Where the principles of the sermon on the mount rule in the dealings between the working man and his employer there is no necessity for the intervention of a third party. The company has made it a rule that when an employe [sic] takes his leave honorably to test other labor conditions he is not discriminated against and is given another opportunity for gaining employment in our company.[30]

Foster's speech exudes confidence in his control over his workers, so much so that the irony of his reference to the Sermon on the Mount was apparently lost on him. The meek would not inherit the earth while in Foster's charge; they could only hope for his continued benevolence. Foster must have also been pleased with the gains in YMCA membership made in Ottumwa between 1904 and 1908, from 638 to 1,065. But then, beginning in 1909, membership at the YMCA declined every year through 1914. Besides, workers seemed to use both the YMCA and company picnics for reasons probably not highly thought of by Foster. The YMCA's athletic leagues drew larger numbers than its religious offerings, and factory health and hygiene talks superseded religious conversions in frequency between 1910 and 1914.[31]

Increasingly, after 1900, Foster was willing to admit that workers did not necessarily share his religious and cultural commitments. During testimony taken to determine if Mayor Thomas J. Phillips should be ousted in 1910 owing to reports of public intoxication, Foster noted that he had never seen Phillips drink, even when he appeared as a guest at the Morrell company picnics. Foster, a public supporter of temperance organizations such as the Modern Woodmen of America, a prominent fraternal organization in southeast Iowa, acknowledged that some employees did consume alcohol at company picnics even though he did not allow it. While testifying, Foster also remarked that the Smoky Row neighborhood near the packing plant was much improved since 1907, when gambling and prostitution flourished there. He did not take direct credit for the improvement, but seems to have made the observation more in the way of supporting Phillips's administration.[32]

Foster's public remarks about Smoky Row and the behavior of his employees and Ottumwa's working people in general suggest that he recognized that his evangelical paternalism was a beacon that some might follow but that few workers could be expected to take readily to heart. More important in terms of labor relations, perhaps, Foster's public remarks about the value of recreation suggest that he did not understand how unskilled workers' seasonal employment at the packing plant crucially affected their ability to embrace either paternalism or unionism. At the 1906 company picnic held in Burlington, that city's mayor noted that Morrell employed about 1,200 "all told," with 500 "dependent" upon its payroll. A time book kept by a foreman in the beef offal department between March 12, and June 25, 1913, also demonstrates how volatile employment was, particularly for unskilled workers. In that department, employees were paid between $1.50 and $3.00 per day. The highest paid workers experienced only two weeks of less than forty hours' work, while the lowest paid workers experienced four weeks of less than forty hours' work in the same two-month period. The cuts in total hours worked per week also did not go as deep for the highest paid workers; the average range between the lowest and highest number of hours worked per week for them was 32 and for the lowest paid workers was 38.5. Consideration of such statistics, even though they represent a narrow slice of the workforce, shed a different light on Foster's remarks at the 1910 company picnic than he probably intended when he said "if a man cannot afford to take a week [of vacation], he at least should take a day occasionally." For unskilled Morrell employees, the problem was not overwork, but the lack of work.[33]

Laying the Groundwork for Unionism

Several crucial changes occurred during the World War I era that would ultimately help to make Ottumwa's meatpacking workers more interested in unionism. In 1915 the demographic profile of the Morrell workforce still shared similarities to that at the turn of the century. The total number of employees was about the same, roughly 1,250 at peak; most workers continued to live in Wards One and Two (56 and 14 percent respectively); and 67 percent of the workers were married (up slightly from 1900). The racial composition was more white than in 1900; the percentage of African Americans employed was down to 8 from 13 in 1900. Women, by then in their tenth year of employment at Morrell, constituted about 7 percent of the workers.

The most telling development since 1900 was the change in workers' nativities. The "new" immigrant surge into the United States in the first two decades of the twentieth century affected Ottumwa only slightly. A handful of eastern Europeans now resided in the city and worked at the plant, but most of the Morrell plant's foreigners were still primarily Swedish, Irish, English, or German, as had been true in 1900. More important, unskilled laborers, butchers, and foremen were now all most often native-born of native-born parents. Even so, foremen still had the most first- and second-generation foreigners in their ranks (47 percent of forty-six total, compared to 26 percent for the unskilled laborers; in 1900 80 percent of the foremen had been foreigners compared to 36 percent of the unskilled laborers). Combined with the decline in nonwhites, these statistics suggest that before World War I, differences among workers in terms of ethnicity, race, and nativity had narrowed and that Ottumwa's workers were becoming more homogeneous. By the World War I period, unlike the cases in either 1880 or even 1900, unskilled workers' perceptions of "foreignness" would be directed at their supervisors rather than at skilled workers. This homogeneity likely increased workers' receptiveness to union organizing. In contrast, among Chicago's meatpacking workers during the World War I era, ethnic factionalism increased between the native-born and older immigrant skilled butchers and the more recent Slavic immigrants who were moving into the unskilled ranks.[34]

Just as crucial to workers' later acceptance of unionism was the death of T. D. Foster on July 20, 1915. With his death came also the demise of the evangelical Christian paternalism that he had espoused during the nonunion era at the Ottumwa plant. In April 1918, following federal judge Samuel B. Alschuler's decision to grant meatpacking workers nationwide more guaranteed hours and a higher base wage rate, Morrell-Ottumwa workers organized AMCBW Local 236. The local gained most of its followers after employees learned that their wages were lower than those in other packing plants. Soon after the local's formation, Morrell ended its annual picnic, revoked its Thanksgiving and Christmas bonuses, and terminated its faithful service pension, formerly given to a few longtime loyal employees. Between 1918 and October 1921, the union enrolled most of the plant's workers. When the local went out on strike on October 19, 1921, two months ahead of the national AMCBW's strike but sparked by the same issues that would prompt it—reduction in the guaranteed workweek and a general wage cut—Local 236 seemed well situated for a long struggle. But intervention by the National Guard beginning in mid-November squelched the strike effort, and Local 236 finally capitulated at the end of December.[35]

After the local union had been smashed, the company introduced a new brand of paternalism, part of the nationwide welfare capitalism movement. These new programs, however, lacked the benevolence and Christianizing components of Foster's paternalism. After John H. Morrell was president from 1915 to 1921, Foster's sons would hold the presidency of the now separate American branch of John Morrell and Company from 1921 to 1953. During the 1920s, under the guiding hand of Thomas Henry Foster, T. D.'s second-oldest son, company picnics would be reintroduced, but they were not paid holidays and were not forums for hard-selling a benevolent view of employer-employee relations. In fact, none of Foster's four sons were as committed to evangelism as he had been. When Foster's sons implemented welfare capitalist programs in the 1920s they were not concerned with the moral and spiritual welfare of workers; they were more concerned with gaining positive publicity, blocking further union efforts, and reasserting managerial authority. In fact, however, the welfare capitalist practices at the Ottumwa plant would actually engender intense feelings of employee animosity toward their employers in a way not evident during the pre–World War I nonunion era.[36]

The World War I period also ushered in changes at the plant that would significantly improve the chances for long-term unionization later on. Morrell constructed several new additions to the Ottumwa plant during the 1920s that resulted in a steady increase in the number of people employed there. Between 1921 and 1931, Morrell-Ottumwa's workforce nearly doubled from 1,500 to 2,500. Seasonal workforce fluctuations, though still a nuisance, would become less severe during the 1920s. Indeed, unlike the years prior to the 1920s when total numbers of animals slaughtered fluctuated normally from one year to the next, after 1928 yearly slaughter totals were remarkably consistent and one-third higher than they were for the highest figures from the pre–World War I period. And, too, the personal evangelical paternalism that T. D. Foster extended to the prewar core workforce of 500 or so became impractical in a plant employing more than 2,000 people.[37]

By 1920, Morrell-Ottumwa's workforce had taken on the composite features, already emerging by 1915, that would characterize it during the New Deal era. Nearly the entire blue-collar component of the labor force was native-born, 92 percent of the total. In the five years following the 1915 census, the portion of foreign-born workers at Morrell had declined dramatically from 16 to 8 percent. The most notable surge into the plant during the war came from native-born whites from Iowa, Missouri, and Illinois (accounting for 62, 11, and 6 percent, respectively, of the total). This farm-to-factory movement reinforced the dominant cultural upland southerner strain that had long existed among the plant's unskilled employees. Even more obvious by 1920 was the division between blue-collar, native-born workers, primarily from Iowa, Missouri, or Illinois, and the foreign (first- and second-generation) white-collar workers. Of the 187 managerial and white-collar workers in the plant in 1920 (including foremen, supervisors, and clerks of various sorts) 79 (42 percent) were foreigners, primarily British, Swedes, or Germans. Resentments stemming from this cultural divide would play an important role in later union-building struggles. Unlike divisions in nativity in the late nineteenth century between skilled and unskilled workers, by the 1920s Morrell's blue-collar employees shared broadly homogeneous cultural backgrounds. The "foreigners" were their supervisors, not their fellow workers.[38]

3

THE WELFARE CAPITALISM OF JOHN MORRELL, 1917–1937

T. D. Foster's death and the new context for labor relations prompted by World War I spelled the end of John Morrell and Company's attempts to mold a compliant workforce at its Ottumwa plant through evangelical paternalism. Just as important, by the time the United States entered the war, Morrell-Ottumwa's employees were largely divided in terms of background between overwhelmingly native-born workers and many foreign supervisors. These native-born workers did not include many who could identify with the evangelical paternalism and English identity of the plant's leaders. In contrast, many among the plant's managerial ranks still did. Moreover, by 1923, only 98 of the plant's 2,300 total employees had worked there since the turn of the century, meaning few actually remembered the heyday of T. D. Foster's evangelical paternalism. When the federal government created the opportunity for unionization during the war, the absence of such ties helped workers jump on the first successful union bandwagon in the plant's history. A violent strike in 1921 further divided workers and managers at Morrell-Ottumwa, and prompted management to try a new form of paternalism, their own brand of welfare capitalism.

A primary facet of the "American Plan" during the New Era, welfare capitalism was "any service provided for the comfort or improvement of employees which was neither a necessity of the industry nor required by law."[1] By a more skeptical definition, it was a movement to maintain workers' company allegiance and the open shop through reform from within an industry. At John Morrell and Company in Ottumwa, it primarily included programs in three areas: employee representation in a company union; establishment of personnel and employment departments that left the power of foremen and superintendents largely intact; and provision for a variety of employee benefit programs. Morrell introduced most of these employee welfare plans from 1922 to 1925, after its victory over a local of the AFL's Amalgamated Meat Cutters and Butcher Workmen of North America (AMCBW) in the 1921 strike. Although comprehensive reform measures were not common in Iowa, managers at Morrell hoped that these programs — most specifically, the company union — would establish a form of "industrial democracy" between management and labor that would keep out industrial unions. Management hoped to inspire workers' identification with their employing company and to make them receptive to the efficiency and productivity of the new scientific management. Indeed, welfare capitalism was part of a larger "reform from above" effort aimed at reducing worker resistance to managerial goals.[2]

Historians have long debated welfare capitalism's ability to control and placate industrial workforces. Traditionally they have disparaged welfare programs. In a highly influential essay, David Brody noted that welfare capitalism might have succeeded in forging strong company loyalties among workers had the wage cuts of the depression not occurred. Others pointed out that distinctions between varieties of welfare capitalism and company unions make generalizations about their adequacies or inadequacies questionable. More recently, Lizabeth Cohen's landmark study of Chicago's workers in the interwar period argued that workers internalized welfare capitalist notions and infused them into their union struggles of the 1930s.[3] A crucial part of this debate has to do with the rising influence of personnel departments. Traditionally, historians have seen these instruments of managerial reform as reducing the power and arbitrary rule of foremen and enhancing the centralized control of plant managers. Where they did not, and the foremen maintained some hold, new welfare programs and employee representation plans were less liable to create industrial harmony.[4] The case of Morrell in Ottumwa supports those who have stressed welfare capitalism's failure to create a stable system of industrial relations. Moreover, Morrell's example suggests that "industrial democracy" was unattainable when foremen still held significant power. Welfare capitalism at Morrell-Ottumwa was a reform facade that did little to improve the plant's labor relations. Indeed, welfare capitalism at the Morrell-Ottumwa plant sparked a rising tide of expectations among workers for better industrial relations that contributed in part to workers' efforts during the 1930s to create an independent union movement.[5]

Smashing Morrell-Ottumwa Workers' Union Experiment

Before 1900, Thomas Dove Foster's Christian paternalism generated three main welfare programs at the Ottumwa plant: the Mutual Aid Association, company picnics, and YMCA work. These programs captured the loyalties of many skilled workers, which in turn disrupted unionization efforts before World War I. In early 1918, however, federal government involvement in the packing industry owing to the desire for peaceful relations between the companies and their workers during the war set the stage for successful union-building in Ottumwa. Fearing strikes, Secretary of Labor William B. Wilson appointed federal judge Samuel B. Alschuler to determine the wages and hours for packing workers during the war period. Swayed largely by the vivid contrasts between workers' living standards and the profits made by the packers drawn by Frank P. Walsh, the AMCBW's legal counsel during the mediation hearings held in Chicago in February 1918, Alschuler established the eight-hour day and guaranteed forty-hour workweek, paid overtime, and equal pay for men and women performing the same work as basic standards in the packing industry. As a consequence, Alschuler's awards in March 1918 not only laid the groundwork for successful union organizing in Chicago, but they spurred the union-building process all across the rural Midwest, including Ottumwa.[6]

Within one month after the Alschuler decision, Ottumwa workers organized AMCBW Local 236. Many joined after learning that Morrell's wages were lower than those in other plants. Unlike his father, Thomas Henry Foster, company vice president at the time and president starting in 1921, was less interested in evangelical paternalism. Like his father, he viewed unionism with disdain and felt the local's formation was an insult. Indeed, other than running the Ottumwa plant with a less obtrusive hand than his father, T. H. Foster was primarily interested in promoting himself as a Shakespeare scholar. Soon after the local formed, Morrell revoked its annual picnic, Thanksgiving and Christmas bonuses, and terminated its faithful service pension given to selected long-time, especially loyal employees. Local union members commented that they were no longer considered faithful servants, just "old" ones.[7]

Morrell employees rapidly joined Local 236 when they realized that the company had now completely shed its older paternalism. In September 1918, Morrell agreed to grant its workers the eight-hour day, forty-hour guaranteed workweek, time and a half for overtime, and seniority rights provided by the Alschuler agreement. One year later, Local 236 claimed 1,065 members out of a total plant workforce of around 1,300. The local proudly noted that 835 members marched in Ottumwa's 1918 Labor Day parade. "For more than two blocks the observant spectator could see nothing but the well appearing division of Local No. 236 with its white caps as the marchers of our local wended their way through the streets of Ottumwa." The erosion of significant nativity differences among workers and federal government support had made such a scene possible.[8]

Although Local 236's total membership vacillated somewhat, over the next two years it did not fall below 800. The first test of the local's solidarity came in March 1921. Morrell, beating the Big Four packers to the punch, reneged on its promise to uphold the Alschuler agreement in January. Local 236 officials requested a meeting with Morrell on March 2 to work out a new compromise. When Morrell refused to meet with the local, 836 members voted to strike. But after union members stayed out of the plant for two days on March 3–4, Morrell officials agreed to reinstate the Alschuler agreement. Within a few days, this enormous victory brought local union membership up to close to 1,300, virtually 100 percent of the plant's workers.[9]

As a consequence, compared to locals in Omaha, Nebraska, and St. Joseph, Missouri, where similar ministrikes had failed, Ottumwa's union faced its showdown with Morrell later in 1921 in much better shape and with much greater confidence. Morrell-Ottumwa's walkout on October 19 preceded the AMCBW's national strike by nearly two months but was brought about by the same factors: Morrell's final rejection of the Alschuler agreement, especially a reduction in the guaranteed workweek from forty to thirty-two hours and a cut in the unskilled labor rate to less than forty cents per hour.[10]

Morrell-Ottumwa's strike began after workers in the beef and hog kill departments walked out in support of a grievance lodged by women workers in the trimming room. In the kill departments, many women who had been doing piecework on high grades of meat had been switched to lesser grades, lowering their wages in the process. When their protests went unheeded, Philip S. Muldoon, treasurer of Local 236, led a delegation that met with plant superintendent Ernest Manns. Manns told the union delegation to "go back to work or 'check out.'" Accordingly, the union called a strike to fight not only on behalf of the women but also for the retention of the hour and minimum wage guarantees and the right to continue collective bargaining through their local.[11]

By October 21, approximately 1,200 of the plant's 1,300 workers had gone out on strike. T. H. Foster halted beef and hog kill operations until new workers could be hired. Commenting on the strike, Cornelius J. Hayes, AMCBW national president, pronounced the Morrell strike to be the most important in the packing industry since the end of the war. Nevertheless, the national union provided little financial backing for Ottumwa workers' efforts.[12]

On October 22, Julius Hillgardner, a butcher representing the local, met with Morrell officials. T. H. Foster asked why the local had not pursued normal grievance procedures. When Hillgardner admitted that the local had ignored them, Foster declared that management would not work with the union.

If union people wanted to be rehired, he said they would have to apply as individuals. Foster proclaimed his word was "final." The result was an impasse that lasted until the eruption of violence between strikers and strikebreakers in mid-November.[13]

Although the strike had been supported by the packing community, Morrell was able to hire strikebreakers almost immediately. Given the lack of union traditions among workers this is not too surprising; union members had probably not given enough thought to how they would man picket lines to keep replacement workers out. The same lack of foresight could not be attributed to Morrell. Company leaders supplemented the scabs from nearby areas with black strikebreakers as well. Alfred Crow, a butcher and union member, claimed Morrell brought blacks to Iowa by train, let them off in Agency, a small town a few miles east of Ottumwa, and then marched them to the city's outskirts and safely across the Des Moines River to Morrell's property. The strikers were unable to stop the flow of replacement labor and by the end of October Morrell announced the resumption of both beef and hog killing. Approximately 600 people were working in the plant by mid-November. Most of them were sleeping in the plant to avoid confrontations with the strikers.[14]

Inexperienced in mobilizing a massive strike effort and frustrated with their inability to halt production, strikers started a brawl with strikebreakers in front of the plant on the morning of November 15. Roughly 200 to 300 people were involved in the fight. Twenty-five people were injured, including T. H. Foster, who was hit in the head with a rock thrown through his car window. A group of prominent Ottumwa citizens, including Foster, the mayor, and the county sheriff, promptly met after the fight. Claiming that Ottumwa's police department had been unable to control the situation, they urged Iowa governor Nathan Kendall to assist in restoring order. On November 16, Kendall dispatched four companies of the Iowa National Guard, totaling about 250 troops, to Ottumwa. This was the first use of national guard troops in a labor dispute in Iowa since the Muscatine button strike of 1911.[15]

Arriving in the city from Des Moines by train, the troops started patrolling the streets around the plant "with their bayonets fixed." They also set up machine guns at important intersections around the plant. In addition, the Wapello County attorney deputized 150 men to aid the state militia in their efforts. Injunctions were also issued forbidding strikers from picketing the plant. Use of national guard troops resulted in sharp rebukes from many prominent Iowans, including John C. "Shady" Lewis, president of the Iowa State Federation of Labor. Lewis wrote the governor and pointed out that the troops were being housed by company officials and transported to the plant in company vehicles. By the time Kendall started to remove the troops about one week later, strikers could no longer halt production. Local 236 continued its strike until Christmas Eve, but their effort collapsed shortly thereafter.

After the strike the company treated returning union workers harshly. Butcher Alfred Crow recalled that the company "had it in for us young guys, they wanted to break us . . . they were very mad." Many demotions occurred; management moved men to the trimming rooms where only lowly-paid women had generally worked before the strike. The company retained or eventually rehired many of the scabs, which increased the bitterness between families of loyal union supporters and those who had crossed the picket lines. Moreover, the strike reinforced the firm antiunion stances of the two major management leaders during the strike, T. H. Foster, soon to become president of the company, and plant superintendent Ernest Manns. It also resolutely shaped management attitudes toward labor during the next two decades. Because of their adherence to old-style worker control, Foster, Manns, and other Morrell supervisors kept the company's excursions into New Era welfare capitalism from changing power relationships or instilling cooperative attitudes.[16]

The Plant Council

In October 1922, to take advantage of the situation that the lost strike created and to follow the lead of the major packers, including Armour, Swift, Cudahy, and Wilson, Morrell introduced its own employee representation plan: the plant council. At the same time, employers were adopting such plans nationwide. Their number had grown from 225 plans covering 500,000 workers in 1919 to 725 plans affecting over 700,000 workers in 1922. This trend reached a peak in 1926 when over 800 plans covered about 1,500,000 employees. Also during the early 1920s, Morrell established personnel and employment departments, a foremen's club, and various other financial and social welfare programs. A group life insurance plan would supplement the already existing Mutual Aid Association, and Morrell offered a vacation plan and the Morrell Credit Union. Among the more socially oriented offerings established were athletic leagues, a company journal (*Morrell Magazine*), company picnics, and the Morrell Male Chorus. Morrell hoped that these programs would forge new ties between employees and the company and thus keep out independent union activity.[17]

Management modeled the plant council on the unicameral Rockefeller (or Colorado) plan which the Colorado Fuel and Iron Company introduced in October 1915. At Morrell it provided for a monthly meeting between equal numbers, usually eleven each, of plant and management representatives. A chairman and secretary from management conducted the meetings, and employees elected plant representatives in either March or September. Each of the plant's divisions, approximately equal in numbers of employees, chose a representative to serve a one-year term. The chairmen would then appoint the elected representatives to serve on one of six standing committees: rules, sanitation, athletics, safety, hours and wages, or grievance. Employees with questions or problems for the plant council were supposed to submit them to their representatives, who would then bring them up at the council meetings. Management could also submit questions and reports. This was "industrial democracy."[18]

The actions of the plant council, however, could not infringe upon management's right to control company properties or to direct the workforce through hiring, transferring, or firing. Its actions could not extend beyond recommendations. These, when passed by a two-thirds majority, were to go to the plant superintendent who could either implement them or refer them to the company president, who also could either implement them or refer them back to the council for reconsideration. An employee, moreover, could file a grievance with the plant council only after conferences with his foreman, the superintendent of his department, and the plant superintendent. An employee could consult the employment supervisor at any time, but often such a consultation was unhelpful. Only after the plant council's consideration could employees appeal their grievances to higher company officials.[19]

Clearly, in the Morrell case, the label "industrial democracy" was a misnomer. Management never intended the council to settle grievances or pass recommendations itself, and it never served as an effective means of labor-management bargaining as Swift's packing plants or the Buckeye Steel Castings Company plant in Columbus, Ohio, came close to achieving. As historian Daniel Nelson has argued, the extent of industrial democracy in the many company unions of the period varied greatly. The Morrell case, however, casts doubt on his view that the longer such unions existed the more liable they were to achieve a degree of democracy. This plant showed that one company union could persist without "innovative plant management and . . . progressive personnel practices."[20]

More applicable to the situation at Morrell is Herbert Feis's characterization of the company union meetings at the Cincinnati, Ohio, plant of Procter and Gamble. There, Feis claimed, the topics of discussion were generally "fix a stairway, arrange for train services, stop leaky roofs, carry off fumes, [and] arrange a summer outing." At Morrell's the most consistently discussed matter of business was the confirmation of vacations, which the strict rules governing vacation allowances necessitated. In addition, meetings regularly interpreted rules regarding Morrell athletic teams and scheduled athletic events. Topics of discussion such as who would play on the Morrell baseball teams, and the towel distribution system, were often the chief items considered, since addressing issues of larger importance was often futile.[21]

According to the *Employee Handbook*, wages and hours were legitimate areas for council concern, and on occasion issues relating to them did come before the council. In no case, however, did they change as a result of council action, and in no respect did the council ever serve as a bargaining agent on such matters. Meetings held in March 1927, April 1928, July 1930, and June 1934, which considered wage readjustments and changes in the plant's workweek, resulted in council recommendations to implement upward adjustments. When management considered the suggestions, it rejected them. Nonetheless, management decreased guaranteed hours and wages in 1931 and 1932, without any kind of council consultation. A major weakness of the Morrell plant council system, then, was management's prerogative to disregard the council's directives.[22]

Another primary weakness of the plant council was its inability to settle employee problems or grievances until after their presentation to the foremen. In various instances where workers complained about the plant environment or mistreatment by foremen, the council refused to consider the grievance unless the complainant had first brought it to the foremen's attention. In this respect the council reinforced traditional methods of handling grievances and traditional work roles. Under these circumstances the workers could expect very little satisfaction and probably some chastisement for complaining. Virgil Bankson said: "You might as well not tell them you got a problem because they'd do nothing for you. It was a big joke, this plant council." Indeed, Art Bankson laughingly recalled that many of the workers chided the representatives about the "ice cream and cake" served to them at the meetings. Gust Hallgren, a foreman in the curing department during the twenties and thirties and a management representative at some of the meetings, when asked about the council, could only smile and concede that it "didn't work."[23]

Employment and Personnel Departments

Initiated at the same time as the plant council were the employment and personnel departments, which together supervised the group life insurance plan, Mutual Aid Association, vacation plan, athletic programs, and events such as the company picnics. These departments, however, did not assume the foremen's and superintendents' traditional power over hiring and firing. Their first director, Nelson G. Rupp, was not a professional personnel specialist of the stature that some New Era companies employed. Morrell had hired him six months earlier as a salesman and had given him his new position because he had a high school coaching background and a short term as personnel director of the DeVilbus Company of Toledo, Ohio. Art Bankson recalled that men seeking jobs usually lined up in front of an employment office in the general office building that had a staff of two men and a "lady secretary." These three people "didn't do anything" to select workers. Plant superintendent Ernest Manns came out of the building every morning and chose the men he wanted, or, as in Bankson's case, beef department superintendent Art Woodman hired him after a personal appeal that Bankson's brother Virgil made for him. Art Bankson also remembered that, on occasion, foremen and superintendents acted as recruiters, and even called discharged or retired butchers on the telephone to offer them temporary employment. Morrell was apparently among the companies that Daniel Nelson describes as having low degrees of commitment to personnel work, and it was clearly among those that historian Sanford Jacoby has identified as leaving the traditional powers of foremen and factory superintendents largely intact.[24]

The power over transfers, clearly stipulated as a managerial prerogative in the *Employee Handbook*, also remained with foremen and superintendents. They continued to exercise it in an arbitrary fashion with little regard for either personnel science or workers' feelings about seniority and job rights. Alfred Crow, Donald Jones, and Virgil Bankson recalled that workers had to do whatever bosses told them, especially during the depression, when management prodded them with the threat that "three or four hundred men . . . [are] out in line ready to take your place." Virgil Bankson felt arbitrarily switched from one department to another and expressed his resentment by walking out on his job when the company promoted ahead of him a man who had worked there less time than Bankson. "I hoped to get a job driving a city delivery truck," he reminisced, "but they pulled another guy out of a department and transferred him to do it." The foremen could and did play favorites. Their influence in discharging workers, although the implementation of the plant council curtailed it somewhat, remained more important than anyone else's. Paul Bissell said, "If a foreman didn't like the color of your eyes you'd be out." Foremen also engaged in harassment, including sexual harassment. Workers resented unreasonable enforcement of the system of tickets and tags that regulated rest room use and the arbitrary measures taken to prevent "cheating" the company out of working time.[25]

In March 1925, Morrell also established a foremen's club, which was one way the company gave the old foremen system a modern and progressive veneer. It became an agency for fostering comradeship and "right thinking" among foremen and for instructing them in techniques to gain greater efficiency and productivity from the workforce. In addition, the club seemed to be a substitute for a centralized planning or engineering department. The Ottumwa plant did not initiate other more "scientific" management schemes, such as time studies, until the 1940s when it did establish an industrial engineering department. Under the club's sponsorship, some men attended courses on foremanship that the Iowa State College Engineering Extension Service offered. At one of the earliest foremen's club meetings, Ernest Manns hypocritically recommended that foremen be "diplomats who get results without the bluster and profanity of other days." These efforts did not change what Sanford Jacoby has called the "drive" methods of foremanship, since foremen continued to rely upon toughness and fear to ensure workers' proper behavior. Many foremen had worked their ways up through the ranks when profanity and intimidation were the accepted methods of ensuring worker effectiveness. Not surprisingly, such men had little sympathy with "scientific" personnel work that challenged both practical wisdom and the validity of their careers. Traditional foremanship caused many of Morrell's smoldering dissatisfactions that surfaced in the unionization drive of the 1930s.[26]

Other Benefit Programs

Morrell's management also implemented welfare capitalist measures in the form of new or expanded benefit programs, including a revised version of the old Mutual Aid Association. This, prior to 1925, had deducted ten cents from each participating employee's weekly paycheck and used the money to provide weekly disability benefits of five dollars or less. Under the new plan, employees earning more than 32.5 cents per hour paid 15 cents per week, while those earning less paid 10 cents. Such proceeds made possible a maximum disability benefit of $1.50 per day for those in the first category and $1.00 per day for those in the second (in each case the employee could receive payments for no more than thirteen weeks). Also available was a death benefit provision applicable to workers who had at least five years of service. It provided payments of $500 for those in the higher-earning bracket and $333.33 for those in the lower one. The amounts paid were not inconsequential and the program was probably important for the one-half to two-thirds of the workforce that participated. The employees themselves, however, were still the only source of funding; the company's role was purely administrative, which may account for the lack of complete employee participation in the program.[27]

The company initiated and funded the group life insurance plan in 1924 and made it available to all employees who had been on the payroll for at least one year. Its minimum death benefit was $500 after the first year, which would increase by $100 increments for each additional year at Morrell to a top figure of $2,000 after fifteen years. In addition, the insurance plan included a total disability clause under which the worker could also receive the full amount accrued. The company clearly intended the plan to induce employees to stay, and together with the Mutual Aid Association fund, it provided family assistance when Morrell employees died or became permanently disabled, injured, or ill. The plant had no pension plan, however, until January 1941.[28]

Judging by the amount of space allotted to it in *Morrell Magazine* and the amount of time devoted to it in plant council meetings, the vacation plan was the most celebrated of the new Morrell programs. Management announced it on September 4, 1923, and made it apply to all employees who had been working since January 1 of that year. Like the life insurance plan, management clearly directed it toward reducing labor turnover rates. "Employees who can be depended upon to be in their places," *Morrell Magazine* announced, "are of much more value to John Morrell and Co., and so are given a week's vacation with pay for each year of uninterrupted service." The company based pay for this week of vacation on a usual forty-eight-hour workweek for the hourly-wage employees or, for piece workers, on the average weekly earnings for the four weeks immediately preceding the vacation. Employees had to take their vacations within twelve months of earning them and at a time convenient for the company. Until August 1928 it was impossible for an employee to keep working and take an added week's pay in lieu of vacation. A matter of great concern about the vacation plan was the amount of time that an employee could miss without ruining an uninterrupted service record. The rules limited this to no more than six hours during the year, which meant that an employee could not miss a full working day.[29]

Needless to say, most employees had difficulty meeting these requirements. In 1925, for example, only 428 of a total of 2,485 employees earned a week of vacation, and in the plan's first three years only 34 employees earned three consecutive vacations. Subsequently, 28 received vacations for four consecutive years, 18 for five consecutive years, 11 for six consecutive years, 9 for seven consecutive years, 6 for eight years, 5 for ten years, and 4 for twelve years. One of the remaining 4, Joseph Hanrahan, had been the plant tour guide. As these figures make apparent, the vacation plan was a benefit that reached only a small number of workers.

Another much more successful financial program came somewhat late in Morrell's years of welfare capitalism. Initiated in 1931, the Morrell Credit Union had 496 members by 1934. In 1935 its membership almost doubled (987), and by the end of the decade 1,344 Morrell employees had joined it. During the depression, credit may have held more attraction than even vacations did.[30]

In addition to the Mutual Aid Association, group life insurance plan, vacation plan, and credit union, John Morrell and Company introduced four social welfare programs. It sponsored athletic teams that were particularly popular, and as early as 1922 employees could participate in baseball and basketball leagues. The company also published its own monthly organ, *Morrell Magazine*, beginning in July 1924 and mailed it free to all workers. It provided some entertaining and educational material on topics such as American cities and vacation spots but primarily attempted to instill cooperative and industrious work habits. In 1925, Morrell revived the company picnic of the prewar years. Though enthusiastic at first, employees' interest declined when management scheduled the picnics on working days and did not reimburse employees for the missed day as it had done before World War I. In 1928, 1929, and 1930 there were no picnics, and when held again in 1931, they occurred after working hours. Finally, the Morrell Male Chorus formed in October 1930, and management supported it as part of public relations. The chorus made numerous appearances in and out of the state. Chorus members received time off with pay and meal money for concerts. Even so, the chorus drew its members chiefly from management and consequently had limited employee participation. Morrell officials used each of these organizations to promote the company's image.[31]

The Failure of Morrell's Welfare Capitalism

Morrell may have hoped that these welfare programs would help unite the plant into one big "family." More likely, Morrell seems to have adopted programs that would cost them little money yet provide positive publicity. Some of the new measures, like life insurance and the credit union, met genuine worker needs. Yet most of Morrell's welfare capitalism was aimed at controlling workers' behavior both on and off the job in a way deemed most beneficial to the company. The plant council was never meant to function as an equal partner or bargainer with management, and traditional foremanship continued. The reforms attempted in these areas did little to create the mutual respect and sense of fairness that might have fostered stable industrial relations. Most of the company's financial and social welfare activities were marginal in effect; they did not touch the most fundamental concerns of aggrieved workers. Essentially, workers wanted to increase their pay, secure more regular employment, better their working conditions, and most important, increase their control in plant affairs.

Most significant about the welfare capitalism of John Morrell in Ottumwa was that it coincided with, and perhaps even increased, workers' expectations for improvements in their lives. By the 1920s, many Morrell workers were at least second-generation company employees; they looked to Morrell not only for employment but for the social and financial benefits the company had long provided the city's working class. Yet during the twenties and thirties Morrell plant employees had the reputation of being the "poorest people in town." Clarence Orman, who had started work in the smoked meat department in

1926, remembered that, with the onset of the Great Depression, "guys delivering groceries" made more money than he did. Virgil Bankson recalled that during the same period many people, including Bankson and his wife, lived in one-room shacks. Many employees had gone to work as soon as they finished grade school, and had taken jobs that, for the most part, only required physical strength and willingness to work hard.[32]

E. L. Thorndike's comparative study of 144 American cities with between 20,000 and 30,000 population in 1930 confirmed these observations about Ottumwa packing workers' relative poverty. His indices highlight the city's poor standing nationwide and statewide in several categories, including homes valued under $1,500, children working outside the home, and average yearly factory workers' incomes. Fully 27 percent of Ottumwa's housing fell below his poverty threshold, a rate more than twice as high as the proportion for other Iowa industrial towns such as Burlington, Clinton, Fort Dodge, and Mason City. As a state low-income housing survey of Ottumwa demonstrated in 1936, much of this substandard housing was concentrated in three primary areas where Morrell employees lived, including the immediate packing neighborhoods in Wards One and Two, the near south side of Ward Five, and the so-called "Central Addition," a neighborhood carved out of land reclaimed from the Des Moines River in the center of the city. Three percent of Ottumwa's boys under sixteen worked outside their homes, primarily at Morrell. This percentage was higher than any comparably-sized Iowa community except Clinton. Ottumwa's factory workers earned the lowest average yearly income ($1,040) of any of the Iowa communities surveyed by Thorndike. Their incomes paled especially when compared to those of Ottumwa's white-collar employees, who had some of the highest incomes. People involved in wholesale trade, for instance, earned $1,410 per year and ranked first in the state in this category.[33]

Morrell's wage cuts of 1931 and 1932 aggravated workers' sense of impoverishment. After the cuts, for example, Virgil Bankson was making only $10.40 per week while Earl Paxson, a department sales manager, was still earning $72 per week (down from $80). Wage cuts were not the whole story, however. Even in the 1920s many of the plant's jobs paid very low wages; indeed, apparently few workers then earned even 40 cents per hour, which had been the minimum wage for unskilled laborers before the 1921 strike. In 1923, for example, Kenneth Ellis hired on as an "off-bearer" at 20 cents per hour; two years later Virgil Bankson made 32 cents an hour in the smoked meat department; and in 1929 Gilbert Baker made 35 cents in the same department. Ira Bartholow, who started at the plant during World War I, recalled that he received only 37.5 cents per hour in 1924 for the arduous task of "beef lugging"—hooking sides of beef, which sometimes weighed close to a quarter of a ton, on racks in the meat cooler. Still lower were the wages paid to male teenagers, some of whom did the same work as adults. Morrell's management did not adhere to the "doctrine of high wages" that for some companies, if historian David Brody is correct, was the essential element of success. Brody's argument that welfare capitalism failed primarily because of the depression's decline in workers' wages does not explain why welfare capitalism failed at Morrell. The company did not pay high wages to its plant employees before the depression.[34]

Although a less severe problem compared to the prewar period, seasonal variations in employment affected many workers through most of the 1920s. Employees often faced layoffs for part of the year since employment was closely tied to the peak hog-killing months of September to January. Many kill and cut department employees were laid off in the spring and summer without any kind of income from Morrell. They then had to look for part-time jobs, such as helping farmers with planting and harvests. Even during peak seasons, as Alfred Crow pointed out, kill department employees often had to compete with "boomer" butchers who traveled from packinghouse to packinghouse "chasing the best jobs." Seasonal layoffs became less severe at Morrell beginning in 1928 when total slaughtering at the Ottumwa plant reached new highs that stayed more constant year-round through the mid-1930s.[35]

Workers became embittered over work conditions, especially when Morrell failed to heed their appeals for improvements. Don Jones recalled that pleas to install fans in the hog kill, for example, were ignored, although the company was willing to sell sponges to the men as an alternative. Moreover, workers had to buy all of their knives, tools, and work clothes from the company. In 1932, the plant council dismissed an appeal to change this rule; rather than "take up the time of the council," it referred the request to the foreman of the department. Workers in the kill departments also faced the danger of jobs such as "shackling," attaching a chain to a hog's leg in order to hoist it onto the conveyor and "sticking," cutting a hog's throat so the blood could drain out while it hung suspended from the conveyor. To perform such tasks, a worker often had to literally battle the animals until they were dead, risking accidental stabbing. Yet management took little of this danger into account as it pressured workers for speed and productivity. For men of skill and pride such situations offered clear evidence of company power and worker helplessness. For kill department employees especially, the improvement of working conditions required actions that would divest them from the company's hegemony.[36]

Although most jobs in a packing plant did not take long to learn, some of the operations in the beef-kill and hog-kill departments required training and some degree of skill. Their practitioners took great pride in their work. The floorsmen in the beef-kill department, for example, had to skin a specified number of cattle per hour. In practice they were the leaders of the beef kill, since their efforts determined the pace of the other operations in the department. To a certain extent, the kill departments also set the pace for the entire plant's operations. Therefore, the people in these departments had to bear the full brunt of the foremen's rantings, ravings, and whistlings to keep up the pace of their work.[37]

By the Great Depression, workers' sense of shared dissatisfaction with their material conditions and low status in the community was directed increasingly against the Foster family and Morrell managerial officials in general. The "foreign" background of the Fosters and many company officials reinforced these sentiments and helped focus workers' resentments. Workers like Paul Bissell and Virgil Bankson conveyed an intense hostility toward the Foster family because of their English accents and perceived haughtiness. The lack of personal contact T. D. Foster's sons had with workers made these feelings all the worse.

In fact, oral history testimony regarding the Fosters' "Englishness" points out the growing gulf between managers and workers. Ralph Ransom, who eventually became George M. Foster's personal assistant and a corporate engineer, reveled in his close association with the Fosters' refinement and the scholarly aspirations of T. H. Foster. Many who assumed managerial positions saw the Fosters' English ways as endearing and signs of gentlemanly demeanor and concern. Most plant workers and even some white-collar employees, steeped in the rural cultures of Iowa, Illinois, and Missouri, viewed the Fosters with suspicion and as patronizing. Donald Schaub, an employee in the plant laboratory, said the Fosters and their English associates saw themselves as better than non-English supervisory personnel. In particular, it irritated Schaub that the Fosters refused to park their cars in the same lot as other white-collar workers. Instead, the Fosters had their own private garages on company property. Earl Paxson, who served as T. H. Foster's personal secretary, scornfully referred to the Foster family as "the rich Englishmen." Virgil Bankson recalled that the Fosters deeply offended company workers when, in 1932, following the hysteria surrounding the Lindbergh kidnapping case, the Fosters posted guards around the perimeter of their houses on the Bluff, an area of architect-designed homes primarily for the Foster family and overlooking the packing neighborhood.[38]

The welfare capitalist measures that John Morrell and Company sponsored from 1922 to 1937 failed to meet the needs of its employees, especially those in the kill departments. Basically, the workers wanted some respect and influence in decisions that affected plant affairs. This is not what they received. The plant council could not deal with grievances directly, nor could it act as a collective bargaining agent for the plant employees. It could only consider minor aspects of the workers' welfare. The personnel and employment departments did not deprive foremen of their traditional power, and the foremen's club neither modernized the exercise of foremanship nor ended its abuses. Indeed, Morrell apparently never intended to make such changes. Although some of the other programs were beneficial, for example, the group life insurance plan and the Morrell Credit Union, they were generally too limited or too peripheral to have much impact on workers' situations. It is not surprising that under the changed circumstances of the Great Depression, workers were ready to organize and reject management domination. Morrell workers wanted greater pay, better working conditions, more control over their jobs, a seniority system, job rights, and restrictions on indiscriminate transfers. Ultimately, such issues sparked Virgil and Art Bankson, Donald Jones, Paul Bissell, and others in the beef-kill and hog-kill departments to seek an organization independent of company control or influence. As Virgil Bankson recalled, the men's basic need expressed by establishing a union was "to have a voice in what you're doing." In the 1930s, the great industrial movement that swept through meatpacking and other industries set the stage for Morrell workers to obtain the "voice" and control they were seeking.[39]

4

BUILDING A "LIVE, WIDE AWAKE UNION": THE CREATION OF MILITANT UNIONISM, 1933–1945

Nothing in Morrell-Ottumwa's history before the 1930s could have predicted the success workers there would have in building a militant union. Before the 1930s, unionism had been episodic at best. A few workers had attempted to form an AMCBW union in 1901, which quickly faded into oblivion. Morrell's decision to abide by the Alschuler agreement sparked workers' efforts in creating a more successful AMCBW union between 1917 and 1921. Yet when Morrell rejected the Alschuler agreement and then smashed the union with the help of Iowa's national guard, this union-building effort ended abruptly. In the failed strike's aftermath, Morrell's welfare capitalism attempted to mold a more compliant workforce in the 1920s and early 1930s, but ultimately failed. It did so in part because of limitations in the company's programs themselves, but more importantly because of workers' growing solidarity. Built on common concerns and resentments as well as demographic and cultural affinities, Morrell workers' solidarity would result in the creation of one of the most dynamic CIO union movements in the meatpacking industry.

In the early 1930s, New Deal labor legislation, including Section 7(a) of the National Industrial Recovery Act (NIRA) and, especially, the National Labor

Relations (or Wagner) Act, inspired workers to attempt to revive unionism in the packing industry in urban and rural locations in the Midwest. As they searched for institutional support, advocates for labor organizing typically looked unfavorably at the AMCBW. Because of its poor reputation stemming from the failed 1921–1922 strikes and its low profile during the 1920s and early 1930s, workers interested in union formation typically scorned the older union. Rejection of the Amalgamated helped to lay the groundwork for acceptance of the Committee, later Congress, of Industrial Organizations (CIO), which broke from the AFL when that body failed to satisfy many union leaders' cries for an aggressive strategy for industrial unionism. Arguably more important than either of these two factors was the willingness of militants, including left-leaning groups such as union leaders in Austin, Minnesota, as well as "straight" trade unionists, as in the case of union leaders in Cedar Rapids, Iowa, to risk company reprisals for the sake of union building. In turn, these militant union leaders drew their support from rank and filers who would no longer accept mistreatment and powerlessness in their places of work. Packing workers in the rural Midwest, drawn especially into the Austin or Cedar Rapids union-building "orbits" between 1933 and 1937, then turned to the CIO because of its success in auto and steel. The result was the formation of the CIO's Packinghouse Workers Organizing Committee (PWOC) on October 27, 1937. A vast array of both urban and rural PWOC locals sprang up between 1937 and October 1943, when the PWOC was transformed into the United Packinghouse Workers of America (UPWA), the CIO's independent, international union for packinghouse and stockyard workers.[1]

By the early 1930s, Ottumwa's packing workers shared a cohesive class and cultural identity. In addition to a collective neighborhood, cultural, religious, and associational identity, their sense of community had also been shaped by a shared sense of grievance about their position in the city relative to its elites. Shared bonds of identity and neighborhood ties among Ottumwa's packing workers had become increasingly evident before World War I, and from the late nineteenth century through the Great Depression roughly one-half to two-thirds of Morrell's workforce resided in the immediate environs of the plant in Ottumwa's east end.

Especially during the 1920s and early 1930s, broader cultural alliances solidified the packing workers' sense of a shared identity. By 1935 almost all the city's Morrell workers were at least second-generation Ottumwans or native-born Americans of English, Swedish, or German descent who had migrated from nearby towns and rural areas of south-central Iowa. During World War I and especially through the 1920s, a significant portion of the rural population of south-central Iowa migrated to Ottumwa and other cities of the region. Between 1920 and 1930, while the counties of Wayne, Lucas, Marion, Mahaska,

Monroe, Appanoose, Davis, Wapello, Keokuk, Jefferson, and Van Buren surrounding Ottumwa in south-central Iowa lost 12 percent of their population, Ottumwa grew by 22 percent. Many Morrell workers had grown up in farming families or had participated in the small-scale coal-mining industry that dotted the region. United Mine Workers of America District 13's headquarters was just twenty-five miles west of Ottumwa in Albia. With nearly 20,000 members during the early 1920s, many of whom worked in both the mines and Morrell during that decade before moving permanently to Morrell after the mines shut down during the depression, the UMWA provided union "schooling" for many meatpacking workers. Donald Harris, CIO-PWOC's first national director, later recalled that "it was the old United Mine Workers, or it was their kids whom they had brought up in a union family and taught the value of trade unionism, [that] had imbedded [unionism] in their minds and souls, if you will." Many future packing union activists, including many involved at Morrell-Ottumwa, got their first taste of unionism in the coal mines of south-central Iowa.[2]

Like residents of Ottumwa and surrounding Wapello County, Morrell's workers were mostly Protestants, particularly Methodists, Disciples of Christ, Lutherans, Presbyterians, and Northern Baptists, with a substantial minority of Catholics. Although census records on religious affiliation indicate that in both 1926 and 1936 residents of Wapello County were about one-quarter Methodist, one-fifth Catholic, and about two-fifths Disciples of Christ, Baptist, Lutheran, and Presbyterian, these official statistics likely undercounted the large numbers of Morrell workers who were fundamentalist Protestants. Such workers attended churches that espoused an evangelical and "ecstatic" Christian message of spiritual conversion. Nine new churches were established in Ottumwa between 1922 and 1939: the Fundamentalist Baptist Church, Community Christian Church, Chapel of the Church of God, Pentecostal Church of God, Church of the Nazarene, North Church of the Nazarene, Central Addition Pentecostal Church, First Church of the Open Bible, and Harding Park Open Bible Church. Each was situated in predominantly blue-collar sections of Ottumwa, with the Nazarene churches belonging to the category of "perfectionist" and holiness splinters from Methodism. The prominence of the Methodist Church in Iowa in the 1930s, second only in total membership to Catholics, and the concentration of blue-collar workers in Ottumwa, those most often converted to "ecstatic" Protestantism, helps to explain the appeal of such churches. Although based on a limited sample, it appears that perhaps 60 percent of Morrell workers in 1935 attended some type of fundamentalist church.[3]

Only a handful of Ottumwa's fraternal organizations catered to workers, but increasing numbers socialized together in the city's Eagles, Moose, and

Odd Fellows lodges. The bulk of these workers continued to live in the immediate packing neighborhood surrounding the plant. Perhaps more important in developing the social fabric among men in the packing community was the informal association provided in the many bars along East Main Street, the main commercial thoroughfare near the packing district, and along Church Street, the city's main south side business street. About half of the city's taverns listed in the 1939 McCoy's *Ottumwa City Directory* were situated in these two sections of the city. Ottumwa's packing district residents were also increasingly bound during the 1930s by the bonds of poverty despite low levels of unemployment among its residents.[4]

Packing workers were also united in a painful awareness of the economic gulf that separated them from the Morrell officials who had long dominated the city's elite. Workers shared a collective sense of disdain for the lifestyles and the perceived haughtiness of their supervisors, particularly the Foster family and other plant executives referred to by workers as "the rich Englishmen." Although owing in part to animosities toward the foreign-born executives living in the city, also crucial were the strains resulting from the company's labor relations policies after 1921. The intervention of Iowa National Guard troops in the violent strike of late 1921 effectively broke the AMCBW local formed in 1918. Following that strike, Morrell introduced welfare capitalist measures, providing a thin veneer of managerial reform while actually allowing for harsher methods of worker control undergirded by fear and profanity. Morrell president Thomas H. Foster and plant superintendent Ernest Manns assumed greater power during the plant's wartime union period and after the war set the tone for the new era of labor relations at the plant. Although creating a façade of managerial reform, Foster and Manns allowed plant foremen and superintendents greater autonomy to set standards and production methods in their individual departments. By the mid-1930s, each plant department was run semiautonomously by the plant's largely English-born supervisory staff. The across-the-board wage cuts of 1931 and 1932 did little to help labor relations as well.

Each of these factors contributed to a growing sense of solidarity among Morrell workers during the 1930s. Although divisions persisted among workers, the rapidity with which Morrell employees jumped on the union bandwagon during the mid-1930s owes a great deal to workers' collective sense of shared identity and concerns. More so than in most other packing plants, with the exception of Chicago, Austin, and Cedar Rapids, Ottumwa's workers took the lead in not only union organizing but also in pursuing CIO affiliation and collective bargaining. These pursuits were derived from the particular plant and community concerns at Morrell-Ottumwa. Although stemming in part from their shared identity and sense of grievance, the local's militancy can be pinpointed to the marked sense of injustice and desire for rapid changes among a core of mostly kill and cut department employees. After winning certification for their CIO local, these hard-core activists enforced solidarity among workers. This became especially true following the 1939 strike and during the World War II period when new workers entered the plant in greater numbers. The local's militancy also remained thoroughly grounded in this local context through the end of the war. Even with the formation of a new international union among CIO packinghouse workers during the war, the militants leading the local were most concerned with reshaping their community's power structure. Only with the emergence of a new generation of local union leaders after the war was the particularly local focus of this militancy transformed into a more genuine sense of shared concerns with other packing and CIO union members.[5]

Establishing a CIO Local Union

The solidarity resulting from the shared culture of the packing community, combined with the impetus to unionization provided by the NIRA, infused the union movement that got under way at the Morrell plant in 1933. Workers initially flocked into a revamped AMCBW Local 236, the local that had existed at the plant between 1918 and 1921. At the first mass meeting of the revived local held on August 18, 1933, 600 employees turned out to hear how the NIRA and the Amalgamated might help them. A meeting on September 22 attracted about 900 plant workers, roughly 40 percent of Morrell-Ottumwa's blue-collar workforce. The Amalgamated's reputation among Ottumwa's plant workers was not as tarnished as it was in other midwestern packing cities. As far as Ottumwa workers were concerned it was the state militia that had broken the union in 1921. Clearly, the large turnouts in 1933 indicated the workers' readiness to participate in an independent trade union movement.[6]

Over the next four years, however, support for the Amalgamated eroded among the city's packing workers. As opposed to some midwestern cities, Ottumwa did not have a powerful AFL central labor union that could support the Amalgamated's activities at Morrell. Because of Ottumwa's largely unskilled and semiskilled employment structure, dominated by Morrell, the city's AFL central union impacted relatively few blue-collar workers other than a handful of building trades unionists, some railroad brotherhood members, and a few UMWA unionists in the area. Furthermore, except for Dain Manufacturing Company, a farm implement maker, no other firm besides Morrell employed more than 100 persons. Instead of turning to the city's minuscule AFL central union, Amalgamated Local 236 early on looked to Amalgamated Local 206 at the Wilson plant in Cedar Rapids, Iowa, for assistance. When Local 206 broke from the Amalgamated in January 1935 to form the Mid-west Union of All

Packing House Workers (MUAPHW), Ottumwa's Amalgamated local drifted alone for the next year and a half.[7]

Local 236's president, Henry F. Hoover, charted a conservative course for the AMCBW local during the mid-1930s. Although attractive early on because of his coal-mining background — like many others in the plant, he dug coal during slack packing periods — and his experience working in a bona fide industrial union, the United Mine Workers, his leadership failed to excite many workers who initially expressed interest in the local. Elected president in 1933, Hoover was a longtime Morrell mechanical department employee. Unlike the Cedar Rapids Amalgamated local that aggressively attempted to secure written contracts from Wilson in 1934, Ottumwa's Amalgamated local was satisfied with oral understandings on a few specific demands, the first of which they apparently received in May 1934. Such verbal agreements were not satisfactory to other activists in the plant. Hoover also squelched a proposed strike supporting Amalgamated Local 304's protests at the Morrell plant in Sioux Falls, South Dakota. The strike there, marked by a nationwide Amalgamated-led boycott of Morrell products and periodic episodes between strikebreakers and strikers, lasted from July 1935 to March 1937. Another factor in many workers' dissatisfaction with the Amalgamated was the desire to eradicate the AFL group's insistence on rigid skill classifications. In the beef kill, for instance, Virgil and Art Bankson, younger men who were hired by Morrell in 1930 and 1933 respectively, claimed that the older core of skilled beef-kill employees were Amalgamated members who would not let younger men learn their trades, particularly the floorsmen position. Floorsmen removed the hide from the beef carcass. Moreover, once the Cedar Rapids local became an independent union, and the Independent Union of All Workers (IUAW), based at the Hormel plant in Austin, Minnesota, became active, many Ottumwa activists were drawn to these union movements. Ultimately both the Cedar Rapids and Austin movements would be drawn into the fledgling CIO. By the late 1930s, many of Local 236's early officers, including Sam Kelso and Lawrence Miner, had become strong CIO supporters. Miner would also serve as the first editor of the early Ottumwa CIO packinghouse worker paper, the *Organizer*.[8]

Beginning in 1936, Ottumwa packing workers interested in unionism turned their attention to the MUAPHW and IUAW. Founded by the ambitious, aggressive, and strongly anticommunist Wilson–Cedar Rapids packinghouse leader, Lewis Clark, the MUAPHW attempted to revive packinghouse unionism throughout the Midwest beginning in early 1935. However, after meeting him during his first visit to Morrell-Ottumwa in October 1936, many later CIO activists among Ottumwa's workers were not impressed. Virgil Bankson, for instance, recalled that Clark and a "slick lawyer" placed more emphasis on making sure Ottumwa workers signed an agreement promising they would reimburse Cedar Rapids for their organizing expenses, instead of emphasizing actual organizing strategies. The "slick lawyer" was probably Finley Bell, a "labor consultant" identified by the IUAW's newpaper, the *Unionist*, as offering packing workers his services in setting up agreements with companies if workers paid him five cents per month along with a twenty-dollar per diem for all meetings held outside Chicago. A group of Sioux City packinghouse workers apparently signed such an agreement with him in December 1936.[9]

Most workers looking for an industrial union eager to organize turned instead to the IUAW in spring 1937. Founded in Austin in July 1933 by former Industrial Workers of the World (IWW) member Frank Ellis, the IUAW was an aggressive industrial union that organized Hormel workers as well as workers in other industries in Austin and other communities in Minnesota, Iowa, and South Dakota. The IUAW had attempted to join forces with the MUAPHW in 1936, but its efforts stalled over issues of union autonomy and jurisdictional rights; the main sticking point was that the IUAW organized all industrial workers, described by historian Peter Rachleff as horizontal community unionism, while the MUAPHW only sought packinghouse union members. In fact, the American Federation of Labor (AFL) central labor union in Cedar Rapids actively discouraged the MUAPHW from joining forces with the IUAW. Austin was much more like Ottumwa in that its AFL central union was weak and ineffective.[10]

The IUAW's success in organizing affiliates in Austin and Albert Lea as well as several southern Minnesota, South Dakota, and northern Iowa cities, including Mitchell, Faribault, and Mason City, encouraged a group of disgruntled Amalgamated members in Ottumwa to ask the Austin group in March 1937 to meet with them about joining their union. At the first meeting, Austin organizers Joe Ollman and Ernie Jacob, both Hormel kill department employees, met with a small group of Morrell workers. After twenty-two men, including Virgil, Art, and Eugene Bankson, paid initiation fees and dues for April, the Morrell workers received a charter from the IUAW. The IUAW had by this time met with representatives of the CIO in Chicago. IUAW representatives assured their affiliates that the CIO was a democratic organization like their group yet was also national in scope. An issue of the *Unionist* emphasized this point by proclaiming that "if and when we affiliate with the CIO we are not giving up anything we have won and there will be nothing to hinder us from winning even more." By May, the prospect of a "live, wide awake union" had inspired five hundred workers at Morrell-Ottumwa to join the IUAW in anticipation of joining the CIO movement.[11]

On May 14, 1937, the CIO chartered the Ottumwa local just four days after it had applied for membership and, ironically, before the CIO granted either the Cedar Rapids or Austin groups charters. In fact, United Packing House

Workers Local Industrial Union No. 32 of Ottumwa was the first CIO charter granted to a packinghouse workforce in the United States. Before the formation of the Packinghouse Workers Organizing Committee of the CIO in October 1937, any charter granted to an industrial workforce was a "certificate of affiliation," a distinction that allowed IUAW-organized groups like those in Austin and Ottumwa to continue to pursue horizontal community organizing. In the next few months, new members flooded into the local, while the Amalgamated made a last-ditch effort to forestall the CIO's success as the prospect of a National Labor Relations Board (NLRB) certification election loomed larger during summer 1937.[12]

Morrell-Ottumwa's rank and file enthusiastically participated in union-building in 1937. They elected William "Bill" Fletcher as the first IUAW president. After gaining CIO affiliation, members then selected him as their first Local 32 president. Fletcher had worked periodically at the Morrell plant as a common laborer since 1924, and had been employed in the beef kill as a "knocker" and "shackler" before being elected president. Known as a "radical" and "hothead," Fletcher wanted quick and decisive gains for his fellow laborers. His union meetings were fiery affairs; he was known to storm out when decisions went against him. Yet his enthusiasm attracted workers in droves. Indeed, Lewis Clark enviously noted that the meeting he attended in Ottumwa on July 19, 1937, garnered a crowd ten times larger than any he had had in Cedar Rapids.[13]

The close-knit character of the packing community in Ottumwa facilitated the union-building process. By mid-June, grievance committees had been organized in eleven plant departments and the union had already stipulated how each grievance should be put in writing and reported to the local's recording secretary. Ten more departments had a grievance committee in place by the end of June and three more were added during July. Workers' close neighborhood ties made this rapid organization possible. Twenty-six of the thirty-four grievance committee members listed in the *Organizer*, the local's brand-new newspaper, in mid-June lived in the immediate packinghouse neighborhood (Wards One and Two). Two months later, nearly all the grievance committee members, totaling seventy, resided in the east end packing neighborhood or just across the river on the south side in Ward Five. Half lived in Ward One with just over a quarter in Ward Five. Reflecting the relatively low numbers of women working in the plant during the 1930s, just three of the seventy grievance representatives were women. Establishment of the grievance machinery effectively maintained discipline within the local by eliminating the settling of grievances through individual "deals" with the company. In fact, by mid-July the union reported that Morrell was no longer willing to listen to grievance reports from the local, was attempting to revive support for the company union, something it had officially dropped in early May, and was opposing the local's call for an NLRB certification election. Since reaching their "oral" understandings with the Amalgamated in 1934, which did nothing except reaffirm Morrell's long-standing tolerance of a small AMCBW membership among its skilled butchers, company officials in Ottumwa, like many industrialists across the United States, had clung to the hope that the Wagner Act would be found unconstitutional. Once the Supreme Court ruled in favor of the act, Morrell moved quickly to finally end its company union, long since moribund anyway, and began to meet with local union leaders affiliated with the CIO. Morrell's attorney, George F. Heindel, issued a "very carefully worded statement" in mid-June 1937 saying that employees "would be granted all the Wagner Act implied." At this point, the company was not as aggressively antiunion as Armour in Chicago, for instance, which hired thugs to beat and perhaps even try to kill union leaders, but Morrell did fire activists who identified themselves as CIO members. Morrell also seems to have offered support to the few workers in the plant who supported the Amalgamated.[14]

Even though they risked alienating their largest business neighbor, much of the small business community in the packing neighborhood, including saloon, restaurant, car dealership owners, and other retailers in the east end gave implicit support to the union's efforts by advertizing in the *Organizer*. Small businesses along Church Street, the main commercial thoroughfare for the predominantly working-class south side, did the same. Early union members recalled that organizational meetings were held in various "beer joints" in the packing neighborhood. The local's parade through the downtown in early June, "to show Ottumwa that a 'live-wire' CIO organization exists," consisted of "at least one hundred marchers," according to the less than supportive *Ottumwa Daily Courier*'s report, and had a decidedly revivalistic spirit, reflective of the packing neighborhood's religious temperament. Everett Boyer, a local evangelical minister and grievance representative in the hog-cut department, spoke at the rally after the march and gave several key speeches at other organizing rallies for the local.[15]

During summer 1937, Ottumwa's packing movement also embarked on a IUAW-style horizontal community union organizing effort. As a direct affiliate of the CIO, Local 32 solicited members from several local businesses. Packing workers led successful union-building drives at the Ottumwa Steam Laundry, Barker Ice Company, and Swift poultry plant, all of whose members joined Local 32. The local's executive board even offered to meet with the management of the laundry on behalf of its workers in their ongoing negotiations. Both reflecting and creating a new sense of democratic commitment, the *Organizer* called for women to join the union, and established a ladies' auxiliary to involve them in supporting the virtually all-male activity of organizing the local. Entertainment and social committees were established to raise funds and foster goodwill. In July, Local 32 issued a call for a music instructor who would be capable of leading a local union band or orchestra. Although there is no indication that any such music group was formed, it seems reasonable to assume that the local patterned this concept on the highly successful company-sponsored singing group, Morrell Male Chorus. The *Organizer* also included a column called "Tattler Tattles" that was not unlike the social news about workers included in the *Morrell Magazine*. From its beginning it seems the local attempted to create a new sense of loyalty to the union that would directly supersede company loyalties. It also did this by reassuring new members from the outset that strikes would be called only as a last resort and that they would not occur unless a democratic majority agreed to them.[16]

The local's sponsorship of a "Mammoth Picnic Celebration" on Sunday, August 15, was an important early attempt to gain broader community support for its efforts. Don Harris, a left-wing organizer with the Hosiery Workers out of Des Moines and soon to be appointed national director of the PWOC beginning in October, had provided organizational leadership for the local's union-building effort, and apparently sparked the idea of the picnic. Harris announced in late July that he had invited John L. Lewis, former Wisconsin Progressive governor Robert LaFollette, and current Farmer-Labor governor Elmer Benson of Minnesota to speak to the local. Within a few days, the list of invited speakers had expanded to include Governor Nelson Kraschel of Iowa, Van Bittner of the Steel Workers Organizing Committee (SWOC) and soon to be the PWOC's first chair, and Homer Martin of the United Auto Workers. The *Ottumwa Daily Courier*, in reporting on the planned picnic, noted that Local 32 not only "holds the oldest packing house charter in the CIO[, but] leaders here see the possibility of Ottumwa becoming [the] national headquarters for the packing house union." While none of these labor or political luminaries accepted their invitations, and the main speaker turned out to be Frank Wilson, president of nearby United Mine Workers District 13, the souvenir program for the event, sold for ten cents, listed an astounding array of social events for the day. Beginning at 9:30 A.M. and not ending until 7 P.M., "several hundred" workers socialized and celebrated with events like a women's shoe-kicking contest, a "fat" (over 200-pound) men's race, and a mind-reading act. The program also noted that in addition to President William Fletcher, Local 32's officers included Tom Hadden, first vice president, Carrie Martin, second vice president, Orval Champ, recording secretary, and Walter Walker, financial secretary.[17]

After the local filed for an NLRB certification election on June 17, 1937, the government agency met in Ottumwa on September 16–17, and finally established October 28, 1937, as the election date. During the intervening time,

Henry Hoover, still president of the Amalgamated local, attempted to disrupt the election while company officials confused workers about the meaning of the Wagner Act and fired anyone openly "advertising" for the CIO. Hoover openly opposed the certification election, seemingly in hopes of ingratiating himself and the small Amalgamated local with Morrell officials. Hoover attempted to reestablish the Amalgamated's use of verbal contracts, a practice the company recognized in 1933–1934. George M. Foster, plant vice president and brother of the plant president, claimed that management could comply with the Wagner Act by granting verbal rather than written contracts. To the CIO activists, however, this would open the way to the favoritism that had characterized preceding labor relations at the plant, which they wanted to remove forever. Before the certification election, management still threatened to fire anyone openly wearing a CIO union button in the plant. Kill-floor workers Paul Bissell and Elmer Cline both recalled wearing their buttons under their overalls for most of the preelection period. They continued to do so until all the union members in the hog kill decided to pin their buttons to their hats during one particular lunch period. After collectively displaying their buttons, the men dared the foremen to fire the whole gang. No one was fired.[18]

With solidarity underpinning the local's foundations, neither management's threats nor Amalgamated opposition deflected the CIO local's success. Neither did threats from individual foremen, such as the type leveled at Elmer Cline, a member of the hog-kill department, that "you better be careful who you vote for, or you won't have a job." When the certification election was held on October 28, just four days after the formation of the Packinghouse Workers Organizing Committee (PWOC) of the CIO, PWOC Local 32 emerged victorious. Local 32 received 991 of the 1,547 votes cast out of 1,764 eligible production workers. The Amalgamated picked up just 241 votes. As evident in Table 4.1, in comparison to certification elections held in several large midwestern packing centers during the 1930s, Ottumwa's CIO victory was among the earliest and nearly as convincing as several others. Yet as events in the next couple of years would make clear, solidarity was not spontaneous or guaranteed. Militant union leaders often needed to instill and create it.[19]

The Militant Foundations of Local 1

Soon after winning the certification election, packinghouse workers began to push for a written contract. Desire for such a contract signified Morrell-Ottumwa workers' commitment to industrial democracy. Formalized relations with the company in terms of wages, promotions, layoffs, and other work rules would replace the informal regulation of such issues that had typified Morrell's long history of paternalism and favoritism evident from the days of T. D. Foster's evangelical paternalism through its welfare capitalism era. Although

Table 4.1. NLRB Certification Election Results in Midwestern Meatpacking Plants, 1937–39[20]

Election Date	Meatpacking Plant	Percent of Vote Won by CIO*
1. August 5, 1937	Armour–Kansas City	58
2. October 28, 1937	Morrell-Ottumwa	56
3. November 28, 1938	Armour–Mason City	?
4. December 12, 1938	Armour–St. Joseph	63
5. December 30, 1938	Armour-Chicago	83**
6. October 3, 1939	Armour-Omaha	51
7. December 12, 1939	Armour-Chicago	ca. 67

Sources: Holcomb, "The Union Policies of Meat Packers"; Horowitz, "Negro and White Unite and Fight!"; and Halpern, Down on the Killing Floor; [Omaha] Unionist, 1 September 1939; and St. Joseph Union-Observer, 16 December 1938.

*Percentages are calculated out of total production workers eligible to vote.

**Note that this figure represents a percentage of less than one-half of the workforce that voted. Since a majority of the workforce did not vote, Armour refused to acknowledge the results even though it is likely that company harassment was the main reason why many workers failed to reach the polling booths. See Horowitz, "Negro and White Unite and Fight!", 77; and Halpern, Down on the Killing Floor, 149–50.

militancy characterized many local unions' formative years during this era, more distinctive about Ottumwa workers' pursuit of formal union relations with Morrell was their ability to sustain this militancy. Moreover, while some labor historians see a dichotomy between the desire for industrial democracy and syndicalist-type worker control efforts, many of Morrell-Ottumwa's early union leaders wanted both formal relations and informal control. Indeed, they used a sustained effort of exerting informal power to support their efforts to gain formalized relations.[21]

As such, Local 1, as it was renumbered in early 1939, is a bona fide example of the shop-floor bargaining that labor historians Rick Halpern and Roger Horowitz argue was characteristic of the PWOC and UPWA. Local 1's early union leaders, like Bill Fletcher, were not only "hotheads," they were committed to the use of "job actions" that would require the company to pay attention to their demands. Work stoppages were used consistently by union militants from the late 1930s through the early 1950s. The goal of this militancy was usually control over production standards. Kill and cut workers, in particular, faced the strongest pressure from the company in terms of speedups and changes in production standards. Cohesion among workers in the various kill and cut departments was necessary for any work stoppage to be effective. Militants often had to enforce compliance among some workers in strategic departments. This alienated some workers from the local union, but the union's leaders regarded such hard feelings as a necessary price.[22]

By mid-January 1938, union and company representatives met to negotiate an initial agreement. Negotiations stalled when Morrell refused to consider the closed shop and dues-checkoff provisions the union desired. Already demonstrating the militance that would emerge more dramatically later, union members in the pork by-products and beef departments stopped work on January 20 to force two nonunion members to join the local. These disturbances allowed Don Harris, PWOC national director, to petition for a U.S. Department of Labor representative to help iron out a contract agreement. In the meantime, former members of Local 32, who were now part of Local 497 of the United Laundry Workers of the CIO employed at the Ottumwa Steam Laundry, staged a sit-down strike on January 19. (When Local 32 became part of the PWOC in October 1937, it had to give up its nonpackinghouse worker members.) These events encouraged Morrell unionists to also consider a strike to force the company to bargain in good faith.[23]

Workers continued their strike threats over the next two months but fell short of taking that step. R. M. Pilkington, representing the U.S. Department of Labor, arrived in Ottumwa on January 22, and immediately joined Don Harris, William Fletcher, Lewis Clark, and Ed Fitzpatrick, an organizer from the Wilson–Cedar Rapids plant, in mediating the conflict at the Morrell plant and at the Ottumwa Steam Laundry. Over 900 Local 32 members met at the Odd Fellows Hall on January 24 to consider a strike vote, but decided against it. The steam laundry sit-down became even more controversial a couple of days later when A. R. Swartz Jr., a local attorney and vice-commander of the Iowa American Legion, broke into the laundry building to retrieve American Legion officers' uniforms. He apparently brandished a gun at the sit-down strikers when they confronted him with "iron clubs." Swartz was charged with assault, but a few days later was found not guilty. In the meantime, the owners of the laundry retained George Heindel, Morrell's attorney, as their legal counsel. Perhaps heeding advice from Heindel, on February 23 the company's owners shut off electricity in the building. Though workers bravely continued their sit-down strike, they were forced to capitulate on March 10. The Ottumwa Steam Laundry reopened at a new location using equipment removed from the building while the sit-down strikers had still occupied it and employed workers who had refused to join the sit-down strike.[24]

Local 32 members' hesitation to call a strike against Morrell may have been directly influenced by the harsh tactics used to break the laundry workers' strike. Heindel's involvement in the laundry workers' strike probably sent a strong message to Local 32 that the company might use similar tactics against them if they tried to strike. Recognizing the union's relative weakness at this stage and Morrell's resolve not to give in on the closed shop and dues-check-off provisions, Local 32 finally settled for a written contract without their key demands on March 21, 1938. The contract protected departmental seniority and, interestingly, given later developments, codified the practice of keeping separate seniority lists for men and women even when both worked in the same department. The contract also specified the grievance process and recognized the union grievance committee's right to represent aggrieved workers before company representatives. In terms of basic policies about hours, overtime, wages, and other benefits, however, the contract represented little more than a rehash of earlier policies. For instance, no employee was eligible for overtime unless they worked more than ten hours per day or fifty-three hours per week, the same policy that had been in effect since the beginning of the welfare capitalist period at the plant in 1923. Nevertheless, union members realized that simply gaining a contract was a significant building block. Most important, the company formally recognized the right of the union to bargain for the plant's workers.[25]

Although its militance was already evident in 1938, Morrell-Ottumwa workers' sustained brand of union militance would emerge in the course of noncontractual battles in the years immediately following their first contract. Workers' militance was used to combat management's efforts and ensure fellow workers' cooperation with the union. From the beginning, workers involved in combating management were most concerned with defining a fair work pace. Workers wanted to wrest a degree of informal control over job loads from plant managers not encompassed in the industrial democracy component of their contractual demands. Virgil Bankson recalled one crucial incident soon after the local's victory in the certification election. Clarence "Bronc" Poncy, a floorsmen (skinner) in the beef kill, started a sit-down strike in the department over the speed of the chain used to regulate how many cattle were being killed per hour. Bankson recalled that during his employment there, the company had always established the rate and that this rate might vary from one day to the next. Morrell generally encouraged a fast pace by paying a "lead-off" floorsman a couple of cents more per hour than the others. Poncy announced one day that this practice would no longer continue. The rest of the men followed suit. Although the foreman, Leo O'Malley, proceeded to ridicule him to keep him moving, Poncy refused to budge. Finally the beef department superintendent, Art Woodman, agreed to talk to Poncy after work. When Poncy brought along the whole gang, Woodman agreed informally to allow floorsmen sixteen beef per hour, a limit that would become the workers' benchmark of a proper pace.[26]

Elmer Cline recalled an effort in the hog kill to wrest informal control from foremen. Morrell attempted to cut the hog-kill gang while keeping the chain speed at the same rate. The following morning when the work day started with fewer men, the gang worked until noon when the hog dropper refused to work. The foreman fired him on the spot, but the department steward came up and argued that he could not do that. According to Cline, the steward said, "Besides, what would you do with all the men sitting down?" Meetings with the department superintendent were quickly held, and even the mayor, police chief, and fire chief were called in to convince the men to return to work, but the men continued their work stoppage. Morrell finally decided to slow the chain speed down to a rate that fewer men could handle. The issue of job loads would in fact remain the most important concern of the kill department workers over the next two decades and the major source of contention between the local and Morrell during the late 1940s and early 1950s. Concern over a proper work pace was the cornerstone of workers' concerns and the major motivating force for workers' use of militant job actions.[27]

Another chief concern persisting since the welfare capitalist period was the behavior of plant foremen. The local used "aggressive solidarity" to secure more acceptable behavior from supervisors. Don Jones, a union steward in the hog kill during the early union-building period and the local union president in 1940, recalled one such defining incident. Cut from the same "hothead" mold as Bill Fletcher, Jones worked episodically for Morrell between 1926 and 1929. He was not hired permanently until 1932, a result he strongly attributed in oral history testimony to plant superintendent Ernest Manns's dislike of him. Much of his aggressiveness seems to have stemmed from this old grudge. Not long after the company granted its first contract to Local 32, Jones requested a meeting with hog kill and cut department superintendent Lyle Mosher and department foreman Oscar Johnson to convey workers' concerns about their abusive managerial styles. Instead of coming alone, as Mosher and Johnson expected, Jones brought the entire department's workforce, over 100 men, to the meeting. Over the course of "two or three hours" the workers kept the two men backed into a corner and finally forced them to apologize to all the workers present. Jones claimed that Mosher was never abusive again and described this technique as "the way we used to have to break them foremen." Workers' solidarity on a departmental level allowed this tactic to work. Such tactics may have also contributed directly to Morrell's decision to retain George Heindel permanently beginning in January 1939 as the head of their new legal department. The fact, too, that many of the more abusive superintendents such as Manns and Mosher retired not long after the union was established enabled unionists to intimidate and influence the new generation of plant managers.[28]

Local union leaders also used their emerging power to discipline new workers and recalcitrant union members into accepting militant solidarity. Indeed, local union leaders created situations where management had to accept this militant solidarity as well. Before the closed shop or dues checkoff was written into the union's contract in 1943, union stewards would shut down operations in a department if an employee had not yet joined the union or was behind in paying dues. Such work stoppages were routine in the union's early years even though they violated the 1938 contract; union leaders felt their means justified the ends desired, and Morrell managers did not try to challenge most of these efforts. In extreme cases, workers who refused to join or pay their dues might find their lockers filled with cutting oil or face the prospect of physical abuse.

Virgil Bankson vividly recalled one of the more extreme cases of instilling solidarity from 1938. He and Bill Fletcher, the local's president, led a shutdown in the beef kill when a worker refused to pay his dues. After futile attempts by the departmental foremen and superintendent to get the man to resume work, Ernest Manns was called in. The reluctant worker asked Manns if he had to pay union dues to work at the plant. Manns said no but his refusal was keeping everyone else from working. Embarrassed with this admission, Manns then turned to Bankson and Fletcher and told them to meet with him after work. At the meeting, Manns, frustratedly "thumping" his fingers on his desk, told them, "You guys don't have no control over these men at all." Fletcher, always the hothead, snapped back, "You don't have no control over them either, and you're the superintendent!"[29]

Paul Bissell was hired by Morrell in 1927 and moved permanently to the beef kill in 1928. A leader of the union movement there in the late 1930s, Bissell claimed that union building caused a lot of friction among workers, and that some had to be forced in. He did not like the pressure tactics used in these early days, but acknowledged their utility. When Morrell hired Dorothy Daeges in the smoked meat department in 1939, she had "no problem" with joining the union. Although describing her decision as voluntary, she did insinuate that other workers, especially those hired during the war years, were sometimes less than excited about union membership. The "average person had to join the union, and [Local 32] did put some pressure on people."[30]

Local 32's leaders' militancy was akin to the "mood of syndicalism" labor historian Bruce Nelson describes among Pacific Coast waterfront workers during the same period. Yet it does not seem appropriate to label Ottumwa's packing workers' aspirations as primarily or, certainly, consciously syndicalist. There is no evidence that the workers involved in the various defining militant job actions in the 1930s and 1940s saw their efforts as a means to dictate Morrell's production standards. Rather, Local 32's militancy was designed to achieve a larger, and fairer, degree of control over the pace of production.

Both informal and formal gains in power — both syndicalist and industrial democracy goals — were part of Local 32's early agenda.[31]

The local's militant solidarity blossomed during mid-1939. Whereas PWOC delegates converged on Chicago in spring 1939 to push the Armour chain for a master agreement, Ottumwa's Local 1 (redesignated to indicate its status as the first packinghouse local to apply for a CIO charter) used this heady climate to push for a better agreement with Morrell. Throughout summer 1939, Local 1 pressed Morrell for a new contract that would guarantee a closed shop, dues checkoff, and overtime pay, but the company was unwilling to concede these provisions. After negotiations failed, four workers intentionally left their places in the plant on August 24 after working eight hours to protest the lack of provisions for overtime pay in the current contract. Morrell reacted as the local anticipated: they suspended the workers for leaving their jobs. Local 1 then promptly called a strike. Unlike the Chicago locals, Ottumwa's militants did not shrink from the threat of prolonged conflict. Local 1 was also the only Morrell-owned packing plant in mid-1939 to have affiliated with the CIO. The Sioux Falls plant was affiliated with the Amalgamated Meat Cutters and Butcher Workmen (AMCBW), and PWOC organization efforts in the Topeka plant only began in October 1939. Consequently, the complications of a master agreement did not interfere with Local 1's strike decision as they did in Chicago.[32]

Mindful of one of the lessons of the 1921 packing strike in Ottumwa, strike organizers carefully prepared their picketers to block all possible entrances into the plant. Picket lines were not just established at the front entrances to the plant. Men and women even kept guard on the banks of the Des Moines River and patrolled the river itself. By the strike's second day, union members had caught strikebreakers trying to cross the river. Art Bankson recalled that they took the scabs to the local union office and gave them the "third degree." Union members also stopped chief engineer Bernard Winger from bringing replacement workers into the plant. They surrounded his car, lifted it off the ground, and let Winger gun the engine to no avail.[33]

As strikers served on the local's mass picket line during the weeklong strike, they listened to a variety of CIO officials as well as religious leaders urge them to maintain their efforts. The two religious speakers on August 28 were Rev. John H. Courtney, pastor of Sacred Heart Catholic Church, located in the packing neighborhood, and Rev. Alpha D. McClure, pastor of the Pentecostal Church of God, one of the many fundamentalist churches that served packing workers in the city.[34]

When negotiations between the local and the company stalled, some union members, fearing a protracted strike, broke ranks. On August 28, union leaders heard rumors that workers formerly affiliated with the Amalgamated had organized a back-to-work meeting. Bill Fletcher, Art and Virgil Bankson, Don Jones, and "a couple of carloads of people" hurried to the meeting. There they found a hall filled with Morrell employees, estimated by Jones to number around 500, listening to Henry Hoover, still representing the Amalgamated, and Carl E. Harding, sheriff of Wapello County. Hoover and Harding urged those present to return to work. Although Harding promised to personally lead them through the picket line, Hoover insinuated that the company would look more favorably on the Amalgamated if workers would behave in a more cooperative manner. Hoover, in fact, had announced on the strike's second day that the Amalgamated's followers would go back to work. Local 1's activists were "surprised to see the different faces in the hall," including many workers thought to be loyal CIO members. They quickly decided that immediate action would return them to the fold. Fletcher promptly marched on stage and proclaimed that he would personally "bash some heads" if anyone tried to go back to work. Surprising even themselves, the Banksons recalled how embarrassed many in the crowd immediately became and how quickly and quietly they dispersed.[35]

Interestingly enough, Morrell "rewarded" Henry Hoover for his actions during the strike one year later by influencing city officials to place him on the city draft board. In October 1940, Local 1 officials asked the PWOC international office if they could use their influence to get Hoover removed from this position since they feared he might unfairly draft CIO activists. The international was not able to remove Hoover. When drafting began, Art Bankson, much to his surprise since he was older and had more children than other Morrell workers not drafted, was ordered to report for military training. Fortunately for him, Morrell interceded on his behalf because they were short of skilled butchers and had the order rescinded.[36]

After the near crisis within the local, the strike ended the next day, August 29. Union and Morrell officials agreed that the four men who walked off their jobs would be suspended for three weeks but that no union members would lose their jobs. Although a new contract did not result from the strike, Local 1 counted their failed effort as a moral victory — Donald Jones later described it as the event that "made the union" because it emerged intact. A union membership meeting held soon after the strike's end attracted a large turnout and wholesale agreement that Sheriff Harding had shown his pro-company colors in pledging to help the back-to-work group.[37]

Local union leaders recalled that efforts to solidify the local's membership redoubled after the strike. Departmental stewards embarked on door-to-door membership campaigns, and gathered at the plant's front gate at "five o'clock in the morning to catch [workers needing to pay their dues]." Elected Local 1 president in 1940, Donald Jones remembered that in this way, "we'd get them all. We'd have some [stewards] cut down the roads [surrounding the plant], clear behind the office [building] and down the [railroad] tracks" to ensure that everyone paid their dues. Jones also noted how the local used spontaneous parades of workers marching through the various plant departments to demonstrate the union's presence and strength. The local's militant leadership shored up workers' solidarity in these ways.[38]

Militancy and Conflict with the International Union

Although its "first" local, Local 1 was not a central force in the mobilization of the PWOC or the new international union, the United Packinghouse Workers of America (UPWA), that emerged in 1943. Although certainly an active participant in some of the central meetings and rallies that solidified the emerging international in the late 1930s and early 1940s, Local 1, as Rick Halpern has generalized for several of the strong Iowa, Nebraska, and Minnesota locals in this period, was "fiercely independent[,] represented an extreme antibureaucratic tendency within the PWOC, [and was] limited by a parochial worldview." Although a bit overstated when applied specifically to Morrell-Ottumwa's militants, who were after all closely involved in the organization and leadership of the state CIO council during these years, as described in Chapter 6, it is generally true that Local 1 members did not involve themselves centrally in the international union's development. Local 1's militant leaders wanted to reshape plant and community relations first and foremost. Indeed, their militance and go-it-alone attitudes from the late 1930s to early 1950s irritated union leaders involved in the international's development.[39]

It may be more accurate to say that Local 1's members involved themselves in the PWOC and budding international union when they felt it might benefit their own interests. Local 1 encouraged 150 members to attend the July 1939 meetings in Chicago focusing on the Armour master agreement and potential strike by paying $1 from the local's small treasury toward each delegate's train fare. Wilson–Cedar Rapids' Local 3 decided to copy this practice. In 1940, the CIO fired Henry "Hank" Johnson, a black organizer out of Chicago and PWOC assistant national director, for supporting CIO maverick John L. Lewis and Republican presidential candidate Wendell Willkie and attempting to divert packinghouse locals in United Mine Workers District 50. Local 1 officials signed the resolution asking for Johnson's dismissal, and thus sided with unions who wanted to continue building a national union. Ottumwa and Fort Dodge unionists in 1941 also backed Austin Local 9 leaders' plan to create a democratic international union structure through national conferences of packinghouse workers who would elect committees of local union delegates who would prepare the international's constitution. At the same time, after electing its new slate of local union officers in July 1941, the membership voted to drop any support for an international union for the time being.[40]

Roger Horowitz has described, in the years from 1939 to 1941, that there was considerable disagreement among locals about the shape of the new international. Much of the controversy focused on resentment toward Van Bittner, the CIO-appointed PWOC national chair, who, following the pattern in his union, the United Mine Workers of America, ruled the PWOC autocratically. For instance, without consulting local union delegates, Bittner decided in August 1939 to avoid a national conflict with Armour and let individual plants sign contracts without obtaining a master agreement. Pressure on the CIO finally convinced Philip Murray to remove Bittner from his PWOC position in May 1940. The new PWOC chair, John C. "Shady" Lewis, placed a more democratic representation of local union leaders in top PWOC positions. Lewis was another longtime United Mine Worker leader, though, and many locals, including Ottumwa's, wanted him out. He finally stepped down in July 1942, only to be replaced by Sam Sponseller, whom even more PWOC local unions did not like. Widespread dissatisfaction pushed a disparate array of locals and district organizations to finally advocate the Austin model. The Constitutional Convention Committee, formed in summer 1943, "allowed packinghouse workers to design their organizational structure and founding meeting outside the CIO's control." Crucial for many packinghouse leaders, they wanted nothing to do with the leadership model provided by the United Steel Workers of America (USWA), founded in May 1942, a model most felt was autocratic and not representative of its various regional and local constituencies. When founded in October 1943, the United Packinghouse Workers of America's (UPWA) district structure and executive board retained a strongly distinctive regional and democratic character.[41]

PWOC's leaders frequently clashed with Local 1's militant leaders during the early 1940s. In January 1941, Lewis J. Clark, PWOC District 3 director and soon-to-be PWOC vice chairman, wrote to John Doherty, current PWOC vice chairman, that "I am satisfied at last that the old line of bickering, discontentment and communist element at Ottumwa, Iowa has been broken down and the workers there are ready to work in a cooperate [sic] manner." He was wrong. John Doherty learned not long after this note that the local's news bulletin included statements that William Houston, U.S. commissioner of conciliation, found to be an "outrage." Houston urged Doherty to chastise the local. Doherty wrote Houston that he agreed that Local 1's efforts were not "very discreet," but that the local was battling for the closed shop, and was using these tactics to accomplish this end. Doherty wrote back to Clark to tell Local 1 to be "a little more diplomatic in the language used in their bulletins" but not to do anything that would "dampen the spirits of our boys in Ottumwa." Relations between Local 1 and the PWOC and new UPWA would remain tense with Clark moving into the PWOC vice chair position, then the UPWA presidency from 1943 to 1946.[42]

The "spirits of the boys" in Local 1 sparked further headaches for the PWOC later in 1941 when Sam Sponseller, PWOC's new District 3 director, intervened to arbitrate a dispute in the beef-kill department. Because Bill Fletcher would not attend what he termed a "kangaroo court," Virgil Bankson met with Morrell's top officials and Sponseller in the general offices building. Bankson recalled that Sponseller tried to reassure Morrell officials that Fletcher, Bankson, and the other men would not misbehave again. When a Morrell official then asked Bankson if he would act the same way again, he claimed he said, "I tell you what, if it was to do over, I'd do it again." He expected to be fired for his insolence, but was not.[43]

The early war years also saw significant gains in Local 1's contractual and formal relations with Morrell. Partly because of the demands for stable industrial relations as well as pressure from the labor movement for union security in the face of new manpower requirements after Pearl Harbor sparked America's defense buildup, the National War Labor Board (NWLB) in early 1942 granted so-called maintenance of membership whereby union members would have to retain their membership during the life of any collective bargaining agreement. Because the NWLB would then govern any such collective bargaining agreements, the PWOC's push for multiplant master agreements within the various packing firms, initiated in 1939 with Armour then restarted in early 1942, occurred under government supervision. The Big Four packing companies signed master agreements with the PWOC in 1942 and 1943.

Continuing the pattern evident in Local 1 from its founding, union leaders were able to sustain their militant job actions to enforce Morrell's industrial democratic contract commitments. In June 1943, just after Morrell signed the first master agreement, hog-kill department workers walked off the job, and were then locked out by the company for the next week. On Tuesday, June 1, 1944, 165 employees in the hog kill walked off their jobs in protest of Morrell's decision to give them Memorial Day off instead of paying them time and a half for holiday pay. In fact, workers would have received double time under the 1943 master agreement because Memorial Day was a stipulated holiday and hog-kill workers would have worked more than forty hours for the week. The employees stopped working immediately after putting in eight hours on Tuesday, when Morrell indicated they wanted them to put in an additional hour of work. Workers were then locked out for three days by the company, who argued the local union had made the action an authorized strike. The NWLB reviewed the decision, however, and found in favor of the employees.[44]

Although such job actions were endemic within the UPWA from 1943 to

1945, the international union's leaders had formally accepted the no-strike pledge that virtually all the organized labor movement had accepted in return for government support of union security, wage stability, and contractual agreements. Roger Horowitz argues that international union leaders "encouraged . . . rather than suppressed, shop-floor unrest." They did so, he claims, because they wanted to maintain the rank-and-file democratic character of the union. Local 1's case during the war years seems to cast some doubt on his claim, though certainly there is no evidence of international union interference in the local's largest wartime strike, which started on April 5, 1945. On that date, the entire plant was shut down after two weeks of periodic job actions stemming from a dispute over job transfers in the fresh meat department that began on March 22. Workers in the department claimed Morrell violated seniority principles in their decisions. After the entire workforce of 3,000 employees stopped work on April 5, local union leaders claimed no knowledge of why this happened, perhaps to avoid NWLB involvement in any sort of authorized strike. Nevertheless, the NWLB was quickly involved along with Ralph Helstein, the UPWA's attorney, in negotiations between Morrell and Local 1. Helstein clearly indicated that the international union would not interfere in the local's decision about continuing its strike. On April 10, Local 1 members voted to end their strike. The subsequent NWLB decision resulted in no sanctions levied against either the company or the union.[45]

Between 1933 and 1945, workers at the Morrell-Ottumwa plant forged a militant union during the course of their CIO organizing. They did so without significant outside help, though direction and inspiration from IUAW members in Austin, Minnesota, was important. This independence proved to be characteristic of Local 32 turned Local 1 during its early CIO period. Although militant solidarity was useful in its shop floor bargaining efforts, it would prove to be a mixed blessing. During and immediately after the war, Morrell became much more aggressive and effective in combating the local's shop floor bargaining efforts. In addition, a new generation of workers would begin to question the purposes and efficacy of militant solidarity in the postwar years.

5

THE EROSION OF MILITANT
UNIONISM, 1946–1963

Beginning in the 1930s, workers' struggles for power at the John Morrell and Company meatpacking plant in Ottumwa, Iowa, created a militant brand of industrial unionism. Morrell workers established United Packinghouse Workers of America (UPWA) Local 1, a strong CIO union built on the bonds of a homogeneous packing community, anger at Morrell's unjust labor relations, and workers' desire to exercise more control in the plant as well as Ottumwa. By the end of World War II, workers had not only won contractual and informal concessions of power from Morrell, they had also established a powerful political presence in the larger community. Union leaders were active in local politics, organizing city and county residents in political contests, mobilizing voting efforts, and campaigning for political offices themselves. Local 1 was also centrally involved in establishing Ottumwa's CIO industrial council. Soon after the war, however, Morrell and the local business community reasserted themselves against Local 1. The struggle for power in plant and community affairs peaked between the nationwide UPWA meatpacking strike of 1948 and the declaration of "Morrell Days" by the company in 1954. This chapter focuses on the power struggle in the plant while Chapter 6 examines how this struggle spilled over into community affairs and state politics.

During the immediate post–World War II years, Local 1 and Morrell battled for control over plant floor decisions. From the mid-1940s to early 1950s, Morrell officials reasserted their prerogatives over production decisions through the creation of an industrial engineering department and appointment of supervisors willing to challenge the union's power. In December 1953, Morrell's board of directors selected a new president, W. W. "Wally" McCallum, the first non-Morrell family member to lead the company in its 126-year history. McCallum was bent not only on wresting power away from Local 1 but also on implementing strategies that would shift production away from the Ottumwa plant. McCallum's financial and production strategies, combined with changes prompted by the transformation of the meatpacking industry in the 1950s and 1960s, undermined Local 1's long history of sustained militancy.

Internal disputes within Local 1 were just as important in the erosion of the union's militancy during the 1950s and 1960s. This discord started during and immediately following World War II when Morrell hired many rural workers to meet their expanded labor needs. These workers, largely unaccustomed to unionism and not part of the packing community traditions of the local's founders, subverted the union's strike effort in 1948. Moreover, these and other workers who started at the plant following World War II were largely unsympathetic to the sentiments underlying Local 1's militancy.

Morrell's more aggressive tactics in combating the union's power and the emerging generational differences among union members undermined Local 1's sustained militancy. Indeed, Morrell increasingly chastised workers in the late 1940s and early 1950s that their frequent job actions disrupted production and made the plant unprofitable. McCallum would especially stress that the union either had to become more compliant or the company would close the plant. The new workers and union leaders of the 1950s and 1960s not only took these company claims to heart, they genuinely believed that the grievances of the older generation of union militants and "hotheads" were no longer justified. They could not support union pioneers who used job actions to punish the company over past injustices or what they felt were petty grievances. Moreover, union militancy became even more difficult to sustain when plant closings and the introduction of new managerial philosophies and technologies revolutionized the packing industry during the mid-1950s to early 1960s.

Local Union Militancy in Action

Morrell workers in Ottumwa received the first CIO packinghouse union charter in the United States in May 1937. UPWA Local 1, the numerical designation the CIO gave its first chartered packinghouse union in 1943 and which members would proudly point out in years to come, emerged out of a close-knit and culturally uniform neighborhood in the immediate environs of the Morrell plant in Ottumwa's east end. As early as 1900, 60 percent of Morrell's workers were native-born of native parents. By the mid-1930s over 95 percent of Morrell's workers were native-born of northern and western European stock. Many attended fundamentalist Protestant churches and belonged to the Eagles, Moose, and American Legion halls situated in the city's blue-collar residential areas, including the east end.

Between 1938 and the end of World War II, Ottumwa's Morrell workers were able to secure favorable informal production rules in key departments of the plant. One of the most important of these agreements concerned the number of cattle killed per hour by the floorsmen. Beginning in the late 1930s, after confrontations stemming from sit-down strikes, the beef department superintendents and foremen agreed to abide by limits proposed by workers in the department. Job load issues were largely resolved this way in many departments throughout the plant at the same time. As a result, the union exercised considerable power. In 1942, however, Morrell took the counteroffensive by introducing a new industrial engineering department that took production decisions away from departmental supervisors who had previously negotiated informal production rules with the local union. In 1947, Morrell also hired a new plant superintendent, Charles L. Campbell, who directly confronted the union over production-related issues through 1952.[1]

From the early 1940s until 1950, Morrell expanded production at the Ottumwa plant. This expansion was most rapid from 1945 to 1949, when the number of production workers increased from 2,350 to 3,430. By 1950, the Morrell plant provided almost two-thirds of all the manufacturing jobs in Ottumwa. Significantly, many of the new workers came from outside the city. Whereas in 1935 almost none of the plant's workers resided outside the city, by 1951 about 27 percent of the plant's workforce lived in small towns or farms as far away as fifty miles. These new workers would figure prominently in the local union's struggles over the next several years.[2]

Between 1947 and 1952, Morrell would severely test Local 1's solidarity and its informal control over work pace. One of these tests surrounded the UPWA's decision to call a nationwide strike in 1948. Arguably the most important strike in the history of packinghouse unionism, 100,000 UPWA members nationwide would walk out for more than two months that year. In planning the strike, the international's leaders "projected stabilizing labor relations and reducing shop-floor disorder in exchange for economic benefits and entrenched union power over the pace and organization of work." Essentially, the strike's results would define the character of the new international union of packinghouse workers. As a consequence, labor historian Roger Horowitz has referred to the 1948 strike as the UPWA's "crucible." Both shaping and reflecting the social democratic aims of other major CIO unions during the period, the UPWA wanted to ensure a leading role for unions in the postwar world, particularly in terms of increasing workers' wages and maintaining union power on the shop floors. The UPWA also wanted to demonstrate that the Taft-Hartley Act, passed in 1947, would not hinder its ability to effectively represent workers' interests. As the strike's impact would demonstrate in Ottumwa, it also proved to be a "crucible" for Local 1. The strike's resolution would strengthen Morrell's decision to combat the union and, as evident later, would prove important in undermining the militants' positions.[3]

Called only two years after the highly successful 1946 strike by both the AMCBW-AFL and UPWA that resulted in sixteen-cent-per-hour wage hikes, the AMCBW did not support the 1948 strike. In advocating an additional twenty-nine-cent-per-hour increase, the UPWA felt its wage demands were consistent with its promotion of an economy of abundance, one of the hallmarks of the UPWA's brand of social democracy. After its participation in the successful and brief two-week strike in 1946, Ottumwa's Local 1 was well prepared and confident of further success in 1948.[4]

Ottumwa's packing community demonstrated its solidarity during the early days of the strike in March by maintaining a picket line six and a half miles long around the plant. Public officials, fearing that the strikers might become violent, began to plan how to combat them. A few days after the strike began in early March, officials closed all the taverns in the packing neighborhood, citing instances of public drunkenness among strikers. On April 5, Local 1 issued a bulletin claiming that Ottumwa safety commissioner Charles Carlson was considering the use of fire hoses on picketers since they "would be better than using gun butts." Carlson denied the statement, but quickly added that fire hoses would be used only if a riot broke out.[5]

Because of the unity strikers exhibited in March, Morrell officials decided in early April to test the union's strength by shipping meat out of the plant. Morrell knew that strikers would interpret such an attempt as an initiation of business activity proscribed during strikes by prior agreements. Jim Collins, a foreman who worked in the plant during the strike, later described the company's plan as "an attempt to break the union by shipping meat out." When Morrell officials attempted to move five railcars loaded with meat out of the plant on April 7 and 8, massed picketers successfully blocked the cars from leaving. On April 9, however, Iowa District Court judge Harold V. Levis issued a temporary injunction that thoroughly undercut the massed unity the strikers had demonstrated. The injunction stipulated that just five people could picket at each picket station (instead of the dozens who had done so previously), and that strikers could not barricade plant entrances and exits or impede employees entering or leaving the plant. In addition, the injunction named 220 union activists who could be charged with contempt if any of the injunction's restraints on picketing the plant were violated.[6]

Apart from painting the words "SCAB MEAT" on the side of some of the railcars involved in the attempt to move meat out of the plant, Ottumwa's packing community had not engaged in any violence before April 9. The injunction, however, changed the strikers' tactics. Because of this legal restraint, Local 1 embarked on a type of "guerrilla warfare" to forcibly dissuade foremen and other supervisors, the only employees the company could persuade to process meat, from carrying on such activities. Strikers either verbally or physically assaulted managerial personnel involved in production during the strike. Typically, strikers would follow foremen and supervisors when they left the plant, and attack them at or near their homes. Virgil Bankson later explained that such "violence was necessary" from the union's perspective; union leaders now felt that they were involved in a life-and-death struggle to save their union. From their perspective, it was the company that had violated earlier agreements by attempting to initiate business activities during the strike. Under the restraint of the injunction, union leaders could not bring the full strength of the packing community's solidarity to bear against Morrell. They therefore condoned a type of "directed" violence in the hope of maintaining their strike effort.[7]

Morrell quickly responded to this guerrilla warfare by targeting for prosecution Local 1 leaders who had participated in such violence. On April 15, Donald Jones, Local 1 president in 1947, was arrested for contempt of the injunction. Jones had allegedly participated in an attack on three foremen. During the following week, four rank-and-file members were arrested on similar charges, but Morrell pressed charges only against Jones. Iowa District Court judge Harold V. Levis heard evidence in the Jones contempt case from April 21 to 27. In the meantime, Levis added an additional 255 strikers' names to the injunction. While the Jones case was under way, the *Ottumwa Daily Courier* left no doubt about its stand on the actions of Jones and fellow strikers. "Evidence is multiplying that lawless goon squads are patrolling the city streets and neighboring highways to terrorize persons connected with John Morrell and Co." Morrell officials, as well as growing segments of the business and professional community, were now adamant that the union's ranks were filled with thugs who condoned criminal activity. The union's opponents charged that its workers were not only lawbreakers; they were lazy as well. President George M. Foster publicly proclaimed, "Our experience with the Ottumwa local has been bad. Within the past five years [roughly coinciding with the beginning of the new managerial policies] there have been 42 work stoppages, slowdowns, or strikes resulting in 67 days lost."[8]

In this emotionally charged atmosphere, the packing community's perspective on the strike and its conduct was increasingly isolated. Ottumwa's packing workers were by no means alone in this respect. Nationally, organized labor's power and prestige were in retreat by 1948, particularly following the passage of the Taft-Hartley Act in 1947. Although historians have since downplayed the effect of the act's restrictions on labor, there is little doubt that both the CIO and AFL then saw it as a blow to their strength.[9]

Locally, the isolation of the packing community was reflected in Judge Levis's decision against Donald Jones. Two other strikers present at the altercation, Jim Hammersley and Bernard Jones, Donald's brother, testified that Donald Jones was not involved in the fight. In fact, both men attested that they verbally confronted one of the foreman, Claude Smith, after he got out of a car that had stopped at the home of another Morrell supervisory employee. Smith then struck Bernard Jones with a flashlight. Smith's assault only prompted both men to attack Smith. Of the nine other foremen present at the scene, only one corroborated Smith's claim that Donald Jones was involved in the fight. Yet on April 28, Judge Levis found Jones guilty of contempt and ordered him to serve sixty days in the county jail. Levis's reasoning in his decision is particularly revealing.

> The circumstances surrounding the whole affair lead to the conclusion that the mission of the occupants of the two cars which followed the Morrell car for a distance of four or five miles across the city was not a peaceable one, but rather, it appears that the occupants of the two cars were acting in concert to follow the Morrell car until it stopped for the purpose of using coercion, intimidation and force upon its occupants.

Levis continued that the union men "*must have* rushed almost *en masse* to the door of the Morrell car" (emphasis added). The resulting confusion would account for the contradictions in the foremen's testimony about Jones's participation in the fight. Jones himself repeatedly insisted in interviews conducted over the following twenty-five years that he had not participated in the fight. Nevertheless, the Iowa Supreme Court upheld Jones's conviction on April 11, 1949, but reduced his sentence to thirty days. The message was clear: public order as interpreted by the company and state and local officials must prevail despite the packing community's perception that their avenues of acceptable action had been undercut by the injunction.[10]

Although labor historians Roger Horowitz and Bruce Fehn have stressed how UPWA locals regrouped rapidly following the strike, in Ottumwa at least the strike had graver long-term than short-term consequences. Local 1 suffered from attacks on its leadership, particularly in the case of Donald Jones, but otherwise lost very few members owing to company reprisals. More crucial, however, was the role of rural workers and their impact on the local's solidarity. After the beginning of May, the company had greater success in attracting replacement workers. Local 1's records showed that just 72 active union members crossed the picket lines, while an additional 139 nonunion members worked in the plant before the strike ended. To be sure, the number of strikebreakers was small. Still, the backgrounds of the replacement workers provide insight into the sources of dissension growing within the local union. Based on information on the addresses of 62 union members who crossed the picket lines, the largest segment (37 percent) lived at rural route addresses or in small farming towns. In comparison, although it was still home to about a third of the plant workers, the immediate packing neighborhood surrounding the plant contributed only 16 percent of the scabs.[11]

Another significant difference between the urban and rural workers was that the rural component did not participate to nearly the same extent in the four largest social organizations for working people in the city: the Eagles, Moose, American Legion, and Veterans of Foreign Wars.[12] Since the 1930s, the packing community situated in the immediate plant environs provided considerable membership in the fraternal organizations that catered to working people in Ottumwa. (The VFW drew significant members only after World War II.) Although the content or programs of these fraternals was not overtly political, they functioned as part of the packing community's range of social ties, both formal and informal, that contributed to its solidarity. The importance of Morrell workers in these fraternals was evident during the 1948 strike when the American Legion post's membership voted to donate $1,500 to Local 1's strike fund. Even though a slightly higher percentage of the rural component's males were veterans of World War II, few of them were willing or able to travel to Ottumwa to belong to the local American Legion or VFW posts. Morrell workers apparently hoped to tap the American Legion as an additional source of financial aid. However, the executive board of the post, which was dominated by business and professional allies of Morrell, turned down the membership's request.[13]

Whereas the urban component of Morrell's workforce was knit closely not only by membership in Local 1 but also by a wider circle of social affiliations, this broader social participation was largely absent from the rural components of the workforce. Thus, although Local 1's leaders had attempted to educate and incorporate the farmers and working-class rural residents of the area into its culture of solidarity of 1948 by organizing a farmer–labor relations committee, these people were not enmeshed in the broader network of social relations that undergirded this culture. Accordingly, they were not sensitive to the traditions and concerns that had prompted the packing community's successful union-building. These attributes help to explain the greater propensity of rural workers to cross the picket line during the strike.[14]

Morrell's strategy in fighting the union's militance in the plant from 1949 to 1951 involved a persistent refusal to recognize Local 1's right to contest production decisions made by the company. Specifically, Morrell introduced job load changes; that is, the company decreased the number of workers in various departments while increasing the pace of production. These changes were established in the wake of time studies undertaken by the company's industrial engineering department (and approved contractually by the union and Morrell in their 1946 agreement), and were enforced by plant superintendent "Mad Dog" or "Do It or Else" Campbell (as the union now referred to him). The changes occurred primarily in the union strongholds of the beef and hog kill and cut departments, where they undermined the informal production arrangements the union had established before the end of World War II.[15]

Between 1949 and 1951, Morrell typically implemented upward adjustments in the job loads, which the union militants believed was meant to intentionally provoke them. The local used wildcat strikes to combat changes in work rules initiated by Campbell and the industrial engineering department. For example, beginning in 1949, Morrell demanded Ottumwa's beef-kill department to slaughter twice as many cattle per hour with the same number of men as worked in the company's Sioux Falls plant. Union officials in Ottumwa complained that Morrell unfairly targeted the Ottumwa's CIO workforce while avoiding antagonizing Sioux Falls's more cooperative AMCBW-AFL workforce. In this case, Campbell told the Ottumwa local that if they did not like the job load situation then "why don't you strike?"[16]

In the face of the company's increased resolve after the 1948 strike to disrupt collective bargaining and reshape community attitudes, the local attempted over the course of 1949–1951 to recapture its prestrike aggressiveness in combating the company. The union adopted a concerted policy of attacking Morrell as the enemy of all working people in Ottumwa. Noting that after the speedups in 1949, 75 workers produced as much as 100 workers had ten years earlier, the *Bulletin*, Local 1's weekly paper, proclaimed, "John Morrell and Company will ruin your health and drive you to your grave 15 years ahead of time. John Morrell and Company is our common enemy. Let's concentrate on an all-out effort to defeating [*sic*] them." Morrell responded to such attacks in what was now their typical post–World War II style: they took out an advertisement in the *Ottumwa Daily Courier*. In reply to the union's outburst, the company rhetorically asked Local 1 in a quarter-page ad to explain what it meant when it said that it wanted to "defeat" the company. "Where will you workers go if the company is put out of business?" Local 1 noted in its own (smaller) ad that, as usual, the company's remarks were meant for public consumption and confused the issues. Although Morrell had praised Local 1 for their "magnificent job" during the war, now, even though overall production had increased, workers were told that the company expected a fair day's work for a fair day's pay! "If the company was fair minded and believed in humanity, they would sit down and work out some fair agreement [involving job loads]." In addition, Edward A. Filliman, a former local union president and chief steward who became a UPWA international representative in 1949, also blamed Morrell for hiring rural workers to break the union's solidarity.[17]

During and immediately following World War II, Edward Filliman became the unofficial leader of the militant faction that dominated Local 1. Indeed, in many respects, Filliman assumed the "hothead" standard-bearer position previously occupied by Bill Fletcher. Son of a south-central Iowa miner and union activist, like so many other prominent Local 1 leaders, Filliman became president of Local 1 in 1944 and was then elected chief steward for the local from 1945 through 1948 before resigning in December 1948. As demonstrated by the walkouts in 1945, Filliman from the beginning was not afraid to use work stoppages to assert workers' control.[18]

These battles reached a peak in 1951 when there were eighty-eight separate walkouts at the Ottumwa plant. On the heels of these repeated and massive walkouts, UPWA District 3 director Russell Bull, at the urging of some segments of Local 1's membership, placed the local under receivership, meaning the district officially oversaw its operation. Although some of the local's leaders had been involved in financial malfeasance a year earlier, the district's main concern was the reoccurring walkouts. Local 1 had a combative relationship with the UPWA international office and District 3 long before the early 1950s.[19]

In particular, following World War II, the UPWA international became disgusted with Local 1's avoidance of its antidiscrimination and civil rights program. A key component of the UPWA's social democratic agenda, the union's antidiscrimination program was expanded following the 1948 strike, and was established in 1950 as a department, headed by Russell Lasley. As Roger Horowitz describes it, the antidiscrimination program stressed three main themes: identification and correction of discriminatory practices in packing plants; elimination of discrimination in the communities surrounding the packing plants; and cooperation with community-based civil rights groups, particularly the National Association for the Advancement of Colored People (NAACP). Although active and successful in many locations, including Kansas City and Waterloo, the UPWA's antidiscrimination efforts probably made the most headway in Chicago. As well as battling problems in the plants, packing union activists successfully fought discrimination in housing and local businesses there. The UPWA's antidiscrimination program was also effective in encouraging women workers to improve their situations. Horowitz and Bruce

Fehn have detailed numerous gains, such as the elimination of men-women pay differentials, made because of women's activism in the 1950s.[20]

Even though there were very few blacks in Ottumwa, the UPWA's international leadership expected active participation from one of its strongest local affiliates in these initiatives. In their report on the problems in Local 1 in 1951, UPWA president Ralph Helstein and UPWA District 3 director Russell Bull focused on the local's inactivity on civil rights issues. "There is no activity or even attempted activity on problems of discrimination." Certainly, many Local 1 leaders were unconcerned about the plight of blacks in Ottumwa. Some union leaders, like Donald Jones, had nothing but scorn for the handful of blacks in the plant. Jones described one of the few African Americans in Morrell-Ottumwa's kill departments, Roy Winston, as a "joke" and someone who did anything the company said. Other union members apparently shared Jones's sentiments. As a consequence, Local 1's publications refused to boost the promising singing career of Roy Winston's wife, Ivory. Instead, Morrell actively promoted her career. Although the union was not obligated to involve itself in a nonmember's music career, to many members Local 1's lack of involvement signaled its fundamental lack of interest in civil rights. The Reverend John Harley Telfer, pastor of Ottumwa's First Congregational Church and a supporter of Local 1's politics since 1945 when he moved to the city, was one interested observer who expressed disgust with workers' failure to take up the civil rights cause. As Filliman duly noted, Telfer could solicit little if any support from workers for a citywide committee on civil rights. Thus, the UPWA district office's attempt to create a more tractable Local 1 stemmed from underlying disagreements with the focus of the local's militancy.[21]

Moreover, Russell Bull had participated in the local's fight against Morrell on the job load issue since 1949 and had grown tired of it. By 1951, local union officials felt neither the international nor district office was willing to continue the job load fight. In the fall of 1952, Bull selected Bud Simonson as deputy administrator of Local 1. Simonson's presence helped to clamp down on the union's militancy. The temporary lull in labor-management conflict that ensued allowed new Morrell president McCallum and Local 1 to fashion a symbolic truce at a communitywide "Morrell Days" in April 1954. Dissension in the local union's ranks had for the time being prompted the union to adopt a less confrontational posture.[22]

To be sure, many UPWA local unions' relations with the international office became strained following World War II. Partly because of the union's losing battle in the 1948 strike, some locals lost their internal cohesion. Many union members were upset with the UPWA's decision following the strike to settle for a nine-cents-per-hour increase after pushing for twenty-nine cents. In Omaha, for example, local union officials expressed ambivalence about the need for a strike even before it began. Once it did begin, workers attacked each other over left-wing ideological issues. Whites often blamed black workers for crossing picket lines. Omaha's packers, especially Wilson, exacerbated internal union tensions by granting replacement workers seniority (so-called "super-seniority") over the UPWA strikers when they returned to work. Other UPWA cities experienced similar internal union problems. Racial antagonisms troubled Local 58 at the Armour plant in St. Joseph, Missouri, during the 1948 strike and long after. Whites only reluctantly worked with blacks in the union. Local 174 in Topeka saw about one-half of its members, most of whom were native-born whites, join a back-to-work movement during the strike, then drop their union membership immediately following its conclusion. The core Topeka unionists, consisting primarily of Volga Germans, blacks, and Mexican Americans, only fitfully pieced their local back together. In Ottumwa and some locals, the UPWA international's antidiscrimination and civil rights programs, implemented in the aftermath of the 1948 strike and aimed at overcoming racial tensions and forging interracial solidarity, further divided whites and blacks instead of creating more harmonious relations.[23]

As Horowitz, Fehn, and Rick Halpern have explained, the success of UPWA's antidiscrimination efforts depended on local activism. In places where local union leaders were hostile or ambivalent about helping blacks and women, there was little or nothing the UPWA's international office could do to enforce compliance with its programs. Relative numbers of blacks and women also was crucial. In cities like Ottumwa, where both blacks and women represented very small segments of the workforce, there was often little impetus for change on the part of white men. Moreover, part of the underlying homogeneity of Ottumwa's workers was their "whiteness." Although it was difficult to assess the full extent and dimensions of their race consciousness, local union militants' attitudes toward the few blacks in the plant reflected an exclusivity about the composition of the packing community based in part on racial and gender considerations. In this sense, as many historians have emphasized for white workers elsewhere, Ottumwa's white male militants behaved in ways that undermined their efforts to promote working-class solidarity.[24]

The New Generation of Union Leaders

In Ottumwa, part of the rank and file's growing discord was the increasing division between the union's pioneers and the men and women who came into the union's ranks during and immediately following World War II. Jack McCoy, for instance, started full-time at the plant in 1949 as a twenty-year-old fresh out of military service. Attributing his motives in part to dislike of hard, physical work, McCoy then got involved in the local's politics in 1950, and became recording secretary for the local in 1953. In 1954, McCoy was selected as one of Local 1's representatives to the Ottumwa Industrial Union Council before being elected that fall to the Iowa House of Representatives to represent Wapello County. He credited the aggressiveness of the older militants in Local 1 to three factors: Filliman's political ambitions, calling him a "junior size John L. [Lewis]"; hotheaded local stewards, some of whom he claimed led walkouts just to go "squirrel hunting"; and the belief that his generation of younger workers simply wanted to work to put bread on the table for their families. In contrast, many prewar union activists viewed unionism as a kind of "religion" that would reshape power relations in the plant and the local community.[25]

A significant subtheme of McCoy's characterization of the pro-Filliman faction was his dislike of their alleged drinking habits. He believed that too often Filliman and his compatriots, including William Fletcher, first president of the local and the local's president again in 1952, and Harold "Cap" (or "Cappy") Carson, a local union officer since World War II, plotted their walkouts from two beer joints, Walker's and Champ's, located across the street from the plant. Indeed, the families of Walter Walker and Orvel Champ ran these bars. Both men had helped to organize the CIO local at the plant and had been among its first officers.[26]

As later events would make more evident, however, McCoy's observations signified deeper (and more damaging) gulfs in attitudes between the remaining core of old-time, militant activists, whose attitudes about Morrell had been shaped in the pre–World War II years, versus the new generation, including workers like McCoy, who had started in the plant during or immediately after the war. In particular, the older, militant unionists feared that any deviation from their hard-line stance against the company would result in a return to the "old days." Years later, men in the older, militant camp, like Virgil Bankson, a longtime chief steward, would describe with an undertone of fear and hatred the arbitrary and calloused treatment they received before the rise of the union. Indeed, especially in the eyes of younger workers who had not experienced the preunion period at the Morrell plant, men like Filliman seemed motivated more by vindictiveness and revenge against the company than by a desire for social justice.[27]

Yet what the new generation saw as vindictive attitudes was essentially an overriding commitment among the older generation to the use of collective power against Morrell. Such attitudes, which were fundamental to Filliman's union commitments, come through in a speech he gave to the delegates at the 1948 Iowa State Industrial Union Council's Constitutional Convention in Davenport. After serving as president of the state council since 1947, Filliman announced his decision to not seek the nomination again after Ben Henry, the CIO's regional director in Iowa, accused him publicly of being an "opportunist." Filliman described how he grew up in a southern Iowa mining camp. His father's union involvement got both him and his mother "kicked out of a company house in a mining town." He recounted how he got into the labor movement to redress injustices that his father had faced, including incurring work-related injuries that left him "crippled." Filliman claimed that each hard-fought grievance settlement won from Morrell, no matter how small, "does me good." He wanted no part of leading a labor organization where those involved "forget about the rank and filers in the plant."[28]

The generational gap also overlapped with differences arising from the urban versus rural workforce contribution. The older, more militant workers tended to still reside in the immediate plant environs of Ottumwa's east end, whereas many more recently hired employees (including younger union officials like McCoy) lived across the river on Ottumwa's south side or outside town. These sources of discord would continue to resonate in the union's internal politics throughout the 1950s, especially in the face of the policies that Morrell's new top official pursued.

When W. W. "Wally" McCallum became president of Morrell in 1953, he was not only the first non-Morrell family member in that position in the company's long history, he was also the first top official since Morrell had arrived in Ottumwa in 1877 who did not make his home there. Consequently, workers could no longer use the comparatively extravagant local lifestyle of its top official as an emotional rallying point as the same issue had long been used against the Foster family. Although McCallum had been Oscar Mayer's accountant and president's assistant since 1938, he also had no real experience toiling with meat or handling packing workers; his financial wizardry was his lone credential. In contrast, the Fosters had always started in the plant for at least a token stint of hands-on experience before assuming top managerial positions. When McCallum met with the local union executive board and stewards soon after his ascension to Morrell's top position, he "stressed the fact that he wishe[d] to see a closer harmony between the employees and the company." Nevertheless, he drew the implicit (and threatening) connection between Morrell's finances and its workers' militancy at the supposedly conciliatory "Morrell Days" celebration in April 1954.

> The Ottumwa plant is, in a sense, at a standstill. We are killing hogs and cattle, processing and selling good meat products, paying wages and so forth — but the plant is losing money — and has been losing consistently over the last six years [that is, since the 1948 strike and its subsequent repercussions in labor-management relations].[29]

McCallum's "solution" for ending company losses was threefold. He began buying plants around the country, moved the company's general headquarters from Ottumwa to Chicago in December 1955, and continued to contest the union's power to influence production decisions. The first two decisions stemmed from McCallum's desire to follow the traditional financial path of the Big Four meatpacking plants: establish a high-volume sales empire of plants controlled from America's central packing hub, Chicago. Swift, Armour, Cudahy, and Wilson had traditionally garnered sizable profits, in an industry typified by very slim profit ratios, by slaughtering and processing meat at as many plants as possible. In hopes of mimicking their success, Morrell purchased thirteen small plants throughout the Midwest and the South between August 1954 and February 1963. Most were nonunion and paid relatively low wages, but they did boost Morrell's total sales from just over $300 million in 1954 to $554 million in 1961. During the same period, Morrell also acquired financial interests in Foxbilt, a livestock feed and hybrid corn producer, and Golden Sun Mill, another livestock feed manufacturer.[30]

McCallum's decision to pursue this strategy would prove to be antiquated, however, once Iowa Beef Processors' revolutionary combination of more isolated, rural slaughtering facilities, nonunion workforces, and streamlined, on-rail, boxed-beef technology rapidly transformed meatpacking (and its profit margins) beginning in 1961. When Currier Holman and Andy Anderson started their Denison, Iowa, plant, meatpacking was still largely typified by urban midwestern locations where animals were shipped on the "hoof," although the transition from urban to rural locations to decrease shipping costs had been gradually occurring since the end of World War I. IBP's real innovations were in the introduction of highly automated, assembly-line production techniques in combination with the development of "boxed" beef. Various firms had introduced automated techniques piecemeal in the 1950s but not in the integrated way that IBP did. Boxed beef referred to the cutting of beef carcass quarters into marketable cuts at the plant instead of having retail butchers handle this step, as had been the traditional practice. Most of the old-line plants were unionized as well, whereas, partly because IBP's technical processes did not require skilled labor, they could hire unskilled workers. Much to Morrell's and other traditional packers' surprise, IBP's integrated production practices soon left them scrambling to innovate or be eliminated as competitors.[31]

Besides choosing outdated financial and production strategies, McCallum exacerbated volatile employee relations at the plant by selecting Harry E. Hansel Jr. to head the confrontational industrial relations department that Charles "Mad Dog" Campbell had led from 1947 to 1952. "Kid" Hansel, as the old-time unionists derisively called him, started working at the Ottumwa plant in 1940, but beginning in 1942 was transferred to the new industrial engineering department. Over the next decade, he helped establish time studies and "gain time" to challenge Local 1's power to control production decisions.[32]

Gain time, in particular, became an effective weapon that management wielded to deflect workers' allegiances away from Local 1. Essentially, gain time was a variation on the old Frederick Winslow Taylor notion of incentive pay (or piecework) that allowed employees to work shorter hours for the same pay as long as they met the production standard for the job. In effect, workers who participated in gain time practiced a self-induced job speedup. Through 1960, when he was transferred away from Ottumwa, Hansel, as operations manager and assistant manager of a revamped industrial relations department, protected the practice of gain time and gain timers themselves wholeheartedly.[33]

McCallum and Hansel's continued assaults on the local union's power to affect workplace decisions resulted in a resurgence of union aggressiveness beginning in 1955. "Cap" Carson, Local 1 president in 1955 and 1956, led a new charge by the old-time militant faction of the workforce against management's directives. In the *Bulletin*, the union's newspaper, leadership waged a propaganda battle, as fierce as the one it had conducted in 1949–1952, against Morrell and its policies. The paper attacked "Kid" Hansel, accusing him of undermining the union contract, including seniority provisions.[34]

During the first half of 1956, virtually the same group of older, militant officers from 1955 continued to press Morrell on gain time. Union officials recalled the period from 1949 to 1952 when workers had been fired for failure to meet new production standards. They urged the rank and file to resist gain time incentives since new standards could result in further job losses and consequent loss of union power. As evidence, Local 1 officials pointed to Morrell's shutdown of the dog food manufacturing department in December 1955 based on time study conclusions. Although the department was small, they believed the same thing would soon happen all over the plant.[35]

Officials also noted the deceit of the company slogan adopted at the 1954 "Morrell Days" celebration, "Morrell Needs You and You Need Morrells," in light of the new company policy of discharging workers or delaying sick pay for absenteeism and tardiness. In fact, union leaders claimed this tactic was simply another union-busting technique. They felt Morrell's underlying attitude was "LET'S BREAK THIS DAMN UNION AND RUN THE COMPANY THE WAY WE SEE FIT."[36]

After many of Local 1's new generation members complained that union militancy was spiraling out of control, UPWA District 3 director Russell Bull again placed the union in receivership. Unlike the case in 1952, however, Bull placed Dave Hart, a prominent member of the new generation of workers at Morrell, in charge as deputy administrator. Although all the 1956 officers were retained for the remainder of the year, the *Bulletin*'s rhetoric became much less antagonistic toward Morrell. Then, in the local's 1957 elections, most of the older militants lost to members of the new generation. Five of the nine local officers were new in 1957 with the two key changes occurring in the president and chief steward positions. Tom Cohagan defeated "Cap" Carson for local union president and Louis Crumes defeated Art Johnson for chief steward. Cohagan and Crumes both won in runoff elections. Crumes had last served as Local 1's vice president in 1953 when, under UPWA District 3 receivership, Dave Hart had served as chief steward, Lester Bishop had been president, and Bob McIntosh had been secretary-treasurer. Bob McIntosh was then elected to the same union office in 1957. In contrast to the new generation of officials, Johnson, like Carson, was a longtime Morrell employee. Born in Blekinge, Sweden, in 1903, he started at Morrell in 1922 and worked in the mechanical department. Also notable about the 1957 officers is that just one of the nine lived in the east end packing district neighborhood, whereas both "Cap" Carson and Art Johnson did.[37]

Local 1's new president, Tom Cohagan, was another prominent member of the new generation of Morrell workers who, like Jack McCoy, wanted more stable relations with management. Born in Knoxville, Iowa, and educated in Des Moines, Cohagan was not part of the union-building struggles at Morrell in Ottumwa during the 1930s. First employed at Morrell in 1939, Cohagan was in military service for a good part of the World War II period. When he returned to the plant, like Jack McCoy, he became active in local union politics. The first indication of his anti-Filliman sympathies occurred in 1951. In one of his weekly UPWA field representative reports, Filliman noted that Cohagan, as Local 1 recording secretary, had been in correspondence with Lewis Clark, a prominent UPWA international officer (as well as a vocal anticommunist) about the current chaos in the Ottumwa plant. Filliman noted with disgust that Cohagan's views were "purely personal" and did not represent the views of all local unionists (including, of course, Filliman's). This clandestine correspondence to Clark seems to have kept Cohagan out of local union offices for the next several years. This held true even during 1953, when many other new generation and less combative workers had first had an opportunity to hold office.[38]

Not surprisingly, Local 1's new officers in 1957 immediately toned down much of the militant rhetoric of the *Bulletin*. For instance, the February 18 issue asked union members to follow the correct sick pay procedures. The spirit of the brief article was that the local union needed to abide more cooperatively with the general provisions of their contract with Morrell. Nevertheless, regarding gain time, the new leadership agreed with the older, more militant leaders' viewpoint. A May 6 article of the *Bulletin* asked the rank and file not to use the incentive system since "greed cuts [your] brothers throat [*sic*]" and denies work to everyone.[39]

By May 1957, the older militants in Local 1 attempted to regain power and raised the issue of the union's continued receivership. At the union's regular membership meeting on May 14, John Bednar, vice president of the local in 1955 and a member of the local's bargaining board in 1956, motioned and Art Johnson seconded a proposal to lift the receivership. The motion carried. A similar proposal carried at a special executive board meeting of the local two days later. Over the next couple of weeks, however, as the UPWA district office stalled on the local's request, the older militants heard rumors that Tom Cohagan, on orders from Dave Hart, was planning to print a detailed plea for retaining the local's receivership. Sure enough, this plea, printed in the June 3 issue of the *Bulletin*, noted that the "old union leaders, many of whom were recently defeated," wanted to lift the administratorship. But, from Cohagan's point of view, without this administratorship, the local would return to the "old days when 87 [*sic*] work stoppages took place."[40]

With Russell Bull himself in attendance, the union's vote that night demonstrated the ascendance of the new generation's views among the rank and file. Their support for retaining receivership carried by a landslide vote of 482 to 170. Although Art Johnson asked that the secret vote be made standing, so each person's position on the internal union struggle would be evident to all, Russell Bull intervened and "demanded a secret ballot." On the surface, Bull's position made sense for restraining what might have become an exacerbated internal union fight. It also suggests the increasing promotion of local union malleability within UPWA District 3 as well as the UPWA international.[41]

Over the next several years, members of Morrell's new generation gradually solidified their dominance in Local 1. After another narrow runoff victory over "Cap" Carson in 1958, Tom Cohagan remained local president until 1963. By 1962, the only members among the nine top officials with ties to the older militants were Virgil Bankson, chief steward, and John Bednar, bargaining board member. Although the *Bulletin* became less combative, especially in regard to production decisions, it nevertheless retained a concern about the corrosive effects of gain time. One general reprimand of "gain timers" suggested that workers used their free time for sexual encounters in the parking lots. The article claimed news of this abuse "could break up many marriages if all the facts were exposed." Hansel was also regularly chided for protecting gain timers even at the risk of sparking "open war with the Union."[42]

Local 1's declining militancy dovetailed with shifts in workers' residential patterns. Morrell's demolition and burning of many remaining, though largely vacant, houses in the near east end during the summer of 1962 epitomized the end of the historic connection between Morrell's militant union tradition and residence in the plant's environs. Morrell proudly described its destruction of the remaining houses next to the plant in an article in the company magazine titled "Urban Renewal." In 1935, 39 percent of Morrell's workers lived in the east end. By 1957, only 22 percent did and by 1965 just 15 percent would live there. On the other hand, the proportion of Morrell employees who lived outside the city limits went from zero in 1935 to 33 percent in 1965. To be sure, by 1962 much of the older tension between the east enders and the out-of-towners was gone, largely because the local union no longer contested company production decisions. Yet local union leaders' irritation about the importation of non-Ottumwa workers was still evident enough in 1962 when the *Bulletin* noted that McCallum had been quoted as saying "[o]ut of towners are more efficient than Ottumwa people if they were hired in the last nine years [that is, since the beginning of his tenure as president]." The irony of the company's "urban renewal" project and the transition in employees' places of residence was evident in the pride with which company officials pointed to the replacement of old east end homes with parking lots. After the demolition and burning, Morrell officials claimed that more than ten acres of parking were available to plant employees![43]

During the two decades following World War II, Local 1's militancy eroded in the face of new company counterattacks and persistent propaganda, tensions between the older generation of union founders and the new workers who joined Morrell's ranks after the war, and concerns generated by plant closings and the rise of new-style, antiunion packing companies across the rural Midwest. Ottumwa's local union, immersed in continuing internal conflicts, most notably between men and women employees, would face a new threat during the mid-1960s: renewed pressure to close the plant. Tragically, the earlier militance and solidarity with which workers won and then hung on to hard-fought gains over crucial aspects of working conditions in the plant were not evident when Morrell pushed for the plant's closing.

However, even though the local's militance eroded during the postwar period, Morrell-Ottumwa's workers participated centrally in a remarkable transformation of Iowa's politics. Whereas the union militants led the initial efforts, their successors were arguably more successful in creating a revitalized Democratic party structure across the state. Though Local 1's power in plant affairs eroded and left little permanent legacy, its contributions to this larger political struggle are evident in Iowa's political scene to this day.

6

LOCAL 1'S UNIONISM AND THE TRANSFORMATION OF IOWA'S POLITICS, 1939–1970

Local 1's militant unionism keyed Iowa's political transformation in the post–World War II years. Morrell workers' CIO movement quickly moved beyond plant organizing and bargaining with the company into a larger political struggle for greater power in city and state politics. Ottumwa's meatpacking workers, together with other blue-collar workers and middle-class residents of the city, became Democratic supporters who precipitated a remarkable transition in partisan politics in Ottumwa, Wapello County, and Iowa as a whole. Indeed, Ottumwa's CIO movement, combined with meatpacking, auto-worker, and farm equipment worker unionism across the state, helped to transform Iowa's political landscape from solid Republicanism to competitive two-party status.[1]

This Democratic transition started in the 1930s but did not culminate until the 1960s. As historian James L. Sundquist describes in *Dynamics of the Party System*, the Democratic ascendancy in Iowa and fifteen other northern states was part of a two-stage realignment that spanned the 1930s to the 1950s. Developments among packing workers in Ottumwa illustrate these findings quite well. The packing community's enthusiasm for unionism in the 1930s did not immediately carry over into support for the Democratic party. From the 1860 presidential election until 1928, Ottumwa and Wapello County were usually dependable Republican strongholds in local, state, and national politics, not unlike most of Iowa's cities and counties. Only during the late nineteenth century and then during World War I had Democrats enjoyed success in Ottumwa and Wapello County. Unlike the situation in other industrial cities elsewhere, the 1928 presidential election results did not presage later Democratic landslides; Hoover drubbed Smith in the packing district's Ward One by a 60 to 40 percent margin. Beginning with the 1932 presidential election, however, Iowa Democrats in both urban and rural areas won by landslide margins in the 1932, 1934, and 1936 national and state elections. As in so many midwestern states, though, Democratic gains largely reflected farmers' protest voting. By 1938, with the New Deal agricultural programs addressing farm problems, Democratic gains declined throughout most of Iowa, even in the industrial cities. Although the Democrats received majorities in Ottumwa and Wapello County during the early 1930s, the packing community did not turn out for Roosevelt to a much greater degree than the rest of the city's voters.[2]

With the 1936 election, though, Ottumwa's industrial workers' selections foretold the significant swing to the Democratic ticket by voters in industrial communities in the state after World War II. Between 1944 and 1972, the original packing district and the south side precincts (where even larger numbers of Morrell workers lived after World War II, and who were joined by workers at the UAW-affiliated Deere plant) averaged 65 and 60 percent majorities, respectively, for Democratic presidential candidates. Even more significant, the residents of Ottumwa and Wapello County as a whole voted solidly Democratic for not only presidential candidates but congressional and state-level politicians as well. From 1932 to 1948, Democrats won 52 percent of Wapello County and Ottumwa's gubernatorial vote. Between 1950 and 1972, Democrats garnered 58 percent of the total vote in Wapello County, and 59 percent of the vote in Ottumwa during the same period. From the Civil War to 1954, only two Democrats had occupied the governor's office in Iowa, Horace Boies in 1889 and 1891 and Clyde Herring in 1932 and 1934. With voters in Ottumwa and Wapello County leading the way and contributing to concerted urban support across the state, Democrats Herschel Loveless, an Ottumwa native with working-class roots, and former trucker Harold Hughes won the governor's seat five times between 1956 and 1966.[3]

Accompanying the transformation of voting behavior was the direct political participation of workers from Morrell and other industries in Ottumwa in city and state politics. From the 1940s to mid-1950s several union members ran for various city, county, and state offices, and assumed leading roles in the union-organizing campaigns of other plants around the region. Union representatives from Ottumwa were especially instrumental in the union drive at the Rath Packing Company plant in Waterloo, a somewhat larger manufacturing city in northeast Iowa. Home to Iowa's two largest factories, Rath and John Deere, both CIO organized, Waterloo would emerge in the late 1940s and early 1950s as the other leading CIO locale in the state. Constituting the largest bloc of union members in the state's CIO council, Waterloo and Ottumwa representatives, working together with other representatives from the state's packinghouse and auto worker unions, would promote the political action programs that would transform Iowa's Republican-dominated political establishment into a much more balanced two-party system by the 1960s.

The transformation of voting behavior and workers' direct political participation were mutually reinforcing in Ottumwa through the 1950s. Union leaders, motivated by the same desire for power and control that had sparked most of their union objectives in the plant in the 1930s and 1940s, also ran for political offices to gain a more direct role in community affairs. For union leaders, achieving greater influence in the community was just as important as it was in plant affairs. Their concerns were also increasingly expressed in the voting behavior of rank-and-file unionists as well as significant segments of Ottumwa's population as a whole. As local union achievements became increasingly linked to those of other unions in the industry and around the Midwest by the mid-1940s, Morrell-Ottumwa workers' political horizons became likewise broader. From the mid-1940s to the early 1950s, as workers battled with Morrell's management for control in key production decisions, they also struggled for power in local and state political arenas.

Local 1 was at the forefront of Iowa's Democratic transition long before the post–World War II years. Beginning in 1940, union members registered large numbers of new voters in Wapello County. Then in fall elections of that year, Ottumwa gave Roosevelt his largest percentage victory among all Iowa's industrial cities.[4] With the organization of the CIO's political action committee (PAC) in 1944, workers participated significantly in local Democratic party campaigns. From 1946 through the 1960s, Ottumwa workers' central role in shaping the Iowa-Nebraska States, later Iowa State, Industrial Union Council's CIO-PAC efforts and then the merged AFL-CIO Iowa State Federation of Labor's state-level political efforts resulted not only in consistent Democratic victories in local and county politics, but also helped to secure Democratic successes at the state and national level by the 1960s.

Building a "Union Politic" in Ottumwa

In 1885, Republican orator, later U.S. senator, Jonathan P. Dolliver claimed that "Iowa will go Democratic when Hell goes Methodist." In fact, Republicans did not dominate Iowa's politics until after the turn of the twentieth century. For much of the late nineteenth century, struggles among the various groups that had settled the state, including Yankees, upland southerners, and foreigners, particularly Germans, over racial equality and Prohibition made Democrats and Republicans fairly evenly matched. Ottumwa generally reflected the state's diverse ethnocultural mix and political heritage from the mid–nineteenth century through the 1920s. Although populated by some Irish and German Catholic immigrants, Ottumwa's Democratic supporters in the late nineteenth century were often American-born with roots in the South, unlike Dubuque, where Irish and German Catholics turned that city into a major center of Democratic party support. Situated in the southern half of Iowa where upland southerners were among the earliest settlers, from its earliest years Ottumwa's working class demonstrated a noticeable tendency to vote more Democratic than the city as a whole. In the 1856 presidential election, Wapello County, like several of the counties in the two southernmost tiers of the state, returned majorities for the Democratic candidate, James Buchanan.[5]

Yet beginning with the 1860 presidential election through 1928, the majority of Ottumwa and Wapello County voters, like Iowa's voters in general, normally turned out for the Grand Old Party. Although Ottumwa's working-class voters, particularly those in the Ward One packing district, did vote more strongly for Democrats between 1888 and 1936, the difference between their turnouts compared to those for the rest of the city's voters was generally only a few percentage points. Ottumwa and Wapello County voters also demonstrated a somewhat higher proclivity to vote for third-party candidates, especially Socialists and Progressives though not Populists, resulting in somewhat lower percentage returns for Republicans than the state as a whole, but otherwise there was little significant difference between Ottumwa, Wapello County, and Iowa in Democratic voting tendencies during this period. The Republican party's dominance in Wapello County before the 1930s is also evident when looking at county elected officials. Between 1898 and 1932, only during the period from 1906 to 1912 were there more Democratic officials than Republicans in Wapello County.[6]

The real watershed in the packing district's voting behavior occurred with the 1936 presidential election. Although the packing district gave 56 percent to Roosevelt in 1932, Wapello County as a whole actually supported Roosevelt at an even higher rate of 57 percent. Indeed, the 1932 and 1934 gubernatorial and 1932 U.S. Senate races demonstrated the same pattern. These results lend credence to Harlan Hahn's argument that Roosevelt's success in Iowa's 1932 presidential election was largely owing to rural protest votes. Across Iowa in 1932, farmers gave Roosevelt 70 percent of their vote compared to just over 50 percent from residents of towns over 10,000. The returns from the packing district from 1936 on, however, were consistently higher for Democrats and markedly greater than that of the entire city or county, though the returns from these larger areas also showed consistently higher returns for Democrats.[7]

The underpinning of this Democratic transition in Ottumwa was the extension of workers' struggles for greater power and control in the Morrell plant to the city as a whole. The 1939 strike and the shop-floor struggles that were endemic in the plant in the late 1930s and early 1940s made the larger political context for workers' local workplace efforts more important. During the 1940s and 1950s, workers' forays into local politics mirrored the struggles within the plant. Workers running for local and state political offices often contested management representatives from the Morrell plant. As a consequence, while Local 1 struggled to gain union shop and dues check-off agreements in the late 1930s and early 1940s, the local also aggressively expanded its presence in Ottumwa's politics and within Iowa's CIO movement.

Over the course of the 1950s, however, as the militants among Local 1's leadership lost favor among the new workers entering the plant, they also failed to capture support in community political contests. The 1953 city elections saw the last attempt by Local 1 militants to contest for city council positions. During the same period, however, several members of the new generation of Local 1 officials, including Jack McCoy and David Hart, along with politically active members of the UAW local organized at the city's growing John Deere plant, especially Jacob "Jake" Mincks, as well as a former Morrell worker, Herschel Loveless, would successfully contest for positions in city, state, and state labor politics. Instead of viewing local and state politics as another means of punishing management and gaining greater control in rapid fashion, as the militants tended to view politics, the new generation of labor leaders were in the fray for the long haul. They were willing to work within the political system to gain benefits for their fellow workers in a way that appeared less combative than the militants' efforts and behavior. In particular, workers who began their tenure at Morrell after World War II saw the new Local 1 leaders as less self-interested and vindictive. This perception translated into a wider appeal among other Ottumwa and Iowa voters when the new generation entered politics.

The central agency of Morrell workers' political involvement was the Ottumwa Industrial Union Council (OIUC) created in 1939 by Local 1. It quickly overshadowed the city's AFL central labor body, the Trades and Labor Assembly (TLA). During the war years, animosity between the PWOC and Amalgamated in the Morrell plant mirrored the competition between the OIUC and TLA in part because Henry Hoover, leader of the small group of Amalgamated members in the Morrell plant and infamous among Local 1 members for his attempted back-to-work movement during the 1939 strike, served as TLA president. In September 1941, for example, competition between the two groups flared into a fierce struggle over union affiliation of the city's truck drivers. Local 1 had urged the members of the AFL-affiliated International Brotherhood of Teamsters (IBT) truckers to join the CIO's Motor Transport Drivers and Allied Workers, led by former IBT (and IUAW) leaders Farrell Dobbs, Carl Nilson, and the Dunne brothers, Trotskyites out of Minneapolis and Duluth, Minnesota, and Frank Cronin, a Waterloo-area organizer who later became a CIO regional director in Nebraska. Local 1 provided picketers at grocers still working with IBT truckers. When Local 1's representatives on the OIUC failed to give unanimous support to the challenge to the IBT, Local 1's membership promptly asked for their representatives' resignations. OIUC president Jack Woodrow, secretary Orvel Champ, Donald Jones, and Harold Whitney, all Local 1 members, then threw their support behind Nilson's CIO efforts, but were nevertheless forced to step down because of pressure from Local 1's membership. Because of developments in Ottumwa, Iowa-Nebraska CIO director Ben Henry pledged to throw the weight of the state union apparatus behind a move of the truckers into the CIO. Despite this support from Local 1 and the state CIO, the AFL won out over the CIO and signed a citywide contract to handle both motor and rail freight. Although unsuccessful, the struggle over the truckers' union affiliation demonstrated the widespread militancy within Local 1 and the local's commitment to larger union and political fights.[8]

Both Local 1 and the OIUC supported candidates for local and state offices beginning in 1940. The experience of the 1939 Morrell-Ottumwa strike convinced union leaders that they needed a more supportive city and county government. In 1940, Charles Sears, president of Local 1 in 1939, ran for a seat on the Ottumwa school board. Sears's candidacy posed a test of union power against one of the incumbents running for reelection, recently retired Morrell superintendent and longtime worker enemy Ernest Manns. In the race to select members for three seats, Manns finished second and Sears came in fourth out of thirteen candidates. Interest in the elections, however, generated the highest turnout in a school board race in twenty years. In the next two months, Local 1 and the OIUC expanded on this interest by helping to boost voter registration in Wapello County before the May 1940 primaries. Their efforts added 1,625 new voters to the county rolls, an increase of more than 10 percent. That fall's elections resulted in the Democrats' sweep of local and state representative slots in Wapello County, a county safely Republican since the late nineteenth century.[9]

The impact of this 1940 voter registration campaign is also clearly evident when the total votes from the 1940 general elections are compared to earlier results. Whereas Ottumwa's population increased by 12 percent between 1930 and 1940, the total vote cast for the president went up 15 percent between

1936 and 1940, and was up nearly 20 percent from 1932. The total number of votes cast for Roosevelt in the same periods was up 16 and 25 percent in Ottumwa. At the county level, although the population had increased by 9 percent between 1930 and 1940, total votes cast for the president in 1940 were up 13 percent over 1936 and 20 percent since 1932. Correspondingly, Roosevelt received 11 percent more votes in 1940 from Wapello County voters than in 1936 and 20 percent more than in 1932.[10]

In addition to entering local political contests and registering voters, Morrell-Ottumwa workers involved themselves early on in a campaign to retain the structure of city government. Local 1 activists saw the city's commission form of government as potentially responsive to working people if labor union members or other union allies could be placed in office. Ottumwa's mayor as well as its streets and public improvements and public safety commissioners each received a salary that allowed them to hold office without needing an additional source of income. This fact also potentially held promise for attracting a working person to run for office. Yet almost as soon as Morrell workers launched themselves into city politics, middle-class groups mobilized to oppose their efforts. Beginning in early 1941, a middle class–dominated Citizens Committee for the Council-Manager Plan proposed that Ottumwa adopt a city-manager plan of local government whereby a salaried city manager would be hired to "administer the city's business." The city council would then consist of unpaid elected officials. Members of the Citizens Committee baldly stated that under the present conditions, namely greater labor union influence, "we cannot ELECT and KEEP men of ABILITY in office." The OIUC led the opposition to the plan, and argued that it was a blatant attempt to remove working people from participating in local political affairs. Using language that echoed workers' desire for power in workplace affairs, the opposition argued that the city-manager plan would mean "ONE-MAN AUTHORITY" and would deprive citizens of "political and personal liberty." The opposition said that Ottumwa residents were being asked to "adopt the dictator plan and have a stranger rule us!" In the union's first true political success in city affairs, the city-manager plan failed in March 1941 by a more than two-to-one vote in the city as a whole and by much wider margins in the working-class precincts. In 1944, however, after racketeering charges resulted in the dismissal of the city's safety commissioner and nearly ended the mayor's tenure, middle-class residents once again attempted to secure passage of the city-manager plan. The Fosters were open proponents of the plan this time around. Once again because of Local 1's and the OIUC's efforts, it fell to defeat by an almost two-to-one margin.[11]

Engaging themselves in local politics during the early 1940s, several leading militants from Local 1 also helped to establish and lead the state's CIO council. The Iowa-Nebraska States Industrial Union Council, CIO, established in Des Moines in April 1938, held its fourth annual constitutional convention in Ottumwa in August 1941. Robert K. Gustafason from Local 1 served as one of the vice presidents. The following year, two members of Local 1 served on the council. Thomas B. Hadden, president of Local 1 in 1941, served as the secretary-treasurer alongside President Ben Henry, and Orvel Champ was one of the vice presidents. In addition, in 1942 Joseph Clark, a member of SWOC's local at the Ottumwa Iron Works, was another vice president. In 1943, Orvel Champ, Local 1's recording secretary that year, then became the secretary-treasurer of the state council with James Provenzano, a member of USWA Local 2134 of the Ottumwa Iron Works, a member of the executive board. Morrell-Ottumwa's local constituted a strong presence in the founding and World War II years of the state CIO council since it was the second-largest CIO local in the state, behind only the UAW-organized John Deere plant in Waterloo. In 1943, after the Rath plant's workforce in Waterloo joined the PWOC-CIO, Ottumwa's Local 1 then constituted the third-largest union in the state council. Indeed, Local 1 was instrumental in providing leaders for the Rath-Waterloo organizing campaign. Lester Bishop, Wilson (Moose) Rogers, and Edward Fitzpatrick all played significant roles leading up to the union's victory there in a November 1942 certification election. A year earlier, Local 1 activists helped Ottumwa's Dain, later John Deere, employees gain their first union contract, and also helped establish the Cedar Rapids Industrial Union Council.[12]

During the World War II years, Morrell-Ottumwa workers continued to run for local political offices. In March 1944, another president of Local 1, Edward A. Filliman, failed in the city's school board elections. The following year, Filliman also lost by a huge margin to Frank Pedrick, a south side hardware merchant, in a race for city riverfront commissioner. In 1944, however, two union members won Wapello County's two seats in the state legislature. Dean Aubrey, a UAW member and John Deere employee, and Wade McReynolds, a bus driver and AFL member, captured those seats in a heavy general election turnout. Voters seemed already to have perceived Filliman's militant credentials as a political liability compared to Aubrey and McReynolds, who did not have the same reputation. As the fall election campaign approached, Ottumwa's packing workers became involved in the newly formed CIO-PAC. Given the organizational and voter registration efforts of the OIUC, Ottumwa-Morrell workers were well prepared to lead local PAC efforts. Local 1 had already formed its own PAC in November 1943, consisting of nine members including Donald Jones, Louis C. May, Virgil and Gene Bankson, and Dean Aubrey. Although the Iowa-Nebraska States Industrial Union Council did not make PAC a permanent part of its committee structure until 1946, the organization did place ten leading union members from across Iowa on its payroll to help with efforts to increase voter registration and distribute national PAC literature. Much of the CIO political action effort across Iowa in 1944 was focused on recruiting farmers into the Democratic party. Lyle Cooper, the UPWA international's research director, specifically commended Ottumwa's Local 1 in this regard as two farmers were elected as Democrats to formerly Republican-dominated county offices. State CIO officials noted that the Iowa legislature also passed a few laws benefiting labor for the first time in twelve years, such as increased workmen's compensation benefits. Nevertheless, though the packing community's Ward One gave Roosevelt 69 percent of its vote, up from 61 percent in 1940, across Ottumwa and Wapello County as a whole votes for the Democrats remained at the same levels as in 1940. Roosevelt received 58 percent from Ottumwa voters and 57 percent from voters in Wapello County.[13]

Nevertheless, at the local political level Democrats already dominated Wapello County's politics by World War II. Except for the period between 1906 and 1912, when the majority of elected county officials were Democrats, Wapello County's elected offices had long been held by Republicans. Beginning in 1932, however, Democrats would prevail in Wapello County elected offices through the end of the 1960s. The only year in which Republicans came close to a majority in the county was in 1942, when there were six Democrats and five Republicans. This dominance would continue long after World War II. From 1956 to 1968, in fact, there were only a total of five Republicans elected for ninety positions in the county.[14]

Through all of its political and welfare efforts by the end of World War II, Local 1 had made significant strides in creating loyalties to union and CIO political goals among a large segment of Ottumwa's working-class residents. As the largest single organization in Ottumwa during the war years, Local 1 became enmeshed in the city's welfare and wartime institutional support network. In 1943, Orvel Champ led the OIUC's War Manpower Commission and Local 1 was the second-largest donor, behind Morrell, to the National War Fund and Red Cross financial campaigns. Local 1 raised $12,000 in 1943, over 15 percent of Ottumwa's entire goal. In 1944, Dean Aubrey served on the board of directors of Wapello County's Red Cross. Local 1 and Morrell together accounted for more than 20 percent of the Red Cross's quota for the county.[15]

At both the state and local level, however, the involvement of Local 1's militants in political efforts often created more controversy and turbulence than success. At the state level immediately following World War II, Local 1 militants were entrenched in positions of power on the Iowa-Nebraska States Industrial Union Council. In 1946, Orvel Champ was the group's secretary,

Donald Jones was the chair of the Legislative Committee, and Edward Filliman was secretary of the Resolutions Committee. With twenty-five votes in
the council, the third largest bloc — behind Waterloo's UPWA Local 46 from
Rath and UAW Local 838 from John Deere — Local 1's delegates supported
the council's establishment of a permanent PAC. Yet Edward Filliman in particular was adamantly opposed to increasing the per-capita tax from four to
five cents to help support PAC activities. Filliman had emerged as Local 1's
leading militant during World War II, and as the local's chief steward from
1945 to 1948, had masterminded many of the local's worker control efforts
against Morrell's speedup campaigns. He attempted to assert the same sort of
control over the state's CIO council. Instrumental in leading the separation of
the Iowa-Nebraska States Council into two separate councils in 1947, he accepted Orvel Champ's nomination to be the first president of the independent Iowa CIO council and won the election.[16]

Filliman's tenure as the state's CIO council president was short and combative. His tenure also coincided with a period of intense factionalism within
Iowa's (and the national) CIO over various issues, particularly the Progressive
party's presidential campaign. Iowa's CIO left-wingers, supportive of the Progressives, were led by Charles Hobbie, head of the United Farm Equipment
and Metal Workers Union (FE). At the 1948 state CIO constitutional convention, Filliman promoted the majority report against third-party candidates in
the fall elections. Even though Hobbie had advocated support for third-party
candidates, he nevertheless nominated Filliman for another term as state
council president, noting that "I have worked with him over a period of time
and found him to be efficient, capable and [an] honest trade union leader." But
because of charges of opportunism leveled on him by state CIO president Ben
Henry and his frustration with the present council's constitution that did not
allow him to "take and formulate and carry out policy," Filliman declined the
nomination.[17]

From 1946 through 1948, however, when Local 1's militants were significant leaders of the state CIO council, they strongly influenced the political efforts the group undertook in conjunction with the national CIO-PAC as well as
the various regional representatives of CIO unions, such as UPWA, UAW, and FE.
At the same time that the UPWA and FE were especially active politically in
Iowa following the disastrous 1946 elections and passage in June 1947 of the
Taft-Hartley Act, the state CIO council urged greater PAC activities and
greater effort in terms of farmer-laborer cooperation. The state CIO council as
well as UPWA, FE, and several other unions brought their members out in
droves to protest a proposed "right-to-work" law for Iowa. On April 21, 1947,
25,000 unionists picketed at the state capitol in Des Moines to no avail; the law

passed Iowa's rural-dominated legislature and Republican governor Robert Blue signed it into law.[18]

Passage of a state "right-to-work" law galvanized both the UPWA and FE into pursuing farmer-labor organizing. Union leaders felt farmers needed to be more sympathetic to the needs of labor and see their common interests. Both unions established full-time farm relations directors in 1946, and began to pursue cooperative efforts with the Iowa Farmers Union (IFU) by the end of that year. The IFU's president beginning in 1945 was Fred W. Stover, a social democrat and devotee of Henry A. Wallace. As was true of many left-liberals and their organizations during the 1940s, Stover and the IFU pushed issues such as full employment, economic planning, expanded social welfare and civil rights programs, higher farm commodity subsidies, and international cooperation with the Soviet Union. Stover's first editorial for the *Iowa Union Farmer* called for closer relations with labor since "[a] sympathetic understanding by farmers of labor and labor organizations is of prime importance if we are to progress as citizens in a democracy." The fact that the IFU was as committed to social democratic programs as either the UPWA or FE greatly helped labor's coalition-building efforts with farmers.[19]

To be sure, the social democracy of the UPWA, FE, and IFU in this period was episodic and, as David Plotke carefully points out about this theme in American liberalism in the 1930s and 1940s, should not be seen as "an autonomous political force" and "had no chance of success" in replacing the Democratic party. Moreover, Ottumwa's workers, as they demonstrated in the 1948 national elections, were not budding social democrats, even if they wanted greater shop floor power. Nevertheless, the social democratic themes and programs of the three organizations captured the imaginations and support, however fleeting, perhaps, of many workers in Ottumwa and industrial cities in Iowa and the Midwest in the period. The UPWA's social democratic programs rested on a vision of labor, capital, and the state cooperating to restructure America's economy and society so that class conflict would be reduced and all Americans would prosper. The UPWA advocated national economic planning or "planned production for abundance," practiced already in Austin, Minnesota, where union members at the Hormel packing plant had won a guaranteed annual wage. The UPWA also supported pay raises, especially those advanced in the union's national strikes of 1946 and 1948, social welfare, farmer-labor cooperation, civil rights and antidiscrimination programs, and local union participation in Democratic community politics.[20]

Ottumwa's Local 1 quickly became one of Iowa's most active UPWA social democratic advocates, especially in regard to farmer-labor organizing. In April 1947, Lee Simon, the UPWA's farm relations director, served as a conciliator along with Local 1 representatives for a four-day Ottumwa milk strike, in which 190 dairy farmers refused to accept the price cut imposed by four area milk distributors. Building on the success of Simon's efforts, Stover, Simon, and the Reverend John Harley Telfer, pastor of the First Congregationalist Church in Ottumwa, elaborated in May on the IFU district conference theme, "Building for Peace and Abundance," by speaking to Ottumwans on "Farmer-Labor Teamwork for Peace and Abundance." Telfer, an Ottumwa resident since July 1945, had already made a name for himself as an outspoken advocate for black civil rights. Educated at the University of Chicago, he had been director of the Milwaukee Federation Forum and Milwaukee Town Hall before moving to Ottumwa. He chaired Ottumwa's Interracial Committee and the People's Flood Prevention Committee, an organization of local farmers and laborers. Beginning in 1947, he became the UPWA District 3's radio show host. The show aired three times weekly and was described by the UPWA as one of the most widely aired labor radio shows in the country.[21]

Soon after the IFU conference, Local 1 formed one of the first UPWA local union farmer-labor committees. Later in the fall, Ottumwa was the site of the UPWA-IFU jointly sponsored Farmer–Labor Day picnic. More than 3,000 people attended the two-day celebration at Wildwood Park on Ottumwa's south side and heard liberal and left-wing farm and labor leaders urge a "political revolt against [R]epublican legislators and congressmen." The picnic was organized by Ed Filliman and Dwight Anderson, a farmer from Agency and local IFU leader, along with a planning committee including five meatpacking workers, five employees of the Deere-owned Dain Company farm implement plant, two employees of the Ottumwa Iron Works, and one machine operator at the Hardscog Pneumatic Tool Works in Ottumwa. Local 1 militants later complained about how AFL groups were notably absent from this and other farm-labor efforts in Ottumwa during the period, but it is difficult to know just how eager they actually were to work with them, given earlier squabbles between the two groups. The FE also held joint meetings with the IFU during summer and fall 1947 at Charles City, home to a large Oliver farm implement plant, and other nearby north-central Iowa locations.[22]

Although the state CIO council was strongly supportive of farm-labor cooperation and political efforts, inviting Fred Stover, Homer Ayres, and Lee Simon to speak on the issue at its 1946 and 1947 constitutional conventions, the state CIO, like the national CIO, was not supportive of third-party candidacies in the 1948 election. Thus, a more decidedly left-wing political impact from the joint efforts of the UPWA, FE, and IFU was limited. This is especially evident in the failure of Henry A. Wallace's presidential bid in 1948. Wallace's emphasis on programs for full employment, economic abundance, and international cooperation with the Soviet Union were attractive for many left-wingers with social democratic concerns. In late 1947 and early 1948, the FE international and Iowa's FE District 5's leadership endorsed Wallace. Some local leaders within the UPWA also lobbied on his behalf. Fred Stover bucked the National Farmers Union to endorse Wallace in the January 1948 issue of the *Iowa Union Farmer*. Yet in 1948, most Americans associated these planks with communism. Accordingly, such efforts were unacceptable to most farmers and laborers. Also crucial in swaying CIO members was the removal of several FE District 5 left-wingers by the state CIO council in August. CIO regional director Ben Henry castigated Hobbie and Stover for their support of Wallace. Despite the support and organizing efforts of the IFU, FE, and some UPWA locals on behalf of Wallace's presidential candidacy, he did not gain many votes in the November election. He only garnered 1 percent more of the total votes in north-central Iowa counties where the IFU had its largest support than his overall nationwide vote total of 2 percent. He did even worse in Ottumwa, where he received less than 2 percent of the votes cast, primarily because Local 1 leaders, such as Edward Filliman, did not encourage their membership to support him.[23]

After 1948 left-liberal farm-labor educational efforts declined noticeably. This was owing in part to conflicts within the IFU, to conflicts between them and the state CIO, and to the virtual absence of support for the popular front in Iowa as a whole. Another significant factor was the loosening of ties between the IFU and the UPWA. Even though UPWA District 3 leadership continued to pass resolutions supporting farm-labor work, they no longer organized farm-labor meetings and conferences. Some of this might be attributed to Lee Simon's death in September 1948. From 1948 to 1950, the UPWA devoted most of its efforts to promoting farm-labor cooperation by distributing leaflets at its booths at county fairs in the Midwest. These efforts were substantial in their own way. In the fall of 1948, for example, UPWA District 3 staffed booths at twelve county fairs in Iowa and at least two 4–H shows, and during the summer of 1949 it increased its allocations for exhibits and literature and even sponsored a group of ballad singers at over thirty local union meetings and county fairs in Iowa and Nebraska. In all, the UPWA visited more than forty fairs in 1949 and expanded its monthly literature mailings to farmers from 14,000 to 100,000 pieces between 1948 and 1949. Yet in 1949 the UPWA no longer was as active in sponsoring farm-labor meetings and conferences, unlike the FE, which merged reluctantly with another outcast CIO international, the United Electrical, Radio and Machine Workers of America (UE). Local 1's farm-labor committee also evaporated during these years. Consequently, after 1948 the FE was the only labor union willing to work in this way with the IFU.[24]

Criticism within the state CIO council during the early 1950s singled out several problems with mainstream CIO farmer-labor cooperative and political efforts. In 1951, Jacob "Jake" Mincks, a member of UAW Local 74 representing Ottumwa's John Deere plant, voiced several concerns as chair of the state CIO council's farm-labor committee about the episodic nature of labor's political efforts. Mincks, though never employed at Morrell-Ottumwa or a participant in the factionalism within Local 1, emerged as the most important unionist from Deere in Ottumwa after starting work there in 1947. He immediately became involved in local union, community, and statewide political causes. Raised on a farm south of Ottumwa, he came to live in the city in 1931 after his father's death. After working at odd jobs and for the Civilian Conservation Corps, he first joined a labor union in 1938 as a Teamster, and then worked at the Ottumwa Iron Works from 1941 to 1947 and joined the local CIO steelworkers union there. Though like the militants who formed Local 1 Mincks was an early CIO supporter, unlike them he apparently never supported militant job actions. He revealed in a later interview that he took pride that Deere had only one significant strike (in 1950) during the long period that he worked there. Although clearly ambitious in his own way, he did not view politics as a forum for punishing employers. Within a year of joining the Deere ranks, Mincks was a clear leader within the UAW local there. He was also one of the UAW's local representatives on the OIUC. In October 1948, he gave a report to the local's membership on PAC efforts, and one month later initiated a motion within the local to have them go on record supporting Ben Henry's purge of the left-wingers within the state's FE. His political involvement at the local level soon carried him into prominence within the state CIO council. He became a consistent voice for more concerted political efforts on the part of the state CIO council. Indeed, Jack McCoy, part of the new generation of Local 1 leaders to move into state-level politics, later described Mincks as "the pusher behind the political activities of all of us [in Ottumwa]."[25]

Mincks thoroughly backed the new leadership of the state CIO council, led since the controversial 1948 elections by president Vernon Dale and secretary-treasurer Kenneth Everhart. Dale, a member of Amalgamated Clothing Workers of America (ACWA) Local 261 in Muscatine, and Everhart, part of UAW Local 838 in Waterloo, were committed especially, like Mincks, to increasing the level of funding for the state CIO council's PAC efforts. This commitment never wavered from the late 1940s through the state council's merger with the state AFL council in 1956 largely because both Dale and Everhart were reelected to their offices each year by acclamation. In 1950 this fact led to an attempt initiated by Filliman to oust them by demanding a secret ballot for the election of officers. Three years earlier, Filliman, along with many other delegates from the UPWA especially, had demanded roll call votes for the election of officers so that local union constituencies could be assured that delegates voted for the candidates they had agreed on before the convention. That motion was narrowly defeated, and so was Filliman's attempt to enforce the secret ballot provision in 1950. Nevertheless, the defeat of this motion caused several local unions, including Local 1, to withdraw from the state CIO council for the next two years. Although Filliman's overt argument all along was the need for democratic process and responsiveness, his efforts also strongly suggested a personal desire for power and control. After the return of most local union delegations to the state's fold by 1953, state CIO delegates no longer were swayed by Filliman or other CIO militants. The two-year absence of the most militant voices effectively muted their voice in the state CIO council.[26]

As articulated by Dale, Everhart, and Mincks, the PAC chair beginning in 1952, effective political efforts demanded more systematic voter registration, more lobbying efforts, especially at the grassroots level, and, more than anything, a greater commitment by local union members to financially support PAC. By 1950, for instance, the national CIO-PAC was working more closely with the state CIO council's PAC, and had committed substantial funding for selected campaigns, especially Albert Loveland's candidacy for the U.S. Senate. Morrell-Ottumwa's Local 1 spent $3,000 of its own funds and expended considerable manpower in canvassing unsuccessfully for Loveland on behalf of PAC. The CIO hoped Loveland would also appeal to family farmers because of his support for the Brannan Plan, a proposal to hike farm supports to higher, fixed levels. Despite winning 67 percent of the First Ward's vote as well as 54 percent of Ottumwa's and 53 percent of Wapello County's votes, Loveland only mustered 45 percent of the state's total tally. Some blamed his poor showing on scathing attacks on the Brannan Plan by the American Farm Bureau Federation, a larger organization representing more prosperous individual farmers and agribusiness interests. More important, because of a lack of more consistent political efforts and money overall, Democratic candidates did not do well throughout the state. This sentiment was voiced by Mincks when he noted in his farmer-labor committee report regarding U.S. House efforts that "We down in Ottumwa can carry Wapello County, but we have four counties in the district down there. How are you going to carry the others?" Another CIO delegate noted that too few county-level PAC committees had been established. In his 1952 president's report, Dale noted that "in the early days . . . too few people tried to do too much. The end result [was] a lot of noise with little accomplished." On a related issue of farmer-labor political strategies, Everhart noted in 1952 that "setting up booths at State Fairs [was not] particularly conducive to good farmer-labor relations in the state of Iowa." Though thoroughly supportive of farmer-labor political efforts, he questioned the tactic of "trying to cram a farm program down the farmer's [sic] of Iowa without knowing what we are talking about." In another debate on political tactics, Everhart and Mincks stressed the need for more direct visits with local legislators.[27]

Again, the underlying need, according to these leaders, was greater funding for the PAC. Before the 1951 state CIO council convention, the militants, led by Filliman, had effectively blocked increases in the per-capita tax. However, without the militants' attendance at either the 1951 or 1952 conventions, Dale and Everhart were able to make the issue a key point of debate. At the 1951 convention, President Dale noted that he was sympathetic to the packing-house workers' delegates' position against a per-capita tax increase, but he stressed that the need for a two-cent increase (from five to seven cents) was pressing. The two-cent increase would be earmarked for PAC's use only. This issue was finally resolved the following year. The 1952 convention passed the two-cent per capita increase after a lengthy debate regarding the reaffiliation of the locals that owed back dues or had walked out over the per-capita issue in 1950. Initially, the Resolutions Committee passed a resolution demanding full repayment before locals were allowed back onto the state CIO council. But Fort Dodge UPWA Local 31 member and UPWA Region 3 director Russell Bull, who had helped to move Local 1 militants out of power during the 1950–1952 period, condemned the resolution for trying to "ring [sic] every last cent of blood" out of locals before letting them back in. Both Dale and Everhart reminded delegates that there was no sense in punishing delinquent locals since the PAC program needed all locals to be present and current in dues for it to function effectively. Everhart clinched support for a more moderate resolution that would give the executive board discretionary power over conditional readmittance by exclaiming that "you make councils out of people, not out of money." Ben Henry made an indirect reference to Local 1 in regard to the local union readmittance and the PAC issue by noting that "one particular local union is in an important spot in this political action program that we are going to try to promote."[28]

From 1948 to 1952, Local 1's militants also made several efforts to assert their power in community politics. But just as occurred within the state CIO council, these efforts all faltered. In their wake, moderate and more conciliatory Local 1 leaders emerged and experienced greater political success. Particularly in the aftermath of the tumultuous 1948 UPWA meatpacking strike, Local 1 militants focused even more attention on controlling city politics. They viewed the 1949 city council elections as crucial to the local's political power in Ottumwa in several respects. On the most basic level, Local 1 hoped to retake the offensive against the city's middle-class community that had largely been unsupportive of its strike efforts. True to their tactics at the shop floor level, Local 1's militants wanted to mobilize union members and other blue-collar Ottumwans to defeat and punish public officials who had hindered the workers' strike efforts. As a consequence, militants even attempted to dissuade workers from supporting friends of labor, in this particular election,

Herschel Loveless, because he and others were seen as not sufficiently militant. Loveless's victory would be another sign of the weakening hold the militants had in Local 1.

Early in 1949, Local 1, the OIUC, and the TLA formed the Ottumwa Policy Committee to focus working-class votes in the upcoming city elections. During the mid-March primaries, the Ottumwa Policy Committee supported David Nevin, Lester Parcell, and Patrick Harden. Each man won enough votes to be entered in the general election. Mayoral candidate Nevin and safety commissioner candidate Parcell both finished a close second. Mayor Herman Schaefer was thoroughly defeated, having won the scorn of not only working-class voters for his role in the 1948 strike, but also having alienated middle-class voters for not having controlled the situation more effectively. Streets commission candidate Patrick Harden won the primary election for this position. Local 1 then embarked on an intensive propaganda campaign during the two weeks preceding the general election.[29]

Local 1 supported Nevin over the other mayoral candidate, Herschel Loveless, because union leaders claimed that Loveless had not joined a union until he needed labor's political support. Born on a farm near Fremont, Iowa, in 1911, Loveless had moved to Ottumwa as a youngster and graduated from Ottumwa High School in 1927. He then worked for the Chicago, Milwaukee, St. Paul and Pacific Railroad through most of the Great Depression. In 1939, he joined Morrell's workforce as a turbine operator in the power plant before returning to work for the Milwaukee Railroad in 1944. On a leave of absence from the railroad, Loveless organized the street and sanitation departments and then served as the city council's emergency chief organizer during the disastrous 1947 flood in Ottumwa. It was in this capacity that he earned widespread support among Ottumwans. Nevertheless, Local 1 accused Loveless of not joining the Railway Clerk's Union until the mid-1940s when he pursued political ambitions.[30]

Local 1 also tried to sway working-class Ottumwans to look unfavorably on Edna Lawrence, Lester Parcell's opponent for safety commissioner in the city election. Lawrence, like Loveless, had considerable support among workers in the city. In 1948, with Local 1 support, she had won a seat in the state legislature but then resigned her office in early 1949 in hopes of winning city office. Local 1 noted that Lawrence had run unsuccessfully for local office many times before and now seemed more concerned about settling old scores than serving Ottumwans on the state level, as she had been entrusted to do. John Meagher, Harden's opponent for streets commissioner, had served in that position during the 1948 strike and had suffered consequently in the primary election. Although his role in the strike had been minor, Local 1 did not spare him, attesting that "[h]is management of office and regard for the [p]ublic [since 1947] has been very poor." Indeed, the local reminded workers of Meagher's positions as well, labeling him a "scab" for having crossed the picket line during Ottumwa's 1922 railroad strike.[31]

Before the general election, Local 1 reminded the packing community and other blue-collar residents to "recall just what position certain members of the City Council took in regards to the strike action at Morrells last year." Yet, just before the election, the Ottumwa Policy Committee alliance of AFL and CIO unions broke down. It is not clear which side initiated the split, but Local 1 was left alone in support of its candidates. It seems fair to speculate, however, that many Ottumwa voters, even among the city's working class, saw Local 1's decision to stick with its candidates as evidence of its combativeness. Most of the other AFL and CIO unions in town supported Loveless over Nevin because of Loveless's help for working-class neighborhoods damaged by the 1947 flood. Lawrence, according to other unions in town, boasted significant prolabor credentials. The other unions supported Loveless, Lawrence, and Meagher. When the votes were counted, only Harden among the Local 1 endorsed candidates emerged victorious. Demonstrating the growing divisions within Local 1, the voting results in different parts of the city suggest that many of Morrell's rank and file ignored their leaders' endorsements. The east end original packinghouse community supported Nevin for mayor while south side residents, where most of the flood damage occurred, solidly cast their votes for Loveless. Thus, despite a tremendous effort on the part of the militant leadership of Local 1 to reaffirm its power, the largest city election turnout in Ottumwa's history underscored the unraveling of this control and of unity within the local's ranks.[32]

After 1949, Local 1's militant leaders had little ability to convince blue-collar residents to support their candidates in local elections. Allegations of sloppy handling of local union funds also bothered voters. Ed Filliman, a UPWA international field representative after 1949, exacerbated tensions within the local by noting that the financial stability of Local 1 in 1950–1951 had been seriously compromised by its officers' predilection for ever-increasing salaries and misappropriations of local union funds. Too many officers, Filliman noted, were "Do-Nothing, Money-Grabbing individuals." Although it is difficult to know how much Filliman's charges were motivated by his sense of declining power, having lost a position in not only Local 1 but also on the state CIO council, he named the local's president in these years, Walter Van Tassel, as a particular culprit. In February 1951, Local 1's trustees, including Donald Jones, seconded Filliman's accusations by filing charges against Van Tassel for drawing pay for lost time at the same time that Morrell paid him for vacation time. As discussed in Chapter 5, to a large degree the fight within Local 1 during these years reflected a power struggle between the older militants and the newer generation of less combative union leaders.[33]

This power struggle created generally poor results for Local 1 in city elections during the early 1950s. In 1951, Van Tassel and Thomas Cohagan, Local 1's recording secretary in 1951 and a prominent member of the new generation of union leaders at Morrell-Ottumwa, ran for city offices and lost. Each candidate not only failed to win but could not gain the support of voters in the packinghouse workers' precincts. Herschel Loveless, however, again won the city's mayoral election soundly with the OIUC's solid support. Two years later, Herschel Loveless was the only one of five OIUC-endorsed candidates in the 1953 election who won versus those endorsed by the middle-class and professional voter-backed "Good Government Association." Van Tassel and Dean Aubrey both lost.[34]

By 1953, internal factionalism within Local 1 had seriously compromised its ability to effectively run its own members or even gain working-class support for its endorsed candidates in city elections. The deleterious impact of this factionalism was starkly illustrated in that year when the "Good Government Association" revived its campaign to implement a council-manager plan of city government. Unlike the case in 1941 and 1944 when Local 1 had stood at the center of opposition to similar plans, in 1953 the local ignored the campaign until after enough petitions were collected by July to put it on the general election ballot. At Local 1's July 21 membership meeting, the rank and file decided to spend between $300 and $500 to fight its passage in a last-ditch effort. On July 26, the council-manager plan passed with 58 percent of voters supporting it. Although voters in the old First Ward immediate packinghouse neighborhood rejected it by a 68 percent majority, packing workers who lived in the city's south side precincts contributed to its victory.[35]

Although factionalism within Local 1 contributed to the losses in community politics in 1953, Ottumwa mayor Herschel Loveless demonstrated his strong commitment to labor in the battle over the council-manager plan in that year. Jack McCoy, an employee of Morrell since 1949 and recording secretary for Local 1 in 1953, noted explicitly how Local 1 and the OIUC counted on Loveless's support:

When the fight over going to a city manager form of government developed, Herschel Loveless came down and visited with Dave Hart and I [sic]. He didn't want to turn over the city government to the Chamber of Commerce crowd. We said we'd do our job at the plant. The damn election was held on a Saturday, and we assigned our stewards to different precincts. They worked hard to try to stop it. The newspaper had been building that up for a long while, and they beat us on it, in spite of the stewards doing a good job. We must have fielded between sixty and eighty stewards that Saturday in the precincts in Ottumwa.[36]

Transforming Iowa's Politics

Although factional conflict within Local 1 diluted the union's political strength in Ottumwa during the late 1940s and early 1950s, the union mobilized sufficient power to transform state politics. By 1953, a new generation of Local 1 leaders, like Jack McCoy and Dave Hart, working closely with Jake Mincks, emerged and began to contribute to the next and more successful stage in this political transformation. In 1952, Mincks became Wapello County Democratic chair and, in 1954, McCoy was selected as one of Local 1's representatives on the OIUC. That fall, along with Ottumwa AFL unionist Wade McReynolds and after borrowing over $1,000 from the OIUC's building fund to finance his campaign, McCoy was then elected to the Iowa House of Representatives, a position he won again in 1956. Beginning in the mid-1950s, with the successful merger of the AFL and CIO at both the local level in Ottumwa and, more important, at the state level, Ottumwa's union leaders contributed centrally to the Democratic party's successes.[37]

The state CIO council's 1953 constitutional convention, fittingly held in Ottumwa, opened after an address by Mayor Herschel Loveless with Iowa CIO president Vernon Dale recognizing Ottumwa's key role in the state's labor movement. Dale noted that "much of the leadership and a great number of the membership of the early days of our organization [came from the city]. Ottumwa and its labor movement contributed much to the growth of the CIO in our state." Dale immediately went on to highlight how he viewed the state CIO council's political action efforts, activities in which Ottumwans Mincks, McCoy, and Hart would all play important roles. Mincks, as he had been since the year before, was chair of the PAC, McCoy was secretary of the credentials committee, and Hart, another prominent member of the new generation of leaders at Local 1, was secretary of the Rules Committee. Born in 1907 in the coal camp town of Hocking, Iowa, just west of Ottumwa, Hart had attended UMWA meetings with his father during the World War I era. He worked at odd jobs in Iowa and Chicago before the 1930s, when he moved to New York City. There, interrupted by military service during World War II, he held a variety of laboring positions. When his father died in 1947, Hart returned to Ottumwa and got a job at Morrell just after the 1948 strike. Quickly selected as a department steward, he became chief steward in 1952 in the wake of Local 1's receivership and most intense period of factionalism.[38]

In his comments on the legislative committee's reports at the 1953 convention, President Dale identified labor's most crucial political objectives. Labor unionists elected to the Iowa legislature, such as Kenneth Everhart and Jack McCoy, hammered away at fellow politicians about the need for passing new unemployment and workmen's compensation legislation and repealing the state's right-to-work law, the so-called Senate File 109. However, everything, according to Dale, hinged on counterbalancing the control that the Republican party, and its key lobbying group, the Iowa Manufacturers Association (IMA), had in the legislature. The way to neutralize this Republican dominance was through reapportionment. Although Iowa's constitution required reapportionment after each census, no legislative reapportionment had occurred since 1886. According to political scientist Charles Wiggins, two state constitutional amendments passed in 1904 and 1928 made reapportionment "virtually impossible." The result, especially in the state house since each county received equal representation, was that urban counties were vastly underrepresented. Dale proclaimed that reapportionment "is the only way that the people in Des Moines, Waterloo, Cedar Rapids, Davenport, Dubuque, Sioux City, and the various other cities of the state can have themselves represented." In his 1952 opening convention remarks Dale had also stressed the problem of disproportionate representation in the state legislature. There were too many "men from smaller community areas, farmers and people dependent upon the farm for their living [as well as] those directly representative of the anti labor groups, the big business boys and their lawyers" who constituted the legislators' membership. PAC chair Mincks emphasized how all the convention's resolutions tied into the need to get "our people into the political parties in this state of ours" and to raise funds for PAC. On the funds, Dale noted that the passage of the two-cent increase in the per capita tax, the so-called citizenship fund, had resulted in much "improved financial condition and ability to carry out needed projects in political action and legislation."[39]

Reporting on the CIO's political efforts over the next two years, Dale noted incremental gains. Although the structure of the PAC program was revamped in 1954 with new full-time representatives appointed and training classes started, Dale exclaimed that "you should be getting damn well fed-up with the spectacle of a labor committee [in the state legislature] headed by a business man [sic] and overloaded by farmers who admittedly do not understand the labor problem." Although Democrats picked up eighteen seats in the House, and Republican governor Leo Hoegh agreed to some favorable appointments to various commissioner positions and made good on promises to provide increases in unemployment and workmen's compensation, labor otherwise "received little or nothing" from the state legislature. Moreover, by 1955 much of the state CIO council's discussion pertained to the more immediate issue of the imminent merger of the AFL and CIO.[40]

To be sure, many veteran Iowa CIO unionists looked skeptically at the merger of the two unions. Many agreed with Ralph Helstein, UPWA president, that the merger was defensive; it was a strategy of effectively combating the strength of growing corporations during a period of national political conservatism while also conserving early gains. At the last state CIO council convention, held in Des Moines on June 26, 1956, much of the convention's debate was devoted to the upcoming merger convention, held the following two days in Des Moines. Mincks was one of the outspoken voices urging acceptance and the necessity of the merger. Indeed, Mincks was the guiding force between Ottumwa's CIO and AFL councils' merger, delayed at the request of the AFL council until after the state's merger. To allay the fears of the smaller AFL central body that its unions would have no voice in the new city labor council, Mincks negotiated a nearly equally partitioned representative council. Ottumwa was in the nearly unique position of having CIO unions outnumber AFL unions. The only other Iowa city where this was true was Waterloo, where a volunteer coordinating council had been active since 1950. When founded in August 1956, Ottumwa's AFL-CIO labor council had four AFL representatives and five CIO representatives, despite the fact that Local 1 and UAW Local 74 together accounted for 75 percent of the city's total labor union membership.[41]

In large part, the merger between the AFL and CIO in Iowa occurred as smoothly as it did because the top CIO council officials, like Dale, Everhart, and Mincks, were not militants but were moderates interested in practical political gains for laboring people. They saw the necessity of the merger primarily for political action purposes. Important, too, was the decision of the state's top AFL officials, most notably Ray Mills, the new AFL-CIO president, to throw their support to the Democratic party. Mills, a lifelong Republican, publicly announced his switch to the Democratic party in 1955 after tiring of the IMA-dominated Republican positions on labor laws in the state. Republican governor Leo Hoegh had promised in his 1954 campaign to support the union shop, for instance, but was unable to sway the conservative forces in the legislature to overturn the state's right-to-work law. By combining forces, AFL and CIO activists could certainly accomplish much more working together in the Iowa legislature than they could separately. Iowa's AFL-CIO merger in 1956 created a more politically unified labor movement at both the state and local levels. At the founding convention, the CIO was now outnumbered by AFL unions in the Iowa Federation of Labor (IFL), AFL-CIO, by 390 to 587 votes. Yet in several respects, the CIO still wielded considerable weight. For instance, both the UPWA and UAW received their own vice presidents because each had more than 10,000 members. UPWA Locals 46 and 1 as well as UAW Local 838 were the largest locals in the new IFL. By the 1957 IFL convention, Mincks, Hart, and McCoy all held prominent positions in the state labor federation. Mincks was the Credentials Committee chair, Hart was Resolutions Committee chair, and McCoy was the new Committee on Political Education (COPE) director. After the death of Russell Bull in 1959, Hart became director of UPWA District 3.[42]

In terms of approaches to political action, the IFL's basic strategy, as well as leading personnel, remained true to the CIO's original plan of attack. Farmer-labor cooperation, for instance, remained a key component of the IFL's approach to political mobilization. IFL leaders worked closely with a new farm group, the National Farmers Organization (NFO), for joint political benefit. Although its organizing strategies differed, for many farmers the NFO filled a void left by the decline of the Iowa Farmers Union, embroiled in communist accusations throughout the 1950s. Formed in 1955 and led by Oren Lee Stanley beginning in December 1956, the NFO focused its strategy for raising farm prices on aggressive organizing and collective bargaining. The NFO gained members who were disillusioned with the strategies of farm cooperatives and who felt leery about the future of the federal farm program. Adopted at its convention of 1958, the NFO's collective bargaining aimed at obtaining master contracts with livestock processors and farm commodity buyers on a "cost-plus" basis. Specifically, according to NFO historian Jon Lauck, the "NFO's plan involved Marketing Area Bargaining Committees, elected by NFO members, presenting offers to meatpackers and promising a steady flow of livestock, all in exchange for contracts for better prices." After signing up over 100,000 members, the NFO began to stage holding actions in 1959 as a first step toward gaining master contracts. One of the first holding actions took place at St. Joseph, Missouri, for an entire week. Packers there were able to break the effort, however, by trucking in livestock from outside the organized area. More successful holding actions took place in April 1961 in the Omaha, Kansas City, and St. Joseph areas, followed by further efforts in these and other areas in 1962–1964.[43]

At the local level, this new form of farm-labor cooperation was most successful in Waterloo after the formation of the Black Hawk Labor Council (BHLC), AFL-CIO, in 1956. Besides Ottumwa, Waterloo was the state's other strong CIO center where the merger with the AFL went smoothly because of several previous years of cooperation between the two unions. Unlike earlier efforts by the UPWA and the FE in the late 1940s, however, the BHLC's farmer-labor efforts resulted in greater political gains in this period because they were not tainted with left-wing activities. The NFO initially approached the BHLC because the farm group's organizers, though enthusiastic, had little actual experience with collective bargaining. As a consequence, the BHLC and NFO came to see each other as natural allies.[44]

The BHLC and NFO's collaboration resulted in the formation of a Farm-Labor Association in 1956. John Cooney, president of the BHLC from 1956 to

1965, described how farmer-labor organizing in Black Hawk County and surrounding areas of northeast Iowa worked:

> Well, what happened, you know, the farmers would have one of their meetings and invite somebody from labor to come there and talk. Maybe they would have a hog roast, and they'd invite so many of us to come there. So finally we sat down and, well, if we can sit and talk here why can't we sit down at the table and talk business. We found out there was very little that we couldn't support that they were passing, and vice versa.

Paul Larsen, executive secretary of the BHLC from 1956 to 1965, elaborated on the origins of the Farm-Labor Association:

> [The NFO] came to various elements of the labor movement wanting to know how to organize, wanting to work with and use the expertise of the labor movement. There were a number of people that were very active in the labor movement at that time that had had prior experience working with organizing farm groups too. [As a result of this collaboration], that was the first time that they came up with the slogan, "Collective bargaining in the marketplace." That was the first time that any farm organization had done really anything toward the idea of bargaining for their prices rather than going in and taking [what] was being offered.[45]

In places other than Black Hawk County, Iowa's farmers and urban laborers were drawn closer together politically during the middle and late 1950s by several specific concerns that ultimately bore fruit for the Democrats in several state races, most notably the governor's race in 1956. After several years of rising surpluses and declining prices, farmers balked at U.S. Secretary of Agriculture's Ezra Taft Benson's proposal to combat the problem with flexible price supports. Even Iowa's Republican governor Leo Hoegh castigated Benson's proposal, which cost Hoegh the support of the Iowa Farm Bureau Federation. The Democratic candidate for governor, Herschel Loveless, benefited not only from this issue, but also two others, namely Hoegh's passage of a half-percent increase in the state sales tax and his strong support for blocking the serving of liquor by the drink. The IMA joined Loveless in criticizing the higher sales tax. Moreover, voters in Iowa's urban areas, where slightly more than one-half of the state's population now lived in 1956, endorsed liberalizing the state's alcohol laws.[46]

With a considerable war chest now available from the state AFL-CIO, combined with Democratic party resources and the support of farmers and anti-tax backers, Loveless carried the election, becoming only the fourth Democrat elected governor in Iowa since the Civil War. Election results confirm that Loveless won his greatest support in cities of 25,000 to 50,000 population and farm townships. The state's medium and large industrial cities were now Democratic strongholds, largely accounting for the second-stage gain that James Sundquist describes for the Democratic realignment in Iowa that peaked between 1954 and 1958. Two years later in 1958, similar issues and the same constituencies propelled Loveless to another term as governor and Democrats even took four of the state's eight U.S. congressional seats. In the state legislature, the Democrats increased their representation in both the house and senate. For Wapello County, Mincks won a seat in the senate, which he would retain through 1966, while Dean Aubrey and Robert Conner, another UAW Local 74 member, won places in the house. Ottumwa Democrat Gene Glenn took over Mincks's seat from 1966 to 1974. In fact, from 1944 to 1972, Wapello County Democrats won twenty-one of the thirty total seats contested for the state house.[47]

Loveless made good on his campaign to repeal the half-cent sales tax increase, and along with increasing state social services and appointing professionals to various state commissions, he then made reapportionment the main focus of his term. In his address to the IFL convention in 1957, Loveless emphasized how urban groups, especially organized labor, must be better represented in state politics. Loveless spoke before the IFL convention every year he was in office, and consistently stressed a similar message underpinned by statistics on the shift in Iowa's population from rural to urban locations. In his 1957 address, for instance, he noted how the twenty-six less heavily populated senatorial districts contained about one-third of Iowa's population while the other twenty-four districts comprised about two-thirds of the population. Unless reapportionment occurred, establishment of union shop contracts and improvements in unemployment and workmen's compensation could not occur. Although not specifically named in this speech, the Farm Bureau, especially, together with the IMA, hoped to blunt the urban shift in reapportionment as much as possible through a proposal referred to as the Shaff Plan, after Senator David O. Shaff of Clinton, that called for a state senate based on population and a house based on area. An attempt by the IFL, the League of Women Voters, the urban press, and the Democratic party to gain reapportionment by making the issue a constitutional convention referendum in 1960 narrowly failed after the IMA and Farm Bureau combined to spend nearly $2 million to campaign against it while the IFL and League of Women Voters spent just $100,000.[48]

Although 1960 was a disappointing year for Democrats in Iowa, especially for Loveless who lost his race for the U.S. Senate after spending more time campaigning for John F. Kennedy than himself, the election results indicated that cities of over 10,000 population were now solidly in the Democratic camp. Historian Harlan Hahn's findings indicate that the traditional role of farm townships in casting deciding albeit protest votes for Democrats from the 1930s to mid-1950s was still present after 1958 but less important than the strong support for Democrats in the larger cities. Jack McCoy, as the IFL's COPE director, also laid the groundwork for Democratic gains in the 1960s by establishing local-level COPE programs that were then integrated with the state's programs.[49]

The fruits of the IFL's political efforts can be seen in the success of Democratic governor, then U.S. senator, Harold Hughes throughout the 1960s as well as in Democratic gains in both the state and national legislature following the IFL's successful leadership in the reapportionment battle. Hughes initially attracted Herschel Loveless's attention through his work with the Iowa Better Trucking Bureau. After changing parties at Loveless's prompting, Hughes successfully ran for one of the state commerce commission seats in 1958. A direct, outspoken, and charismatic trucker turned politician, Hughes won the 1962 gubernatorial election by calling for action on the issues of reapportionment and liquor by the drink. In addition to weak stands on liquor reform, Republican governor Norman Erbe had irritated urban Democratic voters by standing by while his lieutenant governor, William Mooty, cast the deciding vote in allowing the passage of the Shaff Plan in 1961. During Hughes's first term, Iowa's liquor laws were repealed and the IFL filed suit in federal court in Des Moines in 1963, challenging the constitutionality of the Shaff Plan's reapportionment scheme. The court refused to act on the plan's constitutionality until after a statewide referendum was held on December 3, 1963. Following a statewide campaign against it by Hughes, organized labor and urban voters in general won an enormous victory when the Shaff Plan was defeated by a margin of 59 to 41 percent. The most overwhelming opposition to the plan came in the seventeen counties containing cities of more than 10,000 population. Wapello, Polk, Woodbury, Linn, and Black Hawk County voters, all home to significant numbers of union members, rejected it by over 80 percent majorities. Farm townships in nineteen predominantly rural counties, in contrast, supported the plan by a 70 percent margin. In a special session of the 1964 state legislature, a new temporary apportionment plan was passed that gave significant increases to urban areas in both the house and senate. A final, more equitable reapportionment plan, mandated by the federal district court in Des Moines, was finally implemented by the state legislature in 1969 and revised by the state supreme court in 1972.[50]

Having deemed reapportionment "the most important project that the Iowa labor movement had ever undertaken," IFL executive vice president Jake Mincks, McCoy's successor as IFL COPE chair, claimed without hyperbole that the Shaff Plan had been defeated because of trade union influence. Certainly labor unionist funding had been vital. Following McCoy's campaign to make

COPE more effective on the local level, the 1962 IFL convention had passed an increase in the per-capita tax, bringing it up to ten cents per member per month. Mincks noted in his 1965 report to the IFL convention that in terms of state and national legislation much had been accomplished. Because of Democratic majorities in the state house and senate — 101 of the 124 seats in the house and 35 of the 53 seats in the senate — "we were able to make gains that we hadn't been able to make in recent years." Among many improvements, Mincks listed a 25 percent increase in the disability benefits of workmen's compensation, positive changes in the unemployment compensation formula and waiting period, and passage of a Fair Employment Practices Act. A bill to legalize the union shop made it through the house but was defeated by four votes in the senate.[51]

In addition to these victories and helped by Democratic control of the state legislature from 1964 to 1968, the IFL and its Democratic allies pushed for and won annual salaries for legislators, encouraged more blue-collar citizens to run for office, and gained a strong workmen's compensation act, unemployment compensation, Iowa's OSHA law, and postcard registration during the late 1960s and early 1970s. Although some members among the IFL blamed Hughes for not pushing harder for the union shop bill, a criticism Hughes strongly rejected in his speech to the IFL convention the next year, in 1965 he helped to settle a UPWA strike at the new Iowa Beef Processors plant in Fort Dodge. At the 1968 IFL convention, Hughes cited some of the gains made for working people during his six years as Iowa's governor, including improvements in workmen's and unemployment compensation, industrial development, greater school aid, property tax relief, abolishment of the death penalty, improvements in state government organization and planning, increased highway patrol and traffic safety programs, and more state facilities for the mentally ill and physically handicapped. Moreover, even when the 1968 elections swept many Iowa Democrats out of state and national legislative offices, the consolidation of the state's Democratic party organization in the late 1960s and early 1970s helped it to bounce back during the 1970s. After Hughes's election to the U.S. Senate in 1968, and establishment of a progressive record there, another progressive Democratic, John Culver, a ten-year veteran of the U.S. House, was elected in his place. Culver's former aide, Dick Clark, was elected to the other Senate seat in 1972. By the mid-1970s, Democrats were also back in control of both houses of the Iowa legislature. Although the Democrats' power has eroded since the 1970s, Iowa remains a competitive two-party state.[52]

By the mid-1960s, labor's political efforts had refashioned local Democratic parties in Iowa's industrial cities. Paul Larsen recalled how "[the BHLC] was very effective politically in endorsing and financially supporting candi-

dates for the . . . state legislative offices. And as a result of that, we were able
to gain a great deal of influence that we had not had with members of the State
Legislature from rural areas." The impact of the BHLC's political activities
"started to show up in the elections of 1958 [when] we started to elect some
people locally to the State Legislature for the first time. This improved in
1960 and 1962." When Black Hawk County went Democratic in 1964 for the
first time since before the Civil War "folks down there thought it was the end
of the world." John Cooney was even more blunt about the impact of organized labor on local Democratic politics:

> Well, as far as I'm concerned, the Black Hawk Labor Council was the local
> Democratic party. We put a lot of money into it. We had good representa-
> tion in this area. We encouraged a lot of people to get mixed into politics
> that had never thought of doing it, simply because, you know, they were
> knowledgeable people.[53]

Cooney also stressed that the BHLC built its Democratic coalition in Waterloo by involving itself in civil rights. Indeed, Waterloo established one of
the first Fair Employment Practice Commissions in the United States during
this period. The BHLC actually built on the antidiscrimination and civil rights
efforts of UPWA Local 46 at Waterloo's large Rath packing plant. Local 46 established its antidiscrimination program in 1950 and especially combated the
segregation of African American women in the plant. The local also fought
segregation in Waterloo beginning in 1953, and when the BHLC was formed,
worked with the countywide labor council to do the same. Besides the establishment of the Fair Employment Practices Commission, the BHLC started the
Martin Luther King Jr. Center for educating blacks of all ages. These antidiscrimination and civil rights initiatives solidified a cross-racial Democratic
base in Waterloo.[54]

Without organized labor's involvement, Iowa would not have become
a true two-party state by the 1960s. Beginning with aggressive local union
efforts during the 1940s in Ottumwa and prompted by the Iowa State Industrial Council's political efforts in the late 1940s and early 1950s, voters in
Iowa's manufacturing centers steadily turned toward the Democrats. Helped
by cooperative efforts with sympathetic farmers, Democrats made steady
gains in state and national representation after the mid-1950s. Despite its national reputation as a conservative farm state, Ottumwa's union leaders along
with the state's CIO movement prompted Iowa's belated participation in the
New Deal political transition and established the state's modern Democratic
foundations.

7

FALLOUT FROM THE "GRUDGE OPERATION": THE MORRELL PLANT'S CLOSING AND ITS AFTERMATH

Local 1's central involvement in local and state Democratic politics was its most enduring legacy. From the 1940s through the 1960s, Local 1's leaders worked with other CIO and AFL activists around the state to create a strong political presence for labor within the state's Democratic party. Yet labor's hard-won political clout did not deter old-line packers from closing plants throughout Iowa during the 1970s. Indeed, labor's clout began to erode almost as soon as it peaked during the 1960s. Despite Local 1's new generation of leaders' efforts to work more cooperatively with the company from the late 1950s through the early 1970s, a wide array of factors stemming from workforce conflicts and the plant's obsolescence as well as corporate consolidation, structural changes in the packing industry, and meatpacking unionism's decline contributed to the decision to close the plant.[1]

For several years following the plant's closing, former Morrell employees gathered annually for a reunion in Ottumwa. I attended the 1982 reunion, and asked people in attendance to fill out a survey on their experiences as Morrell employees. One of the former workers effectively summed up the feelings of many workers in his response to my question about the impact of the plant's closing on Ottumwa.

[It was] very bad. Moral[e] was low. And people with as much as 30 years with [the company] had to start a new [sic] or leave town. The city lost a lot of revenue as the payroll was cut drastically. These people were very bitter about it. Of course the city lost quite a bit of population. They felt let down. They figured Morrell could operate here and make money. People still figure it was a grudge operation and that the wrong plant was closed.[2]

It seems quite likely that nearly every former Morrell-Ottumwa employee expressed very similar sentiments at one time or another in the years following the plant's closing. Most former Morrell employees stayed in the Ottumwa area. Others who left town to transfer to other Morrell facilities found their way back to Ottumwa in fairly short order. In the years following the Morrell plant's closing, Ottumwa was a decidedly poorer, less populated, and more dispirited and anxious city than it had been before the closing. In these respects the city joined the ranks of many other cities in a deindustrializing Midwest.[3]

To the surprise of many, the plant's closing was quickly followed by the opening of a new packing facility in the shadow of Morrell's dead hulk. George A. Hormel and Company, which had borrowed $75,000 from Morrell in 1903 because of the close personal ties between T. D. Foster and George Hormel's brother, Rev. William Henry Hormel, pastor of the East End Presbyterian Church, returned the long overdue "favor" to Morrell and opened a new plant in Ottumwa in 1974. Following a trend typical of the makeover of the modern meatpacking industry, Hormel would never employ as many people as Morrell had, and would leave town in the wake of labor problems nearly as quickly as it had arrived. Another "disposable" packer, Excel, would take over Hormel's facilities and remains in town today. Yet even as Excel continues to hire more workers, Ottumwans know from experience that the company could pick up and leave at any time. Paying industry-standard low wages and employing a much more transient workforce, Ottumwa's blue-collar population is now as dispirited and soulless as Morrell-Ottumwa's workforce was militant and powerful during Local 1's heyday. In part, this is the case because Ottumwa's packing workers since the 1960s have been dispersed throughout the city and region; they could no longer rely on a supportive packing community. As the relative number of available and interested blue-collar workers has declined, Ottumwa has also started to receive an influx of Hispanic workers, a pattern now typical throughout the Midwest. Two decades after closing its plant in Ottumwa, Morrell would even reach out to hurt its former employees in one last tragic event. In 1995, the company decided to forgo its longstanding commitment to provide health insurance benefits for retired workers. This last indignity provides a telling end to the long saga of the company's relationship with Ottumwa's workers.[4]

The Final Years of the Morrell Plant

The decisions that led to the Morrell-Ottumwa plant's closing began early during W. W. McCallum's tenure as company president. McCallum repeatedly proclaimed that Local 1's unionism clouded the plant's future. Though meant to secure its financial viability, he also initiated technological and production innovations that would ultimately undermine the plant's existence. The consequences of Morrell's use of new technologies in combination with gain time on the number of people employed in the Ottumwa plant had been lurking since the early post–World War II years. Yet wholesale job losses at the Ottumwa plant did not cause widespread tension among workers until the early 1960s. Although 28,200 jobs were eliminated in meatpacking throughout the United States between 1956 and 1961, union membership at Morrell through most of the 1950s remained constant. Morrell picked up the pace of technological innovation with consequent job losses in the early 1960s as did many other "old-line" meatpackers. Paul Bissell, who started in 1930 to work his way up through the ranks in the beef kill to beef department superintendent beginning in 1956, recalled that new technologies transformed the Ottumwa's beef killing process only after 1961. Until that date "as far as beef operations were concerned, little had changed back to the '30s."[5]

Although the *Bulletin* emphasized losses in traditionally male-dominated departments like the beef kill, some of the hardest hit departments, such as sliced bacon, had been predominantly female. This created numerous problems. Among them was the system of departmental seniority used by Local 1 as well as most UPWA locals. As historian Bruce Fehn has argued, most union pioneers in packing in the 1930s wanted departmental, as opposed to plant-wide, seniority to prevent management's arbitrary transfer of workers, particularly union activists, from department to department. Then, because most packing departments were sex segregated, this meant that women had little ability to "bump" into male-dominated departments once technological innovations eliminated many women's jobs.[6]

By 1964–1965, more layoffs and continued pressure from longtime women employees presented Local 1's leadership with a true dilemma. How could they help women union members without alienating male workers, especially when men had long dominated the plant's workforce and were its most ardent union activists? In 1935, women constituted just 9 percent of Morrell's workforce compared to 15 percent in 1951 and 14 percent in 1957. Only one woman had ever been elected an official of Local 1 (Mary Shoemaker from the sausage department). Moreover, most of the local's union leaders held conventional views toward women and work. Jesse Merrill, a hog-kill worker and president of Local 1 from 1967 to its closing, claimed he had long believed "if the man's head of the house he should have the job." Virgil Bankson, Local 1's chief steward during the 1960s, was even more adamantly against giving women "men's jobs," claiming that "there's more divorces over women taking men's jobs than anything else." Consequently, though women started attending local union meetings en masse in 1964–1965 to protest the union's departmental seniority, they made little headway with union leaders.[7]

After getting nowhere with the local, thirty women contacted the Equal Employment Opportunity Commission (EEOC) in Washington, D.C. The Washington office told them to approach David Dutton, a Waterloo attorney and civil rights movement activist. Dutton then contacted the UPWA international. He threatened a lawsuit on the women's behalf if Local 1 did not follow the guidelines established by the 1964 Civil Rights Act's Title VII prohibiting sex discrimination. UPWA international officials promptly pressured Local 1 to adopt the so-called ABC seniority plan. "A" jobs were the most physically demanding and thus of interest mostly to men. "B" jobs were women's tasks — light work in relatively clean conditions. "C" jobs were open to both men and women. When the new seniority system was finally put into place in March 1966, however, men either refused to cooperate with it or conspired to undermine women's efforts to tackle "C" jobs. After two weeks, many women concluded that union officials were hindering the implementation of the new plan. Twenty-one women then asked Dutton to move ahead with a formal lawsuit in Des Moines's federal district court in April 1966 under Title VII of the Civil Rights Act.[8]

Less obvious to many outsiders and subsequent observers of the battle of sexes at the Morrell plant was the local union's concern that management, especially the union's old nemesis, Harry Hansel, hoped to use this issue to splinter the union. After a two-year stint from 1960 to 1962 as manager of Morrell's plant in Philadelphia, Hansel moved to the main offices in Chicago as a member of the corporate personnel and public relations department. In 1965–1966, when the ABC plan was debated and the women's grievances were aired, Morrell sent Hansel to negotiate with Local 1 officials. Indeed, Ethel Jerred, chief steward in the sliced bacon department, later recalled that "Harry Hansel tried to help [the women]" but that union officials, especially Merrill and Bankson, blocked his efforts. Yet Jerred also revealed the company's lackluster commitment to the women's efforts by noting that "the company would prefer to hire new people from outside town rather than move women with as much as twenty-eight years seniority" into open jobs.[9]

Historian Dennis Deslippe has further contended that UPWA international officers were sexist in defending the ABC seniority plan. In Deslippe's view, UPWA president Ralph Helstein "still embraced . . . protective labor laws for women" since Helstein argued that women could not handle the physical aspects of many packing jobs. The federal district court in Des Moines effectively sidestepped the discrimination debate when it threw out the women's case on a technicality. The court then gave Morrell time to reach a settlement with the women. On July 12, 1968, the court found Morrell in compliance with Title VII and Morrell settled with each of the twenty-one women for $450.[10]

Despite ongoing harassment from men, Local 1 women activists continued to push for greater access to more jobs with some success. By the late 1960s, however, the women's employment issues had become submerged in more dramatic discussions about the plant's likely closing. Although McCallum's 1954 "Morrell Days" speech established an ominous tone about the company's future in Ottumwa, serious rumblings among workers about the plant's possible closing did not begin to reverberate until the early 1960s. The 1961 contract negotiations saw the first instance of Morrell threatening to close the Ottumwa plant if the union did not back off on some of its demands. The 1964 contract negotiations included similar threats. For the first time, union leaders also openly criticized McCallum's financial strategy as well.

> Who do you think you are kidding by buying all of these small plants and hiring these people for wages that are ridiculous. Not too long ago in a meeting with Harry Hansel, a statement was made to the Bargaining Board, [sic] the Company was making arrangements to transfer the work out of the Ottumwa Plant and distribute it to other Plants. I might say this is already been [sic] done in some instances.

Still, very few workers felt that the company would actually close the plant. Many employees would later recall that threats about closing the plant abounded during the company's last twenty years in Ottumwa, especially around contract time. For workers hired after the early 1950s, warnings about the possibility of a closing were standard background noise.[11]

All this changed in 1967 when AMK, formerly American Seal-Kap, purchased Morrell in what *Fortune* termed the "financial coup of 1967." As part of the largest "merger mania" in American history since 1900 (before the even bigger "merger mania" period that began at the end of the 1970s), the late 1960s saw Ling-Temco-Vought (LTV) acquire Wilson, Greyhound buy out Armour, and Swift become the conglomerate Esmark by buying Vickers Petroleum, Platex, and STP in the 1960s and 1970s. AMK took over Morrell by buying 33 percent of its overvalued stock. Eli Black, president of AMK, later claimed "we bought a dollar for 25 cents." Consequently, AMK, originally a producer of milk bottle caps with sales in 1967 of $40 million, took over a company with $800 million in sales. (AMK scored an even bigger financial coup in 1968 when it purchased the giant United Fruit Company, producer of Chiquita bananas.)[12]

Although McCallum's purchase of numerous small packing plants and re-location of Morrell's headquarters from Ottumwa to Chicago may have di-verted much-needed funds from further modernizing the Ottumwa plant, at least while Morrell remained independent it had not taken active steps to close the Ottumwa plant. AMK had no such qualms, though. AMK vice president Morton H. Broffman explained the company's policies in regard to Morrell as "tough-minded management action." President Eli Black criticized McCal-lum for his outdated production planning methods and for using each of Mor-rell's plants as "individual profit centers" with "no central plant control."[13]

AMK's message to the Ottumwa plant was modernize or else, and the rank and file felt compelled to respond cooperatively. Local union leaders initially balked when Harry Hansel came to Ottumwa in fall 1969. They were skepti-cal of Hansel's announcement that Morrell would modernize the plant for $6.5 million if the union would freeze its severance pay. After some debate, however, they finally agreed to this. Further dramatizing how far the union had strayed from its militant traditions, the leaders of Local P-1 (the "P" sig-nifying the packinghouse locals after the 1968 merger of the UPWA into the AMCBW) agreed to train their own people in time study methods for the first time in its history so they could abide by Morrell's modernization (and layoff) plans. In contrast, Jack Moses, a veteran industrial engineer at the plant, later noted that the chief steward at Morrell's Sioux Falls, South Dakota, plant, a longtime AMCBW stronghold, had always been trained in time studies meth-ods. "He even checked his own men with a stopwatch." During late 1970 and 1971, the union also agreed to company plans for wholesale layoffs in the sliced bacon, canning, beef, and pork divisions. About 600 people were laid off in the pork division alone in 1971.[14]

By early 1973, however, word was out that the Ottumwa plant would close in July. Jesse Merrill and Harold Trimble, chief steward in 1973, conveyed their utter frustration with Morrell and its new president, Elias Paul, in a frank letter to Patrick Gorman, secretary-treasurer of the AMCBW.

In 1970, we thought, the Company was sincere in trying to make the plant go, so we conceded to freeze our severance pay rate and credited service at the 1970 level, only to find out their intentions weren't honorable. We gave them 11 percent more kill, cutting of hogs [that is, a faster pace in the kill and cut departments], beef with modernization, and lost people besides. God knows we tried and we find him [Paul] crying on your shoulder for more concessions. . . . If people like him make it to heaven, than [*sic*] we know there is no one in hell and it is a myth.

Gorman responded in patronizing fashion; Paul "was not crying on my shoulder"—he seemed sincerely saddened by the imminent closing. Moreover, Merrill and Trimble should be ashamed for writing him in a way that suggested they did not "care a hoot whether the plant closes or not." Paul's letter to Gorman was even more revealing. Although Paul noted in passing that he was "concern[ed] about the impact on the employees at Ottumwa and the impact on the town of Ottumwa" if the plant closed, he went on to excuse Morrell of ultimate responsibility for its demise.

> John Morrell and Co. has been taking money from other locations for most of these past twenty-five years and putting it into Ottumwa in an attempt to turn the [plant's losses] around. There is little point in pursuing the wisdom of this past action at this later date, but I believe we all would agree the company has tried hard to solve a difficult problem. I'm sure that the company's patience with this trying situation has always been tempered by the effects that any drastic action would have had on the welfare of the community and on the individual employees involved.[15]

One is left to wonder about the precise meaning of Paul's statement about the "company's patience with this trying situation." Yet it seems likely that in part he was castigating Ottumwa's militant union tradition. To this day, veterans of Ottumwa's long post–World War II labor-management struggles continue to debate the real reasons for the plant's closing. Many management and union leaders agree that the Ottumwa plant by the 1960s was clearly outdated in terms of design efficiency. Lawrence Reedquist, a long-time Morrell traffic engineer, emphasized the irony that Morrell had built the plant to last "one hundred years" without knowing that new-line packing companies like Iowa Beef Processors by the 1960s were building plants to last "no more than 40 years." Though it was equipped with the most up-to-date system of elevators and internal conveyance systems, the Ottumwa plant by the 1960s consisted of dozens of separate, multistory buildings that defied modern processes of packing disassembly. Many workers had to be employed simply to truck products between the various buildings. Still, Jack Moses, another long-time Morrell supervisor, pointed to Morrell's continued operation of its (now seriously downsized) packing plant in Sioux Falls. There, with buildings nearly as old as the Ottumwa facility, Morrell continues to turn out millions of dollars' worth of meat products. As Mickey Lauria and Peter S. Fisher point out in their study of plant closings in Iowa, "any given plant cannot be said to be obsolete in any absolute sense; it could be made efficient at some cost." Moses, as well as many former Ottumwa workers, believed Morrell kept the Sioux Falls plant open because its AMCBW-affiliated workforce had long been more cooperative on production issues.[16]

Although the exact reasons for Morrell's decision to close the Ottumwa plant remain veiled in secrecy, it is plausible that the ascendancy of a new generation of more cooperative leaders in Local 1 (and P-1) allowed Morrell to decide the fate of the plant without much opposition. Although it is doubtful that militancy as practiced by Bill Fletcher or Edward Filliman would have helped, a more aggressive attempt by Local P-1's leadership to apply pressure on Morrell, city, and state authorities to keep the plant open may have helped. Local P-1 and other Ottumwa union members formed the Greater Ottumwa Labor Development (GOLD) Corporation in 1969 to push for greater involvement by labor in Morrell's future as well as the city's post-Morrell plans. Yet by 1972 GOLD members complained that their occasional requests for information and input had usually been ignored by Ottumwa and corporate authorities. Ottumwa's predicament contrasted noticeably to Waterloo's case in the late 1970s when public officials and local union members worked diligently to keep the Rath packing plant open.[17]

Although not evident to the participants in the struggle to save the Morrell plant, the ongoing structural revolution of the meatpacking industry, led by Iowa Beef Processors Inc., later renamed IBP, also undoubtedly contributed to its closing. Since 1961, when IBP built its first plant outside Denison, Iowa, oligarchy has reigned in meatpacking and effective unionism has been largely banished. In fact, despite the complete turnover in the companies constituting the dominant packers, beef packing is as oligarchical now as it was at the turn of the twentieth century during the heyday of the Big Five. In 1900, Swift, Armour, Cudahy, Morris, and Wilson slaughtered about 75 percent of the nation's cattle. In 1988, the modern "Big Three," IBP, ConAgra, and Excel, a division of Cargill, killed 67 percent of the cattle in the country. Recent estimates put the Big Three's percentage of the cattle slaughter industry at more than 80 percent. The same Big Three also slaughtered one-third of the nation's hogs in the late 1980s. Between the early 1960s and mid-1990s, dozens of old-line, medium- and large-city midwestern, unionized plants closed. IBP, ConAgra, and Excel replaced them with new, nonunion beef and pork processing facilities in smaller towns in more isolated, rural Great Plains locations. The new Big Three can be seen in this respect as the most successful practitioners of the direct-buying marketing pattern among meatpackers that dated back to the turn of the twentieth century. They were able to finally "subdue" the old-line terminal market packers by procuring animals directly from farmers through grower contracts, consolidating the cutting and packaging operations in the same plants that killed animals, and by eliminating through advanced technology much of the skilled knife work that used to accompany the killing and cutting processes. The new technology also has created a much faster work pace. Increasingly dependent on immigrant, transient labor for these deskilled positions, meatpacking has become a low-wage industry characterized by the highest rate of injury, especially repeated trauma disorders like carpal tunnel syndrome, of any industry in the United States.[18]

This structural revolution greatly weakened meatpacking unionism across the state and nation, which also hurt Local P-1's effort to keep the Morrell-Ottumwa plant open. After the UPWA and Amalgamated's merger in 1968, the new Amalgamated Meat Cutters and Butcher Workmen, AFL-CIO, maintained previous master contract agreements, but had little success in organizing workers in new plants and, particularly, securing favorable contracts with IBP. The new Amalgamated's successor, the United Food and Commercial Workers (UFCW), formed in 1979, has had even less success with IBP, ConAgra, and Excel. IBP's hard-line labor relations policies have been a major facet of its total managerial strategy of low-wage labor at all costs. From its inception, IBP refused to grant master contracts and rejected costly benefit packages. Until June 1988, when IBP's Joslin, Illinois, beef plant's 1,700 workers joined the UFCW, only four of its plants, including one closed by then, had voted for union affiliation. Its flagship Dakota City, Nebraska, plant's UFCW union struck IBP five times between 1969 and 1988. The 1969 strike, led by the Amalgamated, was especially violent; the eight-month impasse included "firebombings, smashed windows and the murder of a sister of a company informant." And in part because so much of the beef and pork slaughtering industry remains unorganized, the UFCW's contracts have been weak. Both ConAgra and Excel have approached labor relations similarly in the modern era.[19]

Ottumwa's plant was one of many victims of meatpacking's "modernization." Between 1972 and 1980, 5,600 meatpacking workers lost their jobs in Iowa. Nearly one-third of those jobs were lost in Ottumwa alone. Many Morrell managers insinuated that the unionized, older-than-average workforce at the Morrell-Ottumwa plant had largely contributed to its closing. In fact, as another management official put it, "had labor donated their entire 'bill' to the company, this plant would have still been in a losing posture." This news would have been small consolation to the workers who left the plant for the last time on July 14, 1973. One worker's words probably summarized the feelings of many that day. "So many of us have given a good chunk of our lives to this place." Strangely understating the devastating economic impact the closing was bound to have on Ottumwa, an *Ottumwa Courier* editorial dismissed the loss as just one of the "cycles in Ottumwa's industrial history" and that "industrial evolution" would supply substitutes for the plant.[20]

Although Morrell workers with sufficient seniority had several plants around the United States where they might transfer, most workers initially chose not to leave the city. Only about 200 of the 1,700 workers at the time of the closing had decided to transfer. Some were able to find jobs with the John Deere plant in Ottumwa, which was expanding throughout much of the 1970s. Others found work with smaller manufacturing firms in and around the city. Quite a few others, especially those not too tightly involved with Local P-1, were hired by Hormel beginning in 1974. Nevertheless, over the course of the next several years, Ottumwa saw many of its workers drift away and, more important, lost younger, blue-collar residents because the city's dominant employer was no longer present. Although Ottumwa's population probably approached 40,000 during World War II, it officially peaked in 1960 at 33,871. By 1970, it had declined to 29,610. It fell to 27,381 in 1980 and dropped even faster ten years later to 24,488.[21]

Other socioeconomic indicators point to an erosion in the city's health since Morrell's closing. In 1971, two years before the company left town, 5,020 of the city's 17,530 workers were employed in manufacturing. Around half of them worked at Morrell, a level down from midcentury but comparable to its turn-of-the-century prominence as the city's major blue-collar employer. Unemployment in Ottumwa was just 5.6 percent. In 1980, the number of manufacturing jobs had declined to 4,000 (out of a somewhat smaller total number employed in the city), and by the mid-1980s, before the closing of the Hormel plant, Wapello County's unemployment reached 11.6 percent in December 1986. Not coincidentally, Ottumwa's political leaders were reduced in the same years to various desperate promotions of the city. The most feeble of these was Ottumwa's claim to be the "video game capital of the world." One year following the Hormel plant's closing, Ottumwa's unemployment was 10.3 percent, the highest figure recorded among Iowa's cities and nearly twice as high as the statewide average of 5.7 percent. The number of manufacturing jobs plunged to 2,500 in September 1987. Following Excel's opening in the fall of 1987, the official jobless rate in Ottumwa fell to 5.6 percent by October 1989. This was still higher, though, than the state average of 3.9 percent and the U.S. average of 5.3 percent. Despite some stability in employment by the late 1980s and early 1990s — unemployment in the county ranged between 3 and 7 percent from 1990 to 1993 — Ottumwa is still suffering economically and socially. In 1989–1990, the city's municipal tax rate was the second highest in the state. During the late 1980s, Wapello County's teen pregnancy rate was consistently above the state average. From 1991 to 1997, Ottumwa High School's annual dropout rate has averaged between 4 and 5 percent, double that of other school districts in Iowa with comparable enrollments. Ninth- and eleventh-grade students' Iowa Tests of Educational Development scores have also fallen in the 1990s relative to levels recorded during the 1980s.[22]

Labor Strife during the Hormel Era

Ottumwa's current precarious socioeconomic health dates to the closing of the Morrell plant and the opening of the first of its "disposable" packing facilities less than a year after the Morrell plant's closing. In April 1974, Hormel, based in Austin, Minnesota, announced they would build a new pork slaughtering and processing facility next to the abandoned Morrell buildings. In September 1974, Charles Nyberg, Hormel's corporate secretary, told an Ottumwa audience that "we think Ottumwa is a heck of a nice town, and we're coming here to stay." A month later, Hormel said it would invest $16.5 million in its new facility, and eventually employ between 400 and 500 people. Plant operations began on October 16, 1974, with 120 employees.[23]

A major reason for Hormel's interest in Ottumwa was the ample supply of experienced packing workers. Although the introduction of new technologies had long eroded most of the traditional skills involved in butchering animals, there was (and will no doubt remain) a need for specialized hog-killing and processing abilities, like scalers, "stickers," and leaf-lard "pullers," that take years of experience to develop. Consequently, by hiring former Morrell employees, Hormel tapped the abilities garnered in meatpacking by dozens of Ottumwa residents, particularly since so many had not left the area. Not suprisingly, Hormel, according to Dan Varner, a prominent union leader at Hormel, did not hire many of the "high profile" former Local P-1 activists. Jesse Merrill, the last president of Local P-1, was one of the most prominent Morrell unionists not hired by Hormel.[24]

Able to increase production rapidly during the mid-1970s because of its highly experienced workforce, Hormel's operations at the Ottumwa plant expanded faster than expected. By early 1977, nearly 500 people were employed at the plant. From the plant's opening, workers, partly because of previous experience in Local P-1, sought union affiliation. After a lengthy jurisdictional struggle between AMCBW Locals P-1 and 431, the latter originally based at Oscar Mayer in Davenport, Iowa, Local 431 won the certification election to represent Ottumwa-Hormel's workers on December 16, 1976. Local P-1 had many allies in its struggle to maintain its Ottumwa identity, including backing by the active and aggressive Hormel locals in Fort Dodge and Austin, but the Amalgamated international office had already started the trend of forming district as opposed to local union locals and threw its support behind Local 431, which had already started on this road. According to Varner, this factor and Hormel's expressed desire of wanting to work with a less militant union than P-1 were the deciding factors in giving Local 431 the upper hand in Ottumwa.[25]

An employee of Oscar Mayer in Davenport from 1967 to 1976, Varner became involved in Local 431 there and was appointed by that district union's leaders to be the first chief steward at Hormel-Ottumwa. Varner later realized that Ottumwa's workers were part of a compromise reached between Amalgamated and Hormel officials. With the addition of several hundred workers to its ranks, Local 431 was able to greatly expand its per capita dues-garnering ability with which it might further expand. In return for Hormel's support in gaining these additional workers, Local 431's leaders gave Hormel officials assurance that the union would not challenge the company's plans for using its Ottumwa plant as a "wedge" against its other unionized plants. That is, Hormel officials wanted to use the Ottumwa plant to create divisions among the various unionized plants on critical contract issues, like contract expiration dates for the union chain. In that sense, Varner claimed, Local 431 "would not be an active part of the Hormel [union] chain." Hormel signed a three-year contract with Local 431 on April 9, 1977. Employment reached higher than anticipated levels that same spring when the Hormel-Ottumwa payroll hit 563 in May.[26]

For much of the late 1970s and early 1980s, the Hormel facility provided many more blue-collar Ottumwans with employment at relatively high wages than anyone would have predicted in the early 1970s. Employment reached 650 in January 1979 and then hit 800 in June 1982. Base pay started at $10.74 per hour under the new three-year contract signed on November 30, 1982. Nevertheless, Varner noted that Hormel made good on its "deal" with Local 431. By denying Ottumwa workers benefits that other workers in Hormel plants had every three years when contract negotiations came up, it "chipped away" at the solidarity of its union chain. In addition, Varner felt Hormel increasingly began to irritate employees in Ottumwa with key supervisory hirings. An important hiring was the selection of "Iron" Mike McLean as the new personnel manager, a young man with an abrasive personality and a tendency to rely on managerial "theory" gained in his college studies. McLean and others reinforced the wedge through "intimidation" of Ottumwa workers. Hormel officials also generated some distress in 1982 when 120 Hormel employees from Fort Dodge with greater seniority bumped 90 Ottumwa workers out of work. Interestingly, after early concerns, Varner felt many of the Fort Dodge workers, who had long union connections themselves, helped to reinforce the union loyalties of the older P-1 members who were able to get work in the plant. Still, labor relations at the plant were relatively peaceful during the late 1970s and early 1980s.[27]

The first decisive indication of problems to come, however, occurred in 1979 when the United Food and Commercial Workers (UFCW) was formed from a merger of the Amalgamated, Retail Clerks International Association, and Boot and Shoe Workers' Union. Most of the new union's leadership came from the relatively conservative Retail Clerks, whose workers had traditionally earned much less than those of the AMCBW-NA. The UFCW's leadership during these years accelerated the Amalgamated's process of reorganizing locals into larger, amalgamated districts. Local 431 not only represented Hormel-Ottumwa's workers in the early 1980s, but also 5,000 other workers from 100 other companies in Iowa and Illinois.[28]

Louis DeFrieze, Local No 431's secretary-treasurer and business agent, "ran the local with a tight fist." Varner described DeFrieze as a good union leader, originally Local 431's steward in the Mayer-Davenport plant's key sliced-pack department, who used his "dynamic" personality and sincere commitment to workers' concerns to catapult himself into local union prominence. As he moved up the union leadership ladder, however, he lost touch with the rank and file. In Varner's words, DeFrieze "put on the suits and became a dictator." In the early 1980s, Local 431 held only one membership meeting per year and Ottumwa had no union officers above the level of chief steward. Meetings tended to be unproductive because the local represented diverse industries' workers with conflicting needs. Indeed, DeFrieze actively discouraged Ottumwa members from meeting with union members in other Local 431 communities by denying them travel funds.[29]

The boom period for Hormel in Ottumwa did not last long. After the opening of Hormel's new $100 million plant in Austin, combined with massive layoffs of the old Austin plant's workforce, UFCW concessions, and significantly higher production standards and lower employment needs in Austin, company leaders, adopting IBP-like managerial tactics, threatened Ottumwa's workers with massive layoffs in February 1984 if they did not agree to wage and benefit concessions. Hormel claimed that it could no longer pay a base rate of nearly $11 per hour when competitors paid much less. Because of the old-time P-1 members in the plant, the infusion of Fort Dodge workers and their strong union ideas, and younger workers' dawning realization of the company's "wedge" intentions for the plant, Ottumwa workers solidly resisted Hormel's demands. Consequently, the company laid off 444 workers in March and announced they would close the hog kill and cut and perhaps the entire plant unless workers granted the concessions they demanded. Realizing that Ottumwa's membership was absolutely crucial to Local 431's future, DeFrieze pressured Ottumwa's union members to accept the concessions. Ottumwa's workers refused and Hormel laid off another 114 workers on May 2, 1984. Following another DeFrieze appeal, a third vote on the concessions was held on May 25. Ottumwa workers finally voted to accept a base wage cut from $10.69 to $8.75. Bonuses were also eliminated. Hormel then recalled all laid off workers on May 26.[30]

This was just the beginning of the Hormel onslaught. Soon after the first major round of concessions, the company indicated that it would roll back wages and benefits even further. Local P-9 at the main plant in Austin led the counterattack among Hormel's unions. P-9 leaders, with the support of Roy Rodgers and his so-called Corporate Campaign, began a concerted informational and boycott campaign to highlight Hormel's threatening strategy. During summer 1984, two major informational rallies convened in Ottumwa and other Hormel cities. Varner, reelected as the Hormel-Ottumwa's plant steward, having left the post in 1977 after having grown increasingly disgusted with the deterioration of the local's position, supported the rallies. Supportive of the rallies, Varner also felt ambivalent about the Austin union's direction of many union efforts in Ottumwa. Specifically, according to Varner, a "core group" of P-9 backers in the Ottumwa plant "organized" by the Austin local led Ottumwa rallies over the next two years. Although Varner felt P-9 used Local 431 as a "pawn" in its struggle, Ottumwa workers greeted P-9 members "like lost relations" and held a particularly enthusiastic informational rally in the city in August. After an NLRB ruling that Local P-9 could not picket Hormel's primary lender, First Bank, since that constituted an illegal secondary boycott, P-9 members nevertheless decided in December 1984 to continue their Corporate Campaign against Hormel's creditors. Ottumwa's union expressed nearly unanimous support for P-9's efforts.[31]

P-9's informational campaign against Hormel accelerated during 1985, and seemed to find increasing support in Ottumwa and around the nation. On February 20, 1985, 200 P-9 members extended their informational pickets to the Hormel plant in Ottumwa. Six months later, on August 17, 1985, P-9 decided to strike against Hormel without the UFCW international's support after rejecting its final contract offer that called for a base wage cut to $10 per hour as well as other concessions. Support for P-9 in Ottumwa increased from that point through early 1986. Hormel opened its Austin plant to replacement workers on January 13, 1986. On January 27, P-9 extended its pickets to Ottumwa and several other Hormel facilities. In a display reminiscent of the early days of Local 1, approximately 2,000 family members and supporters of Hormel workers marched through Ottumwa's downtown on January 29 before demonstrating in front of the plant. Ottumwa's Democratic mayor Jerry Parker, long supported by Ottumwa's working population since first elected to that position in 1980, participated in the demonstration. On January 31, Hormel then fired 458 Ottumwa workers. Local 431 received support from a broad spectrum of Ottumwans, including church leaders and many local merchants.[32]

Enthusiasm for the strike began to wane in Ottumwa during early February. On February 5, Hormel temporarily suspended slaughtering operations in Ottumwa, and by February 9, the number of discharged Local 431 members was up to 507. Church leaders and local business groups, supportive of the strike a few weeks earlier, began to urge a return to normalcy. Notably, Mayor Parker continued to support Local 431. Also, municipal employees refused to cross the picket lines to thaw out the plant's frozen sewer pipes. Nevertheless, Hormel-Ottumwa began hiring replacement workers on February 17. Four days later, P-9 officials decided to pull its roving pickets after five weeks. Between 600 and 700 Local 431 members and supporters marched down Iowa Avenue to the Hormel plant to reclaim their jobs only to find that they had been locked out. Hormel continued to run the plant with about 200 scab laborers. Compounding the strikers' predicament, in early March an Iowa Job Service hearing panel decided to deny the strikers unemployment benefits since they had acted improperly in supporting the strike. Almost two months later, however, the chief hearing officer, William C. Yost, reversed this finding and allowed workers to receive retroactive jobless pay. Hormel quickly appealed Yost's decision to the Employment Appeals Board. Its members took Hormel's side, and workers had to return up to $5,000 each in benefits or have their unemployment docked as overpaid until their slates were clean. Iowa's supreme court affirmed this decision in November 1988, arguing that workers knew the UFCW had not authorized their sympathy strike.[33]

During spring 1986, violence escalated at the Hormel plant in Austin. The UFCW moved to place P-9 under trusteeship, and the NLRB sought an injunction against P-9 picketing at the Austin plant. By the summer, Austin strikers had been permanently replaced. In Ottumwa, however, arbitrator Bert Luskin returned the 507 fired Hormel workers to their jobs by mid-September. The workers were denied back pay. Only about half of these workers, however, were actually recalled in September. In addition, in a separate arbitration proceeding, Local 431 chief steward Dan Varner was fired by Hormel for "aiding and encouraging the Austin pickets." In Varner's words, he was fired for "being the root of all evil." On September 17, Hormel announced that they were "considering selling, closing, or expanding (!)" the Ottumwa plant in the wake of the strike.[34]

Despite an intense letter-writing campaign, Hormel began laying off production workers at its Ottumwa plant during fall 1986 through early 1987. Slaughtering was permanently suspended on December 15, 1986. Hormel chairman Richard Knowlton responded to the pleas of Ottumwans by saying "knowing that [another labor dispute] could happen again is a major deterrent to our continuance in Ottumwa." On February 23, 1987, Hormel announced that it would close the Ottumwa plant on August 22, 1987.[35]

Even before the official closing announcement, many Ottumwans started pointing their fingers at P-9. Mayor Parker, undoubtedly suffering from pressure put on him by Hormel officials and other community leaders, said "Local P-9 wasn't invited, and we did everything to get them to leave." When Parker was reminded that he had participated eagerly in the support marches one year earlier, he claimed his "involvement was just participating in a couple marches and [giving] a couple fiery labor speeches." Although strongly rooted in Ottumwa's post–World War II Democratic political traditions, having worked his way up the ranks in Ottumwa's political circles by starting as a laborer in the Parks Department (not unlike Herschel Loveless's humble origins), Parker behaved much like other city leaders across the country regardless of party affiliations during the recession-mired 1980s. He hoped to save Ottumwans' jobs. Yet Parker's change of tune on the strike neither forestalled the plant's closing nor saved his own job; he would be voted out of office soon after. City council member Dale Gottschalk said he thought the strike had "erased everything that had been done to improve Ottumwa's image," a slightly veiled reference to the ongoing effort to dispel the image of Ottumwa as a strong labor union town. Unlike its nonchalant position on Morrell's closing in 1973, the *Ottumwa Courier* deemed Hormel's closing a "crime." Hormel's official pronouncements about the plant's closing blamed "overcapacity" in pork slaughtering, IBP's competitive wage advantage, and changing dietary trends as well as Local P-9 and its Corporate Campaign.[36]

Excel's Opening and the Modern Era of Disposable Workers

Within a few days of Hormel's closing, Cargill-subsidiary Excel Corporation, based in Wichita, Kansas, a low-wage follower of IBP's managerial strategies, announced its plan to lease the Hormel-Ottumwa facility. Within one day of their announcement, Ottumwa's Job Service of Iowa office reported that 1,225 people had applied for 450 openings. After three weeks, over 3,000 had filled out applications. These applicants were not put off by the company's starting wage scales: $5.50 per hour for new workers and $6.50 for workers with Hormel experience. Excel claimed it would employ around 800 people within two years and slaughter about the same number of hogs per day as Hormel had. Although Excel claimed it would give preference to former Hormel workers, city and state leaders would not hold Excel to this promise despite giving them a $500,000 grant through the Iowa Department of Economic Development.[37]

Excel eventually hired a mostly new workforce. Many former Hormel employees were apparently put off by the low wages. Within a year about 20 percent of Hormel's former employees had been hired, but many workers with strong union backgrounds, especially former Local 431 officers, were not. By mid-October 1987 the Excel plant had enough workers to begin slaughtering operations. At year's end, 485 workers were slaughtering and processing pork under Hormel's label. UFCW officials quickly began organizing these workers. On July 14, 1988, Local 230 was certified as the legal bargaining agent. In October of the same year, Excel-Ottumwa employees signed a contract, albeit a much less lucrative one than workers had had either under Morrell or Hormel. Base pay started at $6.80 per hour regardless of past experience with Hormel. The contract stipulated that the base wage would increase regularly within the next two and a half years to $8.50 per hour, the average figure in the industry. Workers would be eligible for two weeks of vacation after three years of employment with the company. In 1990, Excel paid the third-lowest starting wage rate, $7 per hour, among Iowa and Minnesota packing plants, behind only the IBP plant in Perry and Dakota Pork's plant in Sioux City.[38]

To date the only significant labor controversy involving Local 230 and Excel-Ottumwa occurred at the end of the initial contract's expiration date in October 1991. When the contract expired on October 5, Local 230 then rejected the new contract and authorized a strike, but decided to continue working until October 13. After ratifying the new contract, the local decided to go ahead with their strike on October 21 because of discrepancies in the contract's language involving official workdays, bonuses paid to probationary workers, and inclusion of suspension letters in employees' permanent personnel files. When the company threatened that "closing the plant 'is certainly on the minds of Excel officials,'" workers took the advice of UFCW officials and called off the strike after two days. However, Excel officials initially suspended workers who tried to return to their old jobs. The company wanted another union vote on the contract's language. Local 230 then voted to allow the company's changes, and workers returned to their jobs on October 28. The local union could exert very little pressure on Excel, especially given the compliance of its international union and the dismay caused by the threat of Excel's closing.[39]

Despite its threats during the 1991 contract dispute, Excel had committed itself more firmly to Ottumwa in August 1990 when it purchased its facility from Hormel. Since then the company has also steadily increased its workforce as well to over 1,000 employees. At the same time, however, the company has kept its low-wage workers on edge by increasing the line speeds — at least double those of Morrell in the post–World War II era — and implementing policies that tend to weed out workers with injuries, particularly carpal tunnel syndrome, which are directly tied to higher line speeds and lower staffing ratios. In 1990, Excel eliminated its multistep firing process and fired three workers, all with carpal tunnel syndrome, after one rule infraction. Across the state of Iowa, meatpacking workers averaged 43 injuries per 100 workers in 1988, well above the national average for workplace injuries. Excel's termination policy change came soon after signing an agreement with UFCW officials to reduce carpal tunnel syndrome; no doubt many people saw this sequence of events as indicative of Excel's less than noble intentions.[40]

Carol Hammersley, an occupational health nurse at the Excel plant until 1998, pointed out that there were about 900 injuries at the plant in 1997. About one-half were "cumulative trauma" injuries; the other half were cuts, scratches, and virtually anything else, including minor problems, that were reported to her. Hammersley believed the company had made genuine progress in implementing more ergonomically sound work practices and technologies into the work process. Indeed, she noted that the rate of injuries was actually down from about 1,350 per year in 1993. Whereas she felt many workers ignored the opportunities for education and rest periods provided by Excel, she also believed the high rate of speed associated with work on the kill and cut lines made cumulative trauma injuries inevitable. Since Hammersley did the prehiring physicals, she also saw many people who quit after working for short stints but returned not long after because there was little else for people with few skills to do in the area. At the same time, she saw few workers past middle age in the plant.[41]

Most recently, Excel has joined the ranks of IBP and other new-style packers in the state by starting to tap into international sources for labor. On March 24, 1998, the Ottumwa Area Development Corporation announced after meeting with Excel-Ottumwa's human resources manager Jim Reimer that "Excel has reached saturation point with the region's available labor supply. Targeted employees could include Russian, Polish, Eastern Europeans, Southeast Asian and/or Hispanic [workers]." Prompted by Excel's desire to add another 500 to 700 employees to the 1,000 already employed, the company admitted that the new hires could create significant new burdens on the local school system, housing market, health care services, and local government services. Like several communities across the state, including Perry, Storm Lake, and Waterloo, the potential influx would contribute to the "explosion of ethnic diversity" that the new-style meatpackers created in Iowa during the 1990s. Although city fathers hailed the potential influx as "bright news" in Ottumwa's ongoing struggle for economic growth, other Iowa cities have not successfully coped with rapid inflows of foreign-born workers.[42]

Although it is tempting to dismiss concerns about the influx of foreigners as nothing more than a revisiting of the nativist refrains of 100 years ago, there are important distinctions between the two periods of intensive immigration. Unlike many other more urbanized places around the United States, Ottumwa and most of Iowa largely missed the "new" immigration of the turn of the twentieth century. Ottumwa has no recent experiences in incorporating newcomers into its population. Further, if experiences in other rural midwestern cities are suggestive, Ottumwans will not feel supportive of expanding services for items like health protection and English as Second Language programs. These likely tensions are magnified by the general economic stagnation present in much of the rural Midwest. Unlike the generally growing economic conditions present earlier while the United States was industrializing, the postindustrial Midwest presents a less inviting environment for short-term positive relations between immigrants and Ottumwa natives.[43]

For most Excel employees in Ottumwa today, the relative glory days of work at Morrell are now almost a full generation removed. The last vestiges of a reminder of those days, the remaining large, abandoned Morrell buildings, were finally removed during 1991. Ottumwa and Wapello County officials began lobbying federal representatives in May 1989 for financial help, and ultimately received nearly $4 million in a federal grant to remove 90,000 square feet of asbestos and demolish the four remaining largest buildings. A last-minute effort sought to preserve the administrative building for its historical significance as "an impressive corporate example of the popular Tudor Revival style." Two other smaller buildings would have also been eligible for the National Historical Register, but had "serious integrity problems." All four major buildings were removed by the end of 1991. The last remaining Morrell structure, used as an auto body shop most recently and for lard rendering, dog food processing, and casing during the Morrell years, was finally removed in 1996. Nearly all city officials and the editors of the *Ottumwa Courier* were overjoyed to see the buildings go. Deemed an "eyesore" and a "hazard," and given the incredible expense that would be required to rehabilitate the administrative building, many Ottumwans agreed that the buildings should best be removed. Once cleared, city officials proclaimed the site could be turned into an industrial park. As of 1999, though, the park has no takers for its wide, empty expanses.[44]

Morrell's Final Indignity

Although its remaining buildings are gone, Morrell is certainly not forgotten or forgiven by most of its former employees. A cruel reminder of the company's legacy created widespread dismay in 1995. On January 25, 1995, over 3,000 Morrell retirees, including several hundred in the Ottumwa area, received notices stating that their medical and life insurance benefits had been canceled. Morrell, the meat division of Chiquita Brands International, had been trying to position itself for sale since 1993. Shedding insurance benefits would cut $15 million in costs and make Morrell "more attractive for potential buyers." Morrell was able to file its case in 1991 in the United States District Court of South Dakota Southern Division in Rapid City because the UFCW had not included all past retirees in contract provisions since 1985 protecting insurance benefits. Judge Richard H. Battey ruled in favor of Morrell on June 24, 1993. Although he later said he was sympathetic to the retirees' plight, he blamed the UFCW for leaving the loophole. According to Battey, "Had UFCW sought permission to bargain for retirees, undoubtedly it possessed the knowledge of how to do so." An appeal was filed with the 8th Circuit Court of Appeals in St. Louis on July 16, 1993, but the court upheld Battey's ruling on October 12, 1994.[45]

Senate Minority Leader Tom Daschle of South Dakota, former Local 1 president and Morrell Retirees Club president Jesse Merrill, and many others moved quickly to stop Morrell's actions, but to no avail. Daschle introduced a bill in the U.S. Senate to stop companies from cutting off benefits while court decisions were still pending and Merrill led the fight for an injunction against Morrell's decision. Both actions were unsuccessful. The 8th Circuit Court of Appeals' decision was appealed to the U.S. Supreme Court, but the high court decided on May 30, 1995, not to hear it.[46]

For the hundreds of Morrell retirees in Ottumwa, cancellation of their medical and life insurance benefits was devastating. Johnny Toopes began working at Morrell-Ottumwa in 1937 at the age of sixteen, worked there until the plant closed in 1973, and then toiled an additional ten years at Morrell in Sioux Falls, South Dakota. Toopes said he paid an additional $11,520 in his last twelve years with Morrell to guarantee that he and his wife would have lifetime insurance benefits. John Bednar, a thirty-seven-year veteran of Morrell-Ottumwa, lived on a fixed income of $500 per month. After the benefits' cancellation, he and his wife faced more than $700 per month in medical insurance and drug prescriptions alone. Bednar, facing the prospect of cutting costs to the bone, said, "I think it's a dirty shame they had to do this to us. Maybe they just want us old people to die." Indeed, on February 5, James Couch shot himself out of despair, according to his son, because he had no idea how he would pay for $300 to $600 monthly expenses in prescriptions for a variety of ailments. Ray Stainer, facing $3,500 yearly for health insurance and prescription costs out of a total income of $11,000, summed up many Morrell retirees' reactions to Morrell's and the Supreme Court's decision: "It's terrible. There's no other place to turn. I guess we've lost and there's just nothing we can do."[47]

Morrell found its happy ending in October 1995. Smithfield Foods bought the company from Chiquita Brands International for $58 million. Ottumwa's packing workers probably could not have cared less. Their future seems far less bright.[48]

8

THE LEGACY OF MILITANT UNIONISM

The prospects for greater power and control among meatpacking and other workers in Ottumwa and much of the rural Midwest today are not favorable. Although unemployment is relatively low, the quality of jobs, especially given the shrinking manufacturing sector, is declining. Ottumwa, and many communities like it, are dependent on a few major corporate employers, usually not community-based, and are increasingly willing to accept whatever opportunities and benefits they offer, even when these are relatively poor. The weakness of unions today, especially in the manufacturing sector and meatpacking in particular, means that workers effectively have little collective means with which to influence corporate strategies. Reflecting on "Iowa's Pride" in the sense of workers' standing in the state today, it is difficult not to feel anything but a sense of despair.[1]

To prevent despondence from turning to indifference, it is important to reflect further on the conditions and causes that allowed Ottumwa's meatpacking workers to gain power and control in the first place. Two external conditions were particularly important. The first was Ottumwa's development as a company town. Already an important direct-buying packing center in Iowa during the Civil War, the establishment of John Morrell and Company's major packing plant in the city in 1877 set Ottumwa on the path to becoming one of the major direct-buying packing centers in Iowa and the Midwest before the turn of the twentieth century. Although this study has explained several negative consequences of the power imbalance exercised by Morrell in Ottumwa's history, the fact that the company was based in the city until the 1950s gave workers, especially when mobilized in Local 1, an ability to affect company labor policies that may be difficult to re-create in the foreseeable future. Given capital's proclivity to flee disgruntled workforces and communities today for others that are willing to accept less, it is difficult to envision a revisiting of the type of sustained militance that accompanied Local 1's rise to power.[2]

The second condition that shaped workers' rise to power in Ottumwa was the development of its packing community or neighborhood. The concerns that sparked workers' desire for unionism during the 1930s were products of collective, long-term disgruntlements among people of broadly similar social demographic backgrounds who lived together in the shadow of the Morrell plant. The divisions that gradually undercut the power of Local 1 after World War II reflected the erosion of this packing community. Over time a smaller percentage of workers lived in close proximity to each other and, accordingly, had fewer opportunities to share workplace or other common concerns. Thus, genuine community bonds eroded. Community dissolution continues in Ottumwa and many other rural industrial locales today. Workers' tendencies to float from job to job as well as corporate strategies to recruit immigrant workers to midwestern cities exacerbate this problem. At least in the short run, greater ethnic diversity such as Iowa experienced in the 1990s for arguably the first time in the twentieth century will probably impede workers' prospects for greater power and control.[3]

Understanding the importance of these two external conditions in Ottumwa meatpacking workers' struggles is crucial if one is to meaningfully ponder labor's situation in the rural Midwest and elsewhere today. Certainly in Ottumwa's case, workers' collective desire to exercise greater control over plant affairs provided the internal dynamic, or agency, that fueled their support for Local 1's sustained militancy from the late 1930s through the early 1950s. However, without the external structure of Ottumwa's status as a company town with its supportive packing community, it seems unlikely that workers could have exercised the power and control they did through Local 1. These structural considerations are largely lacking in the rural Midwest today and will make workers' efforts to regain power and control very difficult.[4]

The legacy of Ottumwa workers' sustained militant unionism is certainly mixed. In Local 1's heyday, from the late 1930s through the early 1950s, the use or threat of militant job actions greatly aided workers. Militant unionism not only cemented industrial democracy, that is, the establishment of contracts that provided fair and orderly workplace procedures, it also ensured Local 1's significant informal power and control regarding aspects of Morrell's labor policies. Yet, as noted, when workers began to lose the security of their company town and packing community, militant unionism served to divide workers. In turn, Morrell was also then able to successfully propagandize new workers and other Ottumwans that militant activities were harmful and selfish.

Militant job actions no longer seem to provide assurance that workers can win either greater power or control or even industrial democracy. In meatpacking, the two great strikes of the past thirty years, the 1969 IBP strike and the 1985–1986 Hormel strike, are the best recent evidence of this. Although impeded by various legal obstacles, the Amalgamated in the IBP strike and Local P-9 and their companion locals in the Hormel strike both used workers' militant solidarity to win some short-term gains, especially in the IBP case, before being smashed in the long run. After signing a contract with the Amalgamated's Dakota City, Nebraska, local union following the 1969 strike and making wage concessions in other plants in the 1970s, IBP stepped up its strategy to close unionized plants and deal only with nonunion labor. As noted in Chapter 7, the UFCW condemned P-9's aggressive Corporate Campaign strategy that also depended on workers' militant solidarity.[5]

Any hope for the successful use of militant union tactics among rural midwestern workers rests on their ability to bridge ethnic and racial divisions. With the growth of ethnic diversity in Iowa and the rural Midwest, white workers in Iowa, often for the first time in their history, will have to work together with immigrant Hispanic and Asian workers in workplaces and their larger communities. Unfortunately, the precedent for such cooperation based on Ottumwa's history is not hopeful in this regard. Indeed, there is a striking degree of tension between Local 1's exclusivity and the inclusiveness necessary for successful union efforts today.[6]

Whereas Local 1's larger political efforts resulted in a revitalized Democratic party in Iowa and a degree of political party competitiveness that is still evident in the state today, labor's ability to shape a favorable political environment for working people has obviously eroded since the 1970s. This is a national problem that reflects shifts in public policy and employer attitudes for which labor unions must accept some responsibility. Although it is a very complicated issue, many studies suggest that the most effective strategy for unions today in regaining political clout is building larger alliances. Local 1's example is, once again, uneven on this issue. Although Local 1's militant leaders created and provided the initial organizational impetus for the Ottumwa Industrial Union Council, the new generation of Morrell workers as well as other unionists in the city were more successful in building larger bases of support in the city for various political efforts. Indeed, the 1949 Ottumwa city elections provide a sobering lesson in how a powerful, militant union can splinter effective coalitions among workers. Organized labor must constantly look for new allies if it is to have any hope of regaining its political voice. Otherwise, as Morrell was able to do with great effect against Local 1's militants, corporations and their allies will be able to charge that unions represent only narrow, selfish interests.[7]

Instead of foreclosing possibilities for renewed power and control among working people, however, this history of Ottumwa workers suggests that such struggle has always been necessary. Certainly no one could have foreseen the rise of labor in Ottumwa before the New Deal era. The obstacles that the fledgling CIO movement faced in Ottumwa and elsewhere were just as great as those faced by labor today despite a much different corporate environment. As in the case of workers in Ottumwa's history, working people will have to continue to struggle mightily to improve their situations.

NOTES

1. Company Town, Packing Community, Labor Relations, and Politics

1. Lawrence Oakley Cheever, *The House of Morrell* (Cedar Rapids, IA, 1948), 81.

2. Lizabeth Cohen, *Making a New Deal: Industrial Workers in Chicago, 1919–1939* (Cambridge, 1990), 7; Gary Gerstle, *Working-Class Americanism: The Politics of Labor in a Textile City, 1914–1960* (Cambridge, 1989); John T. Cumbler, *A Social History of Economic Decline: Business, Politics, and Work in Trenton* (New Brunswick, 1989); and Tamara K. Hareven and Randolph Langenbach, *Amoskeag: Life and Work in an American Factory-City* (New York, 1978).

3. See, especially, Roger Horowitz, "'It Wasn't a Time to Compromise': The Unionization of Sioux City's Packinghouses, 1937–1942," *Annals of Iowa* 50 (Fall 1989/ Winter 1990), 241–68; Shelton Stromquist, *Solidarity and Survival: An Oral History of Iowa Labor in the Twentieth Century* (Iowa City, 1993); and Bruce Fehn, "'The Only Hope We Had': United Packinghouse Workers Local 46 and the Struggle for Racial Equality in Waterloo, Iowa, 1948–1960," *Annals of Iowa* 54 (Summer 1995), 185–216. The availability of the Iowa Labor History Oral Project (ILHOP) collection to the general public has greatly aided the study of Iowa's labor movement especially since the 1930s. Recent histories of meatpacking unionism include Roger Horowitz, *"Negro and White, Unite and Fight!": A Social History of Industrial Unionism in Meatpacking, 1930–90* (Urbana, IL, 1997); and Rick Halpern, *Down on the Killing Floor: Black and White Workers in Chicago's Packinghouses, 1904–54* (Urbana, IL, 1997). More pertinent to Iowa's meatpacking union and labor relations history is Deborah Fink, *Cutting Into the Meatpacking Line: Workers and Change in the Rural Midwest* (Chapel Hill, 1998). How-

ever, given the contemporary focus of Fink's book, its historical perspectives are not systematic.

4. Glenn B. Meagher and Harry B. Munsell, *Ottumwa: Yesterday and Today, 1848–1923* (Ottumwa, IA, 1923); Chris D. Baker, *In Retrospect: An Illustrated History of Wapello County, Iowa* (Virginia Beach, VA, 1992), 105, 117–23; State of Iowa, Bureau of Labor Statistics, *Ninth Biennial Report*, 1899–1900 (Des Moines, 1901), 76–87, 464–67, 104–5; U.S. Bureau of the Census, *Seventeenth Census of Population* (1950), vol. 2 (Washington, DC, 1952); *List of Firms in Iowa Employing 50 or More Persons*, 1 January 1949 (Des Moines: Iowa State Bureau of Labor, 1949); *Iowa Firms with 25 or More Employees*, 1951 (Des Moines: Iowa State Bureau of Labor, 1951); and *Work Force, Employment and Unemployment, Iowa: Statewide and Areas, 1971–1972* (Iowa Employment Security Commission, July 1973), 111.

5. U.S. Bureau of the Census, *Twelfth Census of Population* (1900) *Manufactures* (Washington, DC, 1902); U.S. Bureau of the Census, *Fourteenth Census* (1920) *State Compendiums* (Washington, DC, 1923–24); U.S. Bureau of the Census, *Fifteenth Census of Population* (1930), vols. 3 and 4 (Washington, DC, 1931–33); U.S. Bureau of the Census, *Fifteenth Census* (1930) *Manufactures* (Washington, DC, 1933); and *Census of Population* (1950), vol. 2. For a more thorough discussion of the development of the two marketing patterns in the midwestern meatpacking industry, see Wilson J. Warren, "The Limits of New Deal Social Democracy: Working-Class Structural Pluralism in Midwestern Meatpacking, 1900–1950" (Ph.D. diss., University of Pittsburgh, 1992), chapter 1.

6. H. H. McCarty and C. W. Thompson, *Meat Packing in Iowa*, Iowa Studies in Business, no. 12 (Iowa City, 1933); *Fifteenth Census of Population* (1930), vol. 3; *Census of Population* (1950), vol. 2; *List of Firms in Iowa Employing 50 or More Persons*, 1 January 1949; *Iowa Firms with 25 or More Employees*, 1951; *Packinghouse Worker*, 11 March 1949; *Austin Daily Herald*, 11 November 1941; "United Packinghouse, Food and Allied Workers, AFL-CIO Average Paid Membership for Twelve Month Period," folder 7, box 497, United Packinghouse Workers of America (UPWA) Records, State Historical Society of Wisconsin (SHSW), Madison; *Sioux Falls Argus-Leader*, 11 September 1949 and 4 January 1950, Sioux Falls Public Library Vertical File; and *Madison East Side News*, 25 November 1954. On the proportion of animals slaughtered by terminal market versus direct-buying packing centers, see *National Provisioner*, "Weekly Inspected Slaughter," totals of the weekly data from 6 January to 29 December 1945.

7. U.S. Congress, Senate, Reports of the Immigration Commission, *Immigrants in Industries*, Part 11: "Slaughtering and Meat Packing," 61st Congress, 2d session, 1910, S. Doc. 633. Other important sources on the social demographics of Chicago's meatpacking industry include Edna Louise Clark, "History of the Controversy between Labor and Capital in the Slaughtering and Meat Packing Industries in Chicago" (M.A. thesis, University of Chicago, 1922); Alma Herbst, *The Negro in the Slaughtering and Meat-Packing Industry in Chicago* (New York, 1932); Fred K. Hoehler, Jr., "Community Action by the United Packinghouse Workers of America-CIO in the Back of the Yards Neighborhood of Chicago" (M.A. thesis, University of Chicago, 1947); James R. Barrett, *Work and Community in the Jungle: Chicago's Packinghouse Workers, 1894–1922* (Urbana, IL, 1987), chapter 2; Halpern, *Down on the Killing Floor*, 23–30; and Horowitz, *"Negro and White, Unite and Fight!"* 61–67. For a more complete treatment of the so-

cial demographic patterns in the midwestern meatpacking industry, see Warren, "Limits of New Deal Social Democracy," chapter 2.

8. The ethnic profiles for the packing communities were compiled through surname analysis of a systematic sampling of city directories from 1935 combined with an analysis of 1940 U.S. Census of Housing Block Statistics. For a more detailed analysis, see Warren, "Limits of New Deal Social Democracy," appendices A and B.

9. See especially Barrett, *Work and Community in the Jungle*, 202–24.

10. See Halpern, *Down on the Killing Floor*, 227–45; and Horowitz, *"Negro and White, Unite and Fight!"* 206–42.

11. On Austin workers' community struggles against the Hormel family, see Fred H. Blum, *Toward a Democratic Work Process: the Hormel-Packinghouse Workers' Experiment* (New York, 1953); Richard Dougherty, *In Quest of Quality: Hormel's First 75 Years* (Austin, MN, 1966); Michael T. Fahey, *Packing It In!: The Hormel Strike, 1985–86* (St. Paul, 1988); Dave Hage and Paul Kaluda, *No Retreat, No Surrender: Labor's War at Hormel* (New York, 1989); Hardy Green, *On Strike at Hormel: The Struggle for a Democratic Labor Movement* (Philadelphia, 1990); Peter Rachleff, *Hard-Pressed in the Heartland: The Hormel Strike and the Future of the Labor Movement* (Boston, 1993); and Horowitz, *"Negro and White, Unite and Fight!"* 37–40. An excellent study that hints at workers' community concerns and struggles in Charles City, Iowa, a community dominated by farm implement manufacturing and similar in structure to the direct-buying meatpacking communities described here, is Mark Finlay, "System and Sales in the Heartland: A Manufacturing and Marketing History of the Hart-Parr Company, 1901–1929," *Annals of Iowa* 57 (Fall 1998), 337–73.

12. Useful for understanding labor's upsurge in the New Deal period is Irving Bernstein, *The Turbulent Years: A History of the American Worker, 1933–1941* (Boston, 1969). The best general treatments of the rise of the CIO are Robert H. Zieger, *American Workers, American Unions, 1920–1985* (Baltimore, 1986), chapter 2; and idem, *The CIO, 1935–1955* (Chapel Hill, 1995).

13. On the importance of federal government legislation and the legal machinery it created to aid workers, see especially Irving Bernstein, *New Deal Collective Bargaining Policy* (Berkeley, 1950); J. Joseph Huthmacher, *Senator Robert F. Wagner and the Rise of Urban Liberalism* (New York, 1971); James A. Gross, *The Making of the National Labor Relations Board: A Study in Economics, Politics, and the Law* (Albany, 1974); David Brody, "The Emergence of Mass-Production Unionism," in Brody, ed., *Workers in Industrial America: Essays on the 20th Century Struggle* (New York, 1980); and Christopher L. Tomlins, *The State and the Unions: Labor Relations, Law, and the Organized Labor Movement in America, 1880–1960* (Cambridge, 1985). Arguably the most intensive study of a "classic" CIO union-building effort is Peter Friedlander, *The Emergence of a UAW Local, 1936–1939: A Study in Class and Culture* (Pittsburgh, 1975). Other important examinations of new immigrant and nonwhite CIO movements in large industrial settings are August Meier and Elliott Rudwick, *Black Detroit and the Rise of the UAW* (New York, 1979); David Brody, "Reinterpreting the Labor History of the 1930s," in Brody, ed., *Workers in Industrial America*, 120–72; Ronald W. Schatz, *The Electrical Workers: A History of Labor at General Electric and Westinghouse, 1923–1960* (Urbana, IL, 1983); Ronald Edsforth, *Class Conflict and Cultural Consensus: The Making of a Mass Consumer Society in Flint, Michigan* (New Brunswick, NJ, 1987); and Cohen, *Making a*

New Deal. On the IUAW and MUAPHW, see Galenson, *The CIO Challenge to the AFL: A History of the American Labor Movement, 1935–1941* (Cambridge, MA, 1960), 350–53; Horowitz, *"Negro and White Unite and Fight!"* 45–52; Peter Rachleff, "Organizing 'Wall to Wall': The Independent Union of All Workers, 1933–37," in Staughton Lynd, ed., *"We Are All Leaders": The Alternative Unionism of the Early 1930s* (Urbana, IL, 1996), 51–71; and Gregory Zieren, "'If You're Union, You Stick Together': Cedar Rapids Packinghouse Workers in the CIO," *Palimpsest* 76 (Spring 1995), 30–48.

14. Zieger, *The CIO*, 43–44; and Halpern, *Down on the Killing Floor*, 190–91. On the character of workers' militance in the Midwest, also see Daniel Nelson, *Farm and Factory: Workers in the Midwest, 1880–1990* (Bloomington, IN, 1995), 125–38.

15. See, for instance, Zieger, *The CIO*, 345–46, 349–51, 373–77; Michael Goldfield, "Race and the CIO: The Possibilities of Racial Egalitarianism during the 1930s and 1940s," with responses by Gary Gerstle, Robert Korstad, Marshall Stevenson Jr., and Judith Stein, *International Labor and Working Class History* 44 (Fall 1993), 1–63; Gary Gerstle, "The Protean Character of American Liberalism," *American Historical Review* 99 (October 1994), 1043–73; idem, "Race and the Myth of the Liberal Consensus," *Journal of American History* 82 (September 1995), 579–86; Arnold R. Hirsch, "Massive Resistance in the Urban North: Trumbull Park, Chicago, 1953–1966," *Journal of American History* 82 (September 1995), 522–50; Thomas J. Sugrue, "Crabgrass-Roots Politics: Race, Rights, and the Reaction against Liberalism in the Urban North, 1940–1964," *Journal of American History* 82 (September 1995), 551–78; and idem, *The Origins of the Urban Crisis: Race and Inequality in Postwar Detroit* (Princeton, 1996). Deborah Fink's *Cutting into the Meatpacking Line: Workers and Change in the Rural Midwest* (Chapel Hill, 1998), especially chapters 3 and 4, describes how white male unionists in Iowa have often undercut unionism's broader appeal by not embracing women or minority members.

16. See Zieger, *The CIO*, 120.

17. Richard Oestreicher, "Urban Working-Class Political Behavior and Theories of American Electoral Politics, 1870–1940," *Journal of American History* 74 (March 1988), 1257–86.

18. On labor's contribution to the postwar Democratic party agenda, see Samuel Lubell, *The Future of American Politics* (New York, 1951); Fay Calkins, *The CIO and the Democratic Party* (Chicago, 1952); J. David Greenstone, *Labor in American Politics* (New York, 1969); and Zieger, *The CIO*. On labor's contribution to Iowa's postwar Democratic party's successes, see Harlan Hahn, *Urban-Rural Conflict: The Politics of Change* (Beverly Hills, CA, 1971); and James C. Larew, *A Party Reborn: The Democrats of Iowa, 1950–1974* (Iowa City, 1980). On the fuller context of labor's role in American politics, see Kevin Boyle, ed., *Organized Labor and American Politics, 1894–1994: The Labor-Liberal Alliance* (Albany: State University of New York Press, 1998).

2. Evangelical Paternalism and Divided Workers

1. Daniel Nelson, *Farm and Factory: Workers in the Midwest, 1880–1990* (Bloomington, IN, 1995), 39–46, quote from p. 45; Ralph Scharnau, "The Knights of Labor in Iowa," *Annals of Iowa* 50 (Spring 1991), 861–91; Shelton Stromquist, *A Generation of Boomers: The Pattern of Railroad Conflict in Nineteenth-Century America* (Urbana, IL,

1987), 223; and Jonathan Garlock, *Guide to the Local Assemblies of the Knights of Labor* (Westport, CT, 1982), 112–29, appendix D.

2. *Ottumwa Daily Courier*, 13 November 1877; Lawrence Oakley Cheever, *The House of Morrell* (Cedar Rapids, IA, 1948), chapters 1–4. See also *The Fruits of 100 Years* (Ottumwa, IA, 1927) for an anecdotal company-sponsored perspective on Morrell's origins.

3. Cheever, *House of Morrell*, 53–54, 71–72; John C. Hudson, *Making the Corn Belt: A Geographical History of Middle-Western Agriculture* (Bloomington, IN, 1994), 101–3; Margaret Walsh, "From Pork Merchant to Meat Packer: The Midwestern Meat Industry in the Mid-Nineteenth Century," *Agricultural History* 56 (January 1982), 127–37; idem, "The Spatial Evolution of the Mid-western Pork Industry, 1835–75," *Journal of Historical Geography* 4 (1978), 1–22; and H. H. McCarty and C. W. Thompson, *Meat Packing in Iowa*, Iowa Studies in Business, no. 12 (Iowa City, 1933), 30. McCarty and Thompson note that "Ottumwa was not the first interior packing point [in Iowa], but it was the first to rise to a position of major importance." On the agricultural origins of industrial development in the Midwest, see Brian Page and Richard Walker, "From Settlement to Fordism: The Agro-Industrial Revolution in the American Midwest," *Economic Geography* 67 (October 1991), 285–315, and David R. Meyer, "Emergence of the American Manufacturing Belt: An Interpretation," *Journal of Historical Geography* 9 (1983), 145–74. For further insight on the seasonality of the packing industry in the late nineteenth and early twentieth century, see James R. Barrett, *Work and Community in the Jungle: Chicago's Packinghouse Workers, 1894–1922* (Urbana, IL, 1987), 28–29.

4. Mildred Throne, "A Population Study of an Iowa County," *Iowa Journal of History* 57 (October 1959), 308; U.S. Bureau of the Census, *Tenth Census of the United States* (1880) *Population*, vol. 1 (Washington, DC, 1883), 449; Stromquist, *A Generation of Boomers*, 158–61, 181.

5. Cheever, *House of Morrell*, 11, 16, 45–46.

6. Ibid., 82; 1880 Manuscript Census. Peter Liddy was listed in the census with an "unknown" birthplace and Alex Crosby was not listed. On Chicago's butcher aristocracy, see Barrett, *Work and Community in the Jungle*, 38–44.

7. *Tenth Census, Population*, 507. The native born included many descendants of the so-called upland South "island" groups described by cultural geographer John Hudson. "Upland southerners" originated in five island areas: the Scioto and Miami Valleys of Ohio, Bluegrass of Kentucky, Nashville Basin of Tennessee, and Pennroyal Plateau along and north of the Kentucky-Tennessee border. Yankees were not influential in the nineteenth-century settlement of the Corn Belt. These upland southerners were not "mountaineers from the Appalachians. They were, instead, farmers from the best agricultural lands of the Ridge Valley and Piedmont." Hudson, *Making the Corn Belt*, 3, 10, 63, 111 (quotation). My information on Morrell-Ottumwa's 1880 workers is drawn from the 117 employees indicated in the manuscript census for that year.

8. Morrell closed its Chicago plant in 1888. *Ottumwa Daily Courier*, articles from 1889 and 1891 issues in John Morrell and Company clipping file, Ottumwa Public Library, and 18 May 1887; *Annual Trade Edition of the Daily and Weekly Ottumwa Courier*, February 1893, p. 10; and Cheever, *House of Morrell*, 88. Ralph Ransom, a plant engi-

neer beginning in the 1920s, stressed how crucial the artesian wells were. Ralph Ransom, interview with author, Ottumwa, 14 August 1981.

9. Barrett, *Work and Community in the Jungle*, 122–27; and David Brody, *The Butcher Workmen: A Study of Unionization* (Cambridge, MA, 1964), 15.

10. *Journal of United Labor*, 1 (February 15, 1881), 95; 1 (April 15, 1881); 3 (June 1882), 246; 3 (October 1882), 320–22; and 4 (October 1883), 579. My thanks to Merle Davis for these references. See also Garlock, *Guide to the Local Assemblies of the Knights of Labor*; U.S. Commissioner of Labor, *Third Annual Report*, 1887, *Strikes and Lockouts* (Washington, Government Printing Office, 1888); U.S. Commissioner of Labor, *Tenth Annual Report*, 1894, *Strikes and Lockouts* (Washington, Government Printing Office, 1896); State of Iowa, Bureau of Labor Statistics, *Third Biennial Report*, 1888–89, "Strikes and Lockouts in Iowa," (Des Moines, 1889).

11. Cheever, *House of Morrell*, 115–16; 1885 State of Iowa Manuscript Census; and 1895 State of Iowa Manuscript Census. The 1895 census identifies religious affiliations. The total number of butchers, skilled, and supervisory personnel identified in the 1895 state census is 90 (26.7 percent) of 337 total Morrell employees. The 13 percent noted includes employees born in Britain or Canada with English ancestry. The main Protestant affiliations are Methodist and Presbyterian.

12. The information on Foster's red hair is from *Ottumwa Daily Courier*, 29 July 1910. Comparing Gilded Age industrialists' paternalism is problematic, but Foster's benevolence differed in character from that of, for instance, George Francis Johnson of Endicott Johnson. Johnson, according to historian Gerald Zahavi, wanted a "direct relationship," with his factory workers based, in part, on a rediscovery of the socialistic values of his youth. See Zahavi, *Workers, Managers, and Welfare Capitalism: The Shoemakers and Tanners of Endicott Johnson, 1890–1950* (Urbana, IL, 1988), 13–16.

13. Philip Scranton, "Varieties of Paternalism: Industrial Structures and the Social Relations of Production in American Textiles," *American Quarterly* 36 (1984), 235–57. Also useful for understanding the coercive nature of Gilded Age industrialists' paternalism is Paul L. Krause, "Patronage and Philanthrophy in Industrial America: Andrew Carnegie and the Free Library in Braddock, Pa.," *Western Pennsylvania Historical Magazine* 71 (April 1988), 127–45.

14. On Moody's prominence, see Paul Boyer, *When Time Shall Be No More: Prophecy Belief in Modern American Culture* (Cambridge, MA, 1992), 92–95. Of 90 butchers and skilled or supervisory employees identified in the 1895 state census, 32 (36 percent) were Presbyterian or Methodist. The next two largest groups were 17 Catholics (19 percent) and 11 with no religious affiliation (12 percent). On the other hand, 72 (29 percent) of the 249 workers identified as laborers or unskilled were Presbyterian or Methodist. An almost equal proportion (27 percent) were Catholic. Another 10 percent were Baptist and 9 percent Lutheran. My list of evangelical Protestant churches comes from McCoy's 1899–1900 Ottumwa City Directory. One of the Methodist churches was an African Methodist Episcopal church, though there is no evidence that African Americans benefited directly from their religious affiliations.

15. R. Ames Montgomery, *Thomas D. Foster: A Biography* (Cedar Rapids, IA, 1930); Sanford Jacoby, *Employing Bureaucracy: Managers, Unions, and the Transformation of Work in American Industry, 1900–1945* (New York, 1985), 49–58; George M. Marsden, *Fundamentalism and American Culture: The Shaping of Twentieth-Century Evangelicalism*,

1870–1925 (New York, 1980), 32–37; C. Howard Hopkins, *History of the Y.M.C.A. in North America* (New York, 1951), 5, 15, 45–46, 106, 109, 179–80, 187–88, 227, and 234; and Stromquist, *A Generation of Boomers*, 247–48. On Presbyterianism's connection to the YMCA movement, see Kenneth McDonald, "The Presbyterian Church and the Social Gospel in California, 1890–1910," *American Presbyterian* 72 (Winter 1994), 241–52. For another detailed examination of an Iowa employer's paternalistic approach to labor relations, including an emphasis on the YMCA, during this period, see Mark R. Finlay, "System and Sales in the Heartland: A Manufacturing and Marketing History of the Hart-Parr Company, 1901–1929," *Annals of Iowa* 57 (Fall 1998), 337–73.

16. Clifford Putney, "Character Building in the YMCA, 1880–1930," *Mid-America* 73 (1991), 49–70 (quote from p. 52); "Annual Reports, YMCA Work," box 43, John Morrell and Company Records, Special Collections, University of Iowa Libraries, Iowa City; *Ottumwa Daily Democrat*, 9 September 1896, 28 September 1901, and 26 October 1901.

17. *Agency Tribune*, n.d. [1886], included in John Morrell and Company clipping file, Ottumwa Public Library.

18. *Ottumwa Daily Democrat*, 13 August 1897; and Cheever, *House of Morrell*, 106, 108–11, 145–46.

19. Cheever, *House of Morrell*, 120–21; State of Iowa, Bureau of Labor Statistics, *Ninth Biennial Report, 1899–1900* (Des Moines, 1901), 76–87, 464–67, 104–5; and *Ottumwa Daily Democrat*, 20 July, 10 August, and 28 December 1901. At the turn of the century, the next largest industrial employers in Ottumwa were coal mining and cigar manufacturing. *Ottumwa Morning Democrat*, 31 March 1903, 1, reported that 361 people were engaged in making cigars, although the number employed in this industry also seems to have fluctuated seasonally.

20. Employee Time Book, 1899, box 24, Morrell Records; 1895 Iowa Manuscript Census; and 1900 U.S. Manuscript Census. The data on the twelve highly paid workers combines information on religious affiliation from the 1895 Iowa Census (available on nine of the twelve) with place of birth and occupational information from the 1900 U.S. Census (available on all twelve).

21. General workforce data for Morrell employees in 1900 was compiled on 1,131 workers who were employed at the plant between February 1899 and June 1900. This compilation includes names and data from the February 1899 time book, 1899–1900 Ottumwa city directory, and the 1900 census data which was collected in June, notably a down time normally in the packing business cycle. On the introduction of women workers at Morrell, the Iowa Bureau of Labor Statistics Biennial Reports for the early 1900s indicate no female employees in Wapello County pork and beef packing until 1905. See *Twelfth Biennial Report*, 252. For statistics for Ottumwa's total population, see U.S. Bureau of the Census, *Twelfth Census* (1900), *Population*, vol. 2, part 2 (Washington, Government Printing Office, 1902). For a detailed breakdown of Wapello County residents' church affiliations, see *Census of Iowa, 1915*, 731–32. Another factor that may have underscored workers' reluctance in the next few years to unionize was the high percentage of married employees; 65 percent of the workforce had spouses.

22. U.S. Bureau of the Census, *Twelfth Census* (1900), vol. 2, part 2, *Population*; 1900 Iowa Manuscript Census data; Dorothy Schwieder, Joseph Hraba, and Elmer Schwieder, *Buxton: Work and Racial Equality in a Coal Mining Community* (Ames, IA, 1987), 40.

Schwieder et al. note that while most Iowa coal mines shut down between April and October, the Consolidated Coal Company's mines near Buxton stayed open. When work slacked off, however, instead of laying off miners they usually used a reduced work schedule. See *Buxton*, 72–73, 83.

23. Hudson, *Making the Corn Belt*, 125; and Schwieder et al., *Buxton*, 180–82, 205; *Ottumwa Daily Democrat*, 14 December 1901; and *Ottumwa Morning Democrat*, 1 April 1903. The *Ottumwa Daily Democrat*, 28 September 1901, noted that Joe Williams of the hog killing department had been "rusticating" during the summer at Buxton but had now returned to work at Morrell.

24. Barrett, *Work and Community in the Jungle*, chaps. 4–5; and Brody, *The Butcher Workmen*, chap. 3.

25. *Butcher Workman*, January 1904, 48–56. Retail butchers were organized into separate meat cutter locals. Outside of Sioux City (Locals No. 363 and 369), the other meatpacking locals in Iowa were located at Cedar Rapids (Local No. 66), Albia (Local No. 263), and Olewein (Local No. 270). Meat cutter locals in Iowa were located in Clinton (Local No. 170), Des Moines (Local No. 187), Cedar Rapids (Local No. 206), Oskaloosa (Local No. 237), Davenport (Local No. 279), Marshalltown (Local No. 281), Dubuque (Local No. 296), and Keokuk (Local No. 350). Austin, Minnesota, a meatpacking-dominated town comparable to Ottumwa, had no meat cutter or meatpacking locals in January 1904. AMCBW Local No. 144 at Ottumwa, classified with the meat cutters' locals, actually included meatpacking workers and retail butchers.

26. See Brody, *The Butcher Workmen*, chap. 3, esp. pp. 46–48; Cheever, *House of Morrell*, 156. The first indication of any beef operations at the plant appears in the 1897 Sanborn Fire Insurance Map with the inclusion of a small addition to the plant's stockyards for cattle.

27. Brody, *The Butcher Workmen*, 38; Ralph Scharnau, "The Labor Movement in Iowa, 1900–1910," *Journal of the West* 35 (April 1996), 19–28; *Ottumwa Daily Democrat*, 3 August 1901; State of Iowa, Bureau of Labor Statistics, *Ninth Biennial Report, 1899–1900* (Des Moines, 1901), 188–89, 200, 350; idem, *Tenth Biennial Report, 1901–1902* (Des Moines, 1903), 230–31; idem, *Eleventh Biennial Report, 1903–1904* (Des Moines, 1905), 182, 200; *Ottumwa Evening Democrat*, 19 August 1904. The *Tenth Biennial Report* noted the average workforce at Morrell in 1902 was 1,115. Carl Thompson's "Labor in the Packing Industry," *Journal of Political Economy* 15 (1907), 98, notes that the Amalgamated did not organize unskilled laborers until 1902, which would seem to further undercut the veracity of the membership figures for Local No. 144 in 1901. Gallagher's quote is from *Ottumwa Daily Courier*, 12 July 1904.

28. Brody, *The Butcher Workmen*, 59–74; Scharnau, "The Labor Movement in Iowa," 21–23; *Ottumwa Evening Democrat*, 5 September 1904; State of Iowa, Bureau of Labor Statistics, *Thirteenth Report of the Bureau of Labor Statistics for the State of Iowa, 1906–1907* (Des Moines, 1908), 210; idem, *Fourteenth Biennial Report, 1908–1909* (Des Moines, 1910), 268; idem, *Fifteenth Biennial Report, 1910–1911* (Des Moines, 1912), 264.

29. Cheever, *House of Morrell*, 130; Richard Dougherty, *In Quest of Quality: Hormel's First 75 Years* (Austin, MN, 1966), 65–66; *Ottumwa Daily Courier*, 25 August 1906; 16 July 1910; and 27 July 1912.

30. *The Ottumwa Daily Courier*, 17 July 1907.

31. "YMCA Work," box 43, John Morrell and Company Records. On workers' uses of company paternalism contrary to the desires of their employers see Curtis Miner, "The 'Deserted Parthenon': Class, Culture and the Carnegie Library of Homestead, 1898–1937," *Pennsylvania History* 57 (April 1990), 107–35.

32. *Ottumwa Daily Courier*, 26 and 29 July 1910.

33. *Ottumwa Daily Courier*, 15 August 1906, 29 July 1910. The timebook kept by Ralph A. Bissell is in the author's possession. His son, another Ralph Bissell, a long-time Morrell employee, graciously allowed me to copy the information.

34. The 1915 Morrell-Ottumwa profile is based on data gathered from the State of Iowa Census of that year plus information from the Ottumwa City Directory. The total database consists of 1,044 workers, 754 of which were from the census. On union fragmentation due to ethnic conflict in Chicago during this period, see Barrett, *Work and Community in the Jungle*, 224–31.

35. On labor union developments in meatpacking during World War I see Brody, *The Butcher Workmen*, 78–83, 88–102; Barrett, *Work and Community in the Jungle*, 188–239; and William C. Pratt, "Advancing Packinghouse Unionism in South Omaha, 1917–1920," *Journal of the West* 35 (April 1996), 42–49.

36. Beginning on December 31, 1915, John Morrell and Company separated into American and English firms with parallel and interlocking directorates. The English side of the business continued to exert great influence on the American company during and after World War I. English personnel continued to be sent to Ottumwa. In 1919 Morrell was the largest American exporter of meat products to Britain, with 31 million pounds. See Cheever, *House of Morrell*, 171–72. T. D. Foster's oldest son was W. H. T. Foster, manager of the Sioux Falls plant, opened in 1909, from 1913 to 1939. T. H. Foster was the American company's president from 1921 to 1944. George Morrell Foster was president of the American company from 1944 to 1952. And John Morrell Foster was president of the American company from 1952 to 1953.

37. See Cheever, *House of Morrell*, 187, for a description of new construction at the plant during the 1920s. The decade of the 1920s saw the number of hogs marketed in Iowa almost double from just over 3 million to about 5.5 million. From 1914 to 1923, Iowa rose from tenth in meatpacking production in the United States to fourth. The state remained in fourth place through 1929, by which time it marketed nearly one-quarter of the nation's hogs alone. See H. H. McCarty and C. W. Thompson, *Meat Packing in Iowa*, 114–16, 120–23. Between 1928 and 1934, the total number of animals slaughtered at the Morrell-Ottumwa plant ranged from 907,000 to 993,000. Between 1896, after the fire of 1893 and the rebuilding and additions to the plant, and 1917, the total number of animals slaughtered at the plant ranged from 395,000 to 702,000. In that period, total slaughter figures fluctuated up and down considerably every year except between 1904 and 1908 when the range was from 631,000 to 696,000. Slaughter totals declined from the 1928–1934 level between 1935 and 1939 before jumping steadily to a range of 1,135,000 to 1,438,000 between 1940 and 1944. See box 21, John Morrell and Company Records. On the movement of displaced farmers to more urban, industrial locations in Iowa during the 1920s, see Grace S. M. Zorbaugh, "Farm Background of Country Migrants to Iowa Industries," *Iowa Journal of History and Politics* 34 (July 1936), 312–18.

38. The 1920 Morrell-Ottumwa profile is based on information compiled on the

1,505 employees indicated in the 1920 U.S. manuscript census. The census takers compiled their information in January, coinciding with the peak packing season.

3. The Welfare Capitalism of John Morrell, 1917–1937

1. Stuart D. Brandes, *American Welfare Capitalism, 1880–1940* (Chicago, 1976), 5.

2. Lawrence Oakley Cheever, *The House of Morrell* (Cedar Rapids, IA, 1948), 194–197; and David Yoder, *Labor Attitudes in Iowa and Contiguous Territory*, vol. 5, *Iowa Studies in Business* (Iowa City, IA, 1929), 82.

3. Robert W. Dunn, *Company Unions: Employers' "Industrial Democracy"* (New York, 1927); Herbert Feis, *Labor Relations: A Study Made in the Proctor and Gamble Company* (New York, 1928), 69–70; Irving Bernstein, *The Lean Years: A History of the American Worker, 1920–1933* (Boston, 1960), 73; Brandes, *American Welfare Capitalism*, 32; Robert H. Zieger, "Herbert Hoover, the Wage-earner, and the 'New Economic System,' 1919–1929," *Business History Review* 51 (Summer 1977), 181–87; David Brody, "The Rise and Decline of Welfare Capitalism," in David Brody, ed., *Workers in Industrial America: Essays on the Twentieth Century Struggle* (New York, 1980), 48–81; Mansel G. Blackford, "Scientific Management and Welfare Work in Early Twentieth Century American Business: The Buckeye Steel Castings Company," *Ohio History* 90 (Summer 1981), 238–61; Gerald Zahavi, "Negotiated Loyalty: Welfare Capitalism and the Shoeworkers of Endicott Johnson, 1920–1940," *Journal of American History* 70 (December 1983), 602–20; idem, *Workers, Managers, and Welfare Capitalism: The Shoeworkers and Tanners of Endicott-Johnson, 1890–1950* (Urbana, IL, 1988); Daniel Nelson, "The Company Union Movement, 1900–1937: A Reexamination," *Business History Review* 56 (Autumn 1982), 335–57; and Lizabeth Cohen, *Making a New Deal: Industrial Workers in Chicago, 1919–1939* (Cambridge, 1990), especially chapter 4. H. M. Gitelman's "Welfare Capitalism Reconsidered," *Labor History* 33 (Winter 1992), 5–31, places the 1920s innovations squarely in the larger context of industrial paternalism and sees little differentiation between the two. Andrea Tone, *The Business of Benevolence: Industrial Paternalism in Progressive America* (Ithaca, NY, 1997) is particularly sensitive to gender dynamics in welfare work.

4. Bernstein, *Lean Years*, 177; James R. Green, *The World of the Worker: Labor in Twentieth Century America* (New York, 1980), 102–10; Nelson, "Company Union Movement," 343–45; Sanford Jacoby, "The Rise of Internal Labor Markets in American Manufacturing Firms, 1910–1940" (Ph.D. diss., University of California, Berkeley, 1981), 504–11; and idem, *Employing Bureaucracy: Managers, Unions, and the Transformation of Work in American Industry, 1900–1945* (New York, 1985), 185, 193–95.

5. On welfare capitalism's creation of rising worker expectations for their employers, see in addition to Cohen's *Making a New Deal*, Paul Street, "The Swift Difference: Workers, Managers, Militants, and Welfare Capitalism in Chicago's Stockyards, 1917–1942," in *Unionizing "The Jungles": Essays on Labor and Community in the 20th Century Meatpacking Industry*, eds. Shelton Stromquist and Marvin Bergman (Iowa City, 1997), 16–50; and Rick Halpern, "The Iron Fist and the Velvet Glove: Welfare Capitalism in Chicago's Packinghouses, 1921–1933," *Journal of American Studies* 26 (1992), 159–83.

6. David Brody, *The Butcher Workmen: A Study of Unionization* (Cambridge, MA,

1964), 78–83, 88–102; James R. Barrett, *Work and Community in the Jungle: Chicago's Packinghouse Workers, 1894–1922* (Urbana, IL, 1987), 198–200; David Montgomery, *The Fall of the House of Labor: The Workplace, the State, and American Labor Activism, 1865–1925* (Cambridge, 1987), 382–85.

7. *Butcher Workman*, March 1919, 5. Thomas Henry Foster published *Shakespeare: Man of Mystery* (Cedar Rapids, 1946). Many of Foster's speeches on the "true" identity of Shakespeare and related topics are included in the John Morrell and Company Records at the University of Iowa Libraries' Special Collections, Iowa City. Foster's obituary in the *Des Moines Register*, 30 December 1951, noted that he owned 5,500 books at the time of his death, including over 400 editions (and several firsts) of *Uncle Tom's Cabin*. He also owned a complete Samuel Johnson dictionary dating from 1755 and two pages of a Gutenberg Bible.

8. *Butcher Workman*, September 1919, 5; and April 1921, 12.

9. Ibid., April 1921, 5, 12.

10. Ibid., November 1921, 3.

11. *Ottumwa Daily Courier*, 19 and 20 October 1921; *Des Moines Register*, 20 October 1921; John Jordan, interview with Paul Kelso, 7 April 1978, Iowa Labor History Oral Project (ILHOP), State Historical Society of Iowa (SHSI), Iowa City; Paul Bissell, interview with author, 10 January 1983.

12. *Ottumwa Daily Courier*, 21 October 1921; *Des Moines Register*, 22 October 1921 and 17 November 1921.

13. McCoy's Ottumwa City Directory, 1920; and *Ottumwa Daily Courier*, 22 October 1921.

14. *Ottumwa Daily Courier*, 28 and 29 October 1921 and 1 and 2 November 1921; *Des Moines Register*, 18 November 1921; Kenneth Ellis and Donald Jones, interview with Paul Kelso, 20 October 1978, ILHOP; McCoy's Ottumwa City Directory, 1922; and Alfred "Pat" Crow, interview with Paul Kelso, 1978, ILHOP.

15. *Ottumwa Daily Courier*, 15 and 16 November 1921; *Des Moines Register*, 16 November 1921; and Kate Rousmaniere, "The Muscatine Button Workers' Strike of 1911–12: An Iowa Community in Conflict," *Annals of Iowa* 46 (Spring 1982), 257–58.

16. Alfred Crow, interview; Cheever, *House of Morrell*, 190; Paul Bissell, interview.

17. On company union formation during this period, see U.S. Bureau of Labor Statistics, *Characteristics of Company Unions, 1935*, bulletin no. 634 (Washington, DC, June 1937), 10, 19, 83, 181. This government survey found that strikes were the greatest relative cause of company union formation between 1920 and 1922. The survey also showed that two-thirds of the employers who had company unions also conducted separate welfare activities. See Brody, *Butcher Workmen*, 99–100; Brandes, *American Welfare Capitalism*, 126–27; Nelson, "Company Union Movement," 338. For a perceptive analysis of the role of company papers during this era in attempting to create company loyalties among workers, see Paul Street, "A Company Newspaper: The *Swift Arrow* and Welfare Capitalism in Chicago's Meatpacking Industry, 1917–1942," *Mid-America* 78 (Winter 1996), 31–60.

18. Brandes, *American Welfare Capitalism*, 123–25. In 1934, Morrell introduced an employee-only council (without management representation) at the Ottumwa plant to meet NIRA specifications. Hence this description of the council's format applies only

to the period from 1922 to 1934. Since the two functioned in a similar manner with similar powers, however, this study considers both as a single entity from 1922 to 1937. See the *Ottumwa Daily Courier*, 16 July 1973.

19. *A Handbook for the Employees of John Morrell and Company* (Ottumwa, Iowa, and Sioux Falls, South Dakota, 1924), 18–21, 23–24, in "Miscellaneous file," box 27, John Morrell and Company Records. The government survey on company unions showed that only one-third of those studied handled grievances effectively. See U.S. Bureau of Labor Statistics, *Characteristics of Company Unions*, 201.

20. Barrett, *Work and Community in the Jungle*, 243–55; Brody, *Butcher Workmen*, 172; and Blackford, "Scientific Management," 247–58. The quote is from Nelson, "Company Union Movement," 336–39.

21. Feis, *Labor Relations*, 69–70; Dunn, *Company Unions*. For the Morrell meetings, see *Morrell Magazine*, June 1926, 11; February 1927, 11; and February 1928, 11.

22. *Employee Handbook*, 18; *Morrell Magazine*, March 1927, 11; May 1928, 11, 20; August 1930, 11; October 1931, 19; March 1933, 24; July 1934, 21; Kenneth Ellis, interview with ILHOP. Sanford Jacoby has noted that foremen still determined wages throughout the 1920s even in plants where personnel departments existed. See Jacoby, *Employing Bureaucracy*, 195. John "Jack" Moses, interview with author, 12 September 1982. Jack Moses started work in the smoked meat department in 1926. In the 1940s, he worked in the newly-formed industrial engineering department and later became a divisional superintendent in the sausage department.

23. *Morrell Magazine*, July 1927, 11; June 1928, 11; July 1928, 11; January 1929, 24; Kenneth Ellis and Donald Jones, interview with ILHOP; Elmer Cline, interview with ILHOP, 25 September 1981; Virgil Bankson, interview with ILHOP; Art Bankson, interview; Gust R. Hallgren, interview with author, 16 April 1983.

24. *Morrell Magazine*, January 1927, 9; May 1927, 6; Art Bankson, interview; Nelson, "Company Union Movement," 343–44; Jacoby, *Employing Bureaucracy*, 185, 193–95. For sources that elaborate on the inroads some personnel departments made into the foremen's traditional realms, see Bernstein, *Lean Years*, 177; Green, *World of the Worker*, 102–10; and Daniel Nelson, *Managers and Workers: Origins of the New Factory System in the United States, 1880–1920* (Madison, WI, 1975), 48.

25. *Employee Handbook*, 23–24, 41–42; Virgil Bankson, interview with ILHOP; Alfred Crow, interview; Frances Calhoon, Donald Jones, and Virgil Bankson, interview with Local P-1, Amalgamated Meat Cutters and Butcher Workmen of North America (AMCBW), SHSI; Violet Bohaty, interview with ILHOP, 15 September 1981. Bohaty commented that arbitrary transfers still occurred in 1936 when she started work in the sausage department. On sexual harassment of women workers, see Shelton Stromquist, *Solidarity and Survival: An Oral History of Iowa Labor in the Twentieth Century* (Iowa City, 1993), 221–22. Gust R. Hallgren, interview; Paul Bissell, interview; Elmer Cline, interview; George Gail, interview with author, 13 January 1983. A beef department employee who began in 1934, Gail recalled that one could only use the rest room once every five hours for only five minutes at a time. He added that it often took five minutes simply to reach a rest room.

26. Jacoby, *Employing Bureaucracy*, 187, 230–31; Cheever, *House of Morrell*, 197; *Morrell Magazine*, April 1925, 6, 21; August 1925, 6; and for Ernest Manns's remarks see June 1925, 3; Jack Moses, interview; Gilbert Baker, interview with author, 4 Au-

gust 1982. Baker started work in the trimming room in 1928 and during the 1940s and 1950s was a draftsman for the industrial engineering department. Indications of the types of careers found among the foremen and superintendents appear in the sketches of John Denefe, Lyle Mosher, and Oscar Johnson in *Morrell Magazine*, November 1926, 7; May 1926, 7; and November 1926, 16, respectively.

27. *Morrell Magazine*, December 1925, 3. The figures of "one-half to two-thirds of the work force" are a rough average of those *Morrell Magazine* gave from 1926 to 1933.

28. *Employee Handbook*, 46–47; *Morrell Magazine*, August 1924, 4; July 1925, 5; January 1941, 2.

29. *Morrell Magazine*, June 1925, 10; September 1928, 11; *Plant Council Bulletin*, 1 October 1923, in "Miscellaneous file," box 27, John Morrell and Company Records. Before July 1926, employees were allowed eight instead of six hours of uninterrupted service. See *Morrell Magazine*, July 1926, 6; December 1924, 9; February 1926, 19; January 1928, 21; May 1931, 11. Not until April 1931 did the company relax the rule somewhat for employees with twenty-five years or more of service. It allowed them to miss three additional days.

30. *Morrell Magazine*, December 1925, 5; March 1933, 24. The 2,485 figure includes employees who worked part-time during the year. The other figures are from *Morrell Magazine*, September 1926, 11; February 1927, 24; February 1928, 6; February 1929, 8; January 1930, 7; January 1931, 6; January 1933, 5; and January 1935, 6. On the credit union, see *Morrell Magazine*, February 1934, 3; February 1936, 6; and February 1939, 4.

31. *Morrell Magazine*, July 1924, 3; May 1930, 10; August 1928, 11; August 1929, 11; May 1931, 11; *Agency Tribune*, 1886; Alfred Crow, interview; Jack Moses, interview. Jack Moses later became a director of the chorus.

32. Elmer Cline, interview; Clarence Orman to Wilson J. Warren, 19 July 1982; Clarence Orman, interview with author, 25 September 1982; Virgil Bankson, interview with ILHOP.

33. E. L. Thorndike, *144 Smaller Cities* (New York, 1940); and "Housing among the Low Income Groups: Ottumwa" (Des Moines, Iowa State Planning Board, 1936), Iowa Collection, Ottumwa Public Library.

34. Virgil Bankson, interview with ILHOP; Kenneth Ellis, interview with ILHOP; Gilbert Baker, interview; Ira Bartholow, interview with ILHOP, 19 October 1978; Earl Paxson, interview with author, 27 June 1982. Paxson began at the Morrell plant in Ottumwa in 1909 as a secretary for T. H. Foster, a position he says he received by exaggerating his secretarial abilities. Since the Morrell plant's opening in 1877, young boys under sixteen had typically worked there as was the case in other packing plants. In 1911, for instance, the state's labor bureau reported that nearly 8 percent of Morrell's workforce consisted of children under sixteen. See State of Iowa, Bureau of Labor Statistics, *Fifteenth Report of the Bureau of Labor Statistics for the State of Iowa, 1910–1911* (Des Moines, 1912). See also George Gail, interview. On the "doctrine of high wages," see Brody, "Rise and Decline of Welfare Capitalism," 61–66, 71–78. Brody (p. 62) cites the average wage of an industrial worker in 1922 as forty-eight cents per hour, while in 1929 it was fifty-six cents per hour. For a position downplaying the doctrine's use, see Bernstein, *Lean Years*, 179–80. Endicott Johnson's welfare capitalist programs, ostensibly much more successful than John Morrell's, included profit sharing, medical

service, free legal aid, and "liberal" wages, as well as the nonfinancial programs. See Zahavi, *Workers, Managers, and Welfare Capitalism*, 41–53.

35. Paul Bissell, interview; Alfred Crow, interview; Elmer Cline, interview; Gilbert Baker, interview. The "boomer" butcher phenomenon seems to have declined by the end of the 1920s as workers became less transient.

36. Donald Jones, interviews with ILHOP and Local P-1; *Morrell Magazine*, August 1932, 21. Larry D. Englemann, "'We Were the Poor People': The Hormel Strike of 1933," *Labor History* 15 (Fall 1974), 491, notes kill department employees' role as leaders of the 1930s union drives in meatpacking plants.

37. Virgil Bankson, interview with ILHOP; Donald Jones, interview with Local P-1; Elmer Cline, interview.

38. Ralph Ransom, interview with author, 14 August 1981; Charles Edward Logan, interview with author, 20 July 1981; Donald Schaub, interview with author, 11 January 1983; Earl F. Paxson, interview with author, 27 June 1982; and Virgil Bankson, interview with author, 26 September 1982.

39. Virgil Bankson, interview with author; *Morrell Magazine*, November 1937, 2.

4. Building a "Live, Wide Awake Union"

1. Although the story of the CIO's break from the AFL can be found in many places, one of the most dramatic and compelling accounts is Irving Bernstein, *Turbulent Years: A History of the American Worker, 1933–1941* (Boston, 1969). On the CIO movement in meatpacking, see Walter Galenson, *The CIO Challenge to the AFL: A History of the American Labor Movement, 1935–1941* (Cambridge, 1960), chapter 10; David Brody, *The Butcher Workmen: A Study of Unionization* (Cambridge, MA, 1964), chapters 8–10; Wilson J. Warren, "The Limits of New Deal Social Democracy: Working-Class Structural Pluralism in Midwestern Meatpacking, 1900–1955" (Ph.D. diss., University of Pittsburgh, 1992), chapters 3–6; Paul L. Street, "Working in the Yards: A History of Class Relations in Chicago's Meatpacking Industry, 1886–1960" (Ph.D. diss., State University of New York at Binghamton, 1993); Rick Halpern, *Down on the Killing Floor: Black and White Workers in Chicago's Packinghouses, 1904–54* (Urbana, IL, 1997); and Roger Horowitz, *"Negro and White, Unite and Fight!": A Social History of Industrial Unionism in Meatpacking, 1930–90* (Urbana, IL, 1997). On the Austin and Cedar Rapids union-building "orbits," see, especially, Horowitz, *"Negro and White Unite and Fight!"* chapter 2; Peter Rachleff, "Organizing 'Wall-to-Wall': The Independent Union of All Workers, 1933–1937," in Shelton Stromquist and Marvin Bergman, eds., *Unionizing the Jungles: Labor and Community in the Twentieth-Century Meatpacking Industry* (Iowa City, 1997), 51–74; and Gregory Zieren, "'If You're Union, You Stick Together': Cedar Rapids Packinghouse Workers in the CIO," *Palimpsest* 76 (Spring 1995), 30–48. Roger Horowitz and Rick Halpern coined the term "orbit" in reference to Austin's union-building movement. See Horowitz and Halpern, "The Austin Orbit," paper presented at the Missouri Valley Historical Conference, Omaha, Nebraska, March 1986.

2. Because of the unavailability of census records for the years since 1925, my assessment of workers' ethnicity and nativity in the 1930s is based on my surname analysis of a random sample of 127 Morrell employees taken from the 1935 McCoy's Ottumwa

City Directory and the information provided by thirty *Ottumwa Courier* obituaries of Morrell workers who had worked at the plant in 1935 and who died between 1988 and 1991. In my analysis of workers' probable ethnic background, I relied especially on two surname dictionaries, Patrick Hanks and Flavia Hodges, *A Dictionary of Surnames* (Oxford, 1988), and Eldson C. Smith, *New Dictionary of American Family Names* (New York, 1973). On the population shift during the 1920s, see Bureau of the Census, *Sixteenth Census of the United States: 1940*, vol. 1, *Population* (Washington, DC, 1942). On the UMWA in Iowa and the coal mining background of many meatpacking union activists, see Donald Harris, interview with Paul Kelso, 8 June 1978, Iowa Labor History Oral Project (ILHOP), State Historical Society of Iowa (SHSI), Iowa City; Roger Horowitz, "'It Wasn't a Time to Compromise': The Unionization of Sioux City's Packinghouses, 1937–1942," *Annals of Iowa* 50 (1989/1990), 247; and Dorothy Schwieder, *Black Diamonds: Life and Work in Iowa's Coal Mining Communities, 1895–1925* (Ames, IA, 1983), 126–56, 169–70.

3. U.S. Bureau of the Census, *Religious Bodies* (1926), vol. 1, *Summary and Detailed Tables* (Washington, DC, 1930); and U.S. Bureau of the Census, *Religious Bodies* (1936), vol. 1, *Summary and Detailed Tables* (Washington, DC, 1941). Obituary information on thirty-four workers who were employed at Morrell in 1935 and who died between 1988 and 1991 revealed 60 percent who attended fundamentalist Protestant churches. A sample of 116 obituaries found for Morrell workers who were employed at the plant in 1951 and who died between 1988 and 1991 uncovered 52 percent who belonged to fundamentalist Protestant sects. On the holiness and "ecstatic" traditions in American Christianity, see Paul K. Conkin, *American Originals: Homemade Varieties of Christianity* (Chapel Hill, 1997), 276–314; and Sydney E. Ahlstrom, *A Religious History of the American People* (New Haven, 1972), 806–22. On the importance of evangelical Protestantism as a radicalizing tenet for workers, see Herbert G. Gutman, "Protestantism and the American Labor Movement: The Christian Spirit in the Gilded Age," in *Work, Culture, and Society in Industrializing America: Essays in American Working-Class and Social History* (New York, 1977), 79–117.

4. Obituary data from the 1935 sample indicates that about one-quarter of Morrell workers belonged to one or more of these fraternals. On the working-class taverns in Ottumwa, *The Organizer*, the CIO local union newspaper for Morrell-Ottumwa included in the United Packinghouse Workers of America (UPWA), Local P-3 Records, Cedar Rapids, Iowa, State Historical Society of Iowa (SHSI), Iowa City, regularly included advertisements from businesses in the packing district, including several taverns. See also McCoy's Ottumwa City Directory, 1939. On the relative poverty of Ottumwa's working class in the 1930s, see "Housing among the Low Income Groups: Ottumwa" (Des Moines, Iowa State Planning Board, 1936), Iowa Collection, Ottumwa Public Library.

5. On the importance of left-wing radicals in the formation of the Chicago packinghouse workers' union movements in the 1930s, see Halpern, *Down on the Killing Floor*, 96–166; and Horowitz, *"Negro and White, Unite and Fight!"* 58–83. Horowitz also discusses the importance of left-wingers in the formation of the CIO packinghouse local in Austin, Minnesota. See *"Negro and White, Unite and Fight!"* 35–57.

6. *Butcher Workman*, September 1933, 1; and November 1933, 1. On the bitter

memories of many packinghouse workers toward the Amalgamated Meat Cutters and Butcher Workmen owing to the failed 1921 strike, see, for instance, Halpern, *Down on the Killing Floor*, 73–74; and Horowitz, *"Negro and White, Unite and Fight!"* 113, 189.

7. Iowa State Bureau of Labor, *List of Firms in Iowa Employing 50 or More Persons*, 1941 (Des Moines, 1941); Minutes of Regular Meetings of 6 June 1934, 21 August 1934, 15 January 1935, and 21 October 1936 of Mid-west Union of All Packing House Workers (MUAPHW), 1933–34, 1935–36, and 1936–37 Minutes Books, UPWA Records, Local P-3, SHSI. On the MUAPHW, also see Brody, *Butcher Workmen*, 161; and Horowitz, *"Negro and White, Unite and Fight!"* 50; and Zieren, "'If You're Union, You Stick Together.'"

8. *Butcher Workman*, September 1933, 1; *Ottumwa Daily Courier*, 14 May 1934; and 17 May 1934; Kenneth Ellis and Donald Jones, interview with Paul Kelso, 20 October 1978, ILHOP; Donald Jones and Virgil Bankson, interview with Leslie F. Orear, 14 January 1974, Local P-1, AMCBW-NA, AFL-CIO Records, SHSI; McCoy's Ottumwa City Directory, 1922–23; Paul Bissell, interview with author, 25 November 1984; Art Bankson, interview with author, 17 May 1983 and 25 November 1984; and *The Organizer*, 5 July 1937, UPWA Local P-3, SHSI. On the Amalgamated's strike at Morrell–Sioux City, see James Rogers Holcomb, "The Union Policies of Meat Packers, 1929–1943," (M.A. thesis, University of Illinois, 1957), 72–87; and Lynwood E. Oyos, "Labor's House Divided: The Morrell Strike of 1935–1937," *South Dakota History* 18 (Spring/Summer 1988), 67–88.

9. Minutes of Regular Meeting of 6 January 1937 of MUAPHW, 1936–37 Minute Book, Local P-3 Records, SHSI; *The Unionist*, 29 January 1937, Local P-3 Records, SHSI; and Virgil Bankson, interview with author, 26 September 1982. Donald W. Harris, the CIO-PWOC's first national director, also recalled that Clark and his union aroused suspicions throughout Iowa by asking for reimbursement before attempting to help organize workers. Harris, interview with Paul Kelso, 8 June 1978, ILHOP, SHSI. Milo Barta, one of the early Wilson-Cedar Rapids unionists, claimed that the Midwest group organized a "little nucleus [in] Ottumwa." Barta, interview with Paul Kelso, November 1977, ILHOP. On Lewis Clark, see Horowitz, *"Negro and White, Unite and Fight!"* 132–40, 152–73.

10. Minutes of Regular Meetings of 21 April 1936, 3 June 1936, 17 June 1936, 2 September 1936, and 7 October 1936 of MUAPHW, Minute Book, 1936–37, UPWA Local P-3 Records. On the history of the IUAW, see Larry D. Engelmann, "'We Were the Poor People': The Hormel Strike of 1933," *Labor History* 15 (Fall 1974), 490–93; and, especially, Rachleff, "Organizing 'Wall to Wall'"; and idem, "The Failure of Minnesota Farmer-Laborism," in *Organized Labor and American Politics, 1894–1994: The Labor-Liberal Alliance*, ed. Kevin Boyle (Albany, 1998), 103–20. Also useful for understanding the larger potential for a horizontal, community union-building movement during the 1930s is Staughton Lynd, ed., *"We Are All Leaders": The Alternative Unionism of the Early 1930s* (Urbana, IL, 1996).

11. "History of Local No. 32 of Ottumwa, Iowa," from CIO Convention Program, UPWA P-3 Records, SHSI; *The Unionist* (official newspaper of the IUAW), 30 April 1937; 7 May 1937; and 21 May 1937, "Scrapbook," UPWA P-3 Records, SHSI; Virgil Bankson, interview with Paul Kelso, 1978, ILHOP; and Art Bankson, interviews with author,

17 May 1983 and 25 November 1984. On the IUAW's budding relationship with the CIO, see also Rachleff, *"Organizing 'Wall to Wall,'"* 61–62.

12. *The Unionist*, 7 May 1937, Local P-3 Records, SHSI; "History of Local No. 32"; and *Des Moines Register*, 16 May 1937. The editors of the *Unionist* in the 21 May issue noted that Austin was the only remaining IUAW local that had not affiliated with the CIO by May 1937. See the *Unionist*, 21 May 1937. The MUAPHW was also urging CIO affiliation during 1937. Meetings indicate that the Ottumwa local sent a letter to the MUAPHW following the October certification election thanking them for mailing letters to members urging votes for the CIO. See Minutes of Regular Meeting, 10 November 1937 of MUAPHW, Unmarked Minute Book, Late 1937 and Miscellaneous, Local P-3 Records, SHSI.

13. "History of Local No. 32"; Art Bankson, interview, 25 November 1984; Paul Bissell, interview, 25 November 1984; and Minutes of Regular Meeting of 21 July 1937 of MUAPHW, Minute Book, 1936–37, Local P-3 Records, SHSI.

14. McCoy's Ottumwa City Directory, 1937; *Des Moines Register*, 7 May 1937; and the *Organizer*, 14, 28 June; and 19 July 1937, Local P-3 Records, SHSI. On Armour's aggressive antiunionism in Chicago, see Halpern, *Down on the Killing Floor*, 148–55; and Horowitz, *"Negro and White, Unite and Fight!"* 73–79.

15. The *Organizer*, 14, 28 June; 5, 19 July; and 2 August 1937, Local P-3 Records, SHSI; and Elmer Cline, interview with Merle Davis, 25 September 1981, ILHOP.

16. The *Organizer*, 14, 28 June; 5, 19 July; and 2 August 1937, Local P-3 Records, SHSI. On the issue of labor unions' attempts in the 1930s and 1940s to create new loyalties among workers by replacing similar company efforts, see Elizabeth A. Fones-Wolf, *Selling Free Enterprise: The Business Assault on Labor and Liberalism, 1945–60* (Urbana, IL, 1994).

17. Brody, *The Butcher Workmen*, 168, 223; Harvey Klehr, *The Heyday of American Communism: The Depression Decade* (New York, 1984), 237; *Ottumwa Daily Courier*, 28 July; 5 and 16 August 1937; the *Organizer*, 2 August 1937, Local P-3 Records, SHSI; and Local 32 Picnic Program, 15 August 1937, Local P-3 Records, SHSI.

18. *Des Moines Register*, 12 September 1937; "History of Local No. 32"; the *Organizer*, 28 June and 19 July 1937; the *Unionist*, 23 July 1937; Paul Bissell, interview; Elmer Cline, interview with ILHOP; and Brody, *The Butcher Workmen*, 168.

19. Holcomb, "Union Policies of Meat Packers," 88–89; and Cline, interview with ILHOP.

20. Five of the twenty-four NLRB certification elections held in meatpacking plants owned by the Big Four packers were determined on the basis of evidence of a majority of workers indicating union affiliation. See Holcomb, "Union Policies of Meat Packers," 103, 126, 141, and 163.

21. Some of the more important historical examinations of the concept of industrial democracy include David Brody, *Workers in Industrial America: Essays on the 20th Century Struggle* (New York, 1980); Nelson Lichtenstein, *Labor's War at Home: The CIO in World War II* (Cambridge, 1982); Christopher Tomlins, *The State and the Unions: Labor Relations, Law, and the Organized Labor Movement in America, 1880–1960* (Cambridge, 1985); Melvyn Dubofsky, *The State and Labor in Modern America* (Chapel Hill, 1994); and Robert H. Zieger, *The CIO, 1935–1955* (Chapel Hill, 1995). Each of these histo-

rians emphasize the importance of workers' pursuit of industrial democracy over a desire on the part of unions for greater control over production decisions.

22. On the nature of PWOC-UPWA shop floor bargaining, a strategy for union power that combined elements of both industrial democracy and workers' control, see Horowitz, *"Negro and White, Unite and Fight!"*; and Halpern, *Down on the Killing Floor*.

23. *Ottumwa Daily Courier*, 19 and 20 January 1938.

24. Ibid., 22, 25, 27 January; 5, 23 February; 2, 10 March 1938. Morrell did not establish a legal department at the plant until January 1939, when George Heindel retired from private practice to head it. Nevertheless, he had been associated with the company's legal work for many years prior to that time. See *Ottumwa Daily Courier*, 5 January 1939.

25. *Ottumwa Daily Courier*, 22, 25 January and 22 March 1938; "History of Local No. 32"; "Agreement, date 21 March 1938," folder 2, box 192, UPWA Records, State Historical Society of Wisconsin (SHSW), Madison; and "Plant Council Bulletin," 1 October 1923, box 27, John Morrell and Company Records, Special Collections, University of Iowa Libraries, Iowa City, Iowa.

26. Virgil Bankson, interviews; Art Bankson, interviews; Paul Bissell, interview; and Harold Poncy, interview with author, 8 December 1984.

27. Cline, interview with author.

28. Donald Jones, interview with Leslie Orear, 14 January 1974, Local P-1 Records, SHSI; and Jones, interview with Paul Kelso, 20 October 1978, ILHOP. Manns retired in 1938 and Mosher retired in July 1941 after twenty-eight years as a departmental superintendent. He had started working in Morrell's trimming room in 1887 at the age of eleven, and became a foreman in 1908. See *Morrell Magazine*, August 1941, 6.

29. Virgil Bankson, interviews.

30. Paul Bissell, interview; and Dorothy Daeges, interview with author, 25 September 1982. Other workers who joined the union in the late 1930s conveyed similar recollections of the union's pressure tactics. See Art Bankson, interviews; and George Gail, interview with author, 13 January 1983.

31. Bruce Nelson, *Workers on the Waterfront: Seamen, Longshoremen, and Unionism in the 1930s* (Urbana, 1988). On the issue of syndicalism among other CIO unions, see also Toni Gilpin, "Left by Themselves: A History of the United Farm Equipment and Metal Workers Union, 1938–1955" (Ph.D. diss., Yale University, 1992), chapters 4 and 5.

32. *Ottumwa Daily Courier*, 24 August 1939; and Donald Jones, interviews. On the PWOC delegate meetings in Chicago in July 1939, see Horowitz, *"Negro and White Unite and Fight!"* 126–27; and Halpern, *Down on the Killing Floor*, 162–63. On PWOC organizing efforts in Topeka, Kansas, see *Kansas Labor Weekly*, 19 October 1939; and Warren, "The Limits of New Deal Social Democracy," 235–45.

33. *Ottumwa Daily Courier*, 24 and 25 August 1939; Art Bankson, interviews; and Virgil Bankson, interview with ILHOP.

34. *Ottumwa Daily Courier*, 29 August 1939; and Polk's Ottumwa City Directory, 1939.

35. *Ottumwa Daily Courier*, 26, 28, and 29 August 1939; Donald Jones, interviews; Art Bankson, interviews; and Virgil Bankson, interviews.

36. Art Bankson, interviews; and Lester Bishop, Local 1, to Van Bittner, PWOC president, 6 October 1940, UPWA Records, folder 1, box 306, SHSW.

37. *Ottumwa Daily Courier*, 29 and 30 August 1939; Exhibit B, "Petition for Review," folder 2, box 192, UPWA Records, SHSW; and Jones, interview with Kelso, ILHOP, SHSI.

38. Bankson and Jones, interview with Orear, Local P-1 Records, SHSI.

39. Halpern, *Down on the Killing Floor*, 190–91.

40. Regular Meeting Minutes, 5 July 1939, "Permanent Record Book," January 1939–December 1942, UPWA Local No. 3 Records, SHSI; "Resolution," [November 1940], folder 11, box 306, UPWA Records, SHSW; Local 1 to Sam Sponseller, PWOC District 3 Director, 8 July 1941, folder 2, box 5, UPWA Records, SHSW; and Horowitz, *"Negro and White, Unite and Fight!"* 128–34.

41. On the formation of the UPWA, see Horowitz, *"Negro and White, Unite and Fight!"* 124–41.

42. Clark to Doherty, 21 January 1941, folder 11, box 306, UPWA Records, SHSW; Houston to Doherty, 8 February 1941, folder 11, box 306, UPWA Records, SHSW; Doherty to Houston, 10 February 1941, folder 11, box 306, UPWA Records, SHSW; and Doherty to Clark, 10 February 1941, folder 11, box 306, UPWA Records, SHSW.

43. Bankson and Jones, interview with Orear, Local 1 Records, SHSI; and Bankson, interview with Kelso, ILHOP, SHSI.

44. *Packinghouse Worker*, 4 and 11 June 1943; "Petition for Review," Morrell and Local No.1 and No. 174 before the NWLB, folder 2, box 192, UPWA Records, SHSW.

45. *Packinghouse Worker*, 12 November 1943; Horowitz, *"Negro and White, Unite and Fight!"* 152–62; *Ottumwa Daily Courier*, 5–16 April 1945.

5. The Erosion of Militant Unionism, 1946–1963

1. *Morrell Magazine*, March 1944, 8; and May 1947, 5; Gilbert Baker, interview with author, 4 August 1982; and Jack Moses, interview with author, 12 September 1982. Baker conducted time-study operations in the industrial engineering department from its founding in 1942 until 1950. Moses worked in the industrial engineering department in the same period, and noted quite bluntly that the department was started as a reaction to the union's emergence. For a recent reassessment of scientific management's function during the New Deal era, see Steve Fraser, "The 'Labor Question,'" in *The Rise and Fall of the New Deal Order, 1930–1980*, ed. Steve Fraser and Gary Gerstle (Princeton, 1989), 55–84.

2. *Packinghouse Worker*, 14 December 1945, 3; John Morrell and Co. Executive Department Announcement, 16 April 1949, folder 7, box 411, United Packinghouse Workers of America (UPWA) Records, State Historical Society of Wisconsin (SHSW), Madison; U.S. Bureau of the Census, *Seventeenth Census of the United States* (1950), vol. 2, *Population* (Washington, DC, 1952–53). The calculations of rural residents employed by Morrell in 1951 are based on my systematic sampling of plant employees from the Polk's Ottumwa City Directory for that year. Although not perfect, in lieu of employee records, city directories provide substantial insight into workers' residences since their criteria for inclusion are based on who *works* in the city as well as who *lives* there. The city directories indicate the city where the employee lived, so it is possible to calculate the distance traveled to work. Some workers commuted from Kirksville, Missouri, about fifty miles south of Ottumwa.

3. Roger Horowitz, *"Negro and White, Unite and Fight!": A Social History of Indus-*

trial Unionism in Meatpacking, 1930–90 (Urbana, IL, 1997), 175–205. The quotes are from pp. 175–76. On the CIO's social democratic vision see Nelson Lichtenstein, "From Corporatism to Collective Bargaining: Organized Labor and the Eclipse of Social Democracy in the Postwar Era," in *The Rise and Fall of the New Deal Order*, 122–52. For further insights on the national dimensions of the 1948 UPWA packinghouse strike, see David Brody, *The Butcher Workmen: A Study of Unionization* (Cambridge, MA, 1964), 232–40; Rick Halpern, *Down on the Killing Floor: Black and White Workers in Chicago's Packinghouses, 1904–54* (Urbana, IL, 1997), 227–45; and Wilson J. Warren, "The Limits of New Deal Social Democracy: Working-Class Structural Pluralism in Midwestern Meatpacking, 1900–1955" (Ph.D. diss., University of Pittsburgh, 1992), chapters 7–10. For a superb analysis of the context and evolution of the 1948 UPWA strike in Iowa, see Bruce Fehn, "Ruin or Renewal: The United Packinghouse Workers of America and the 1948 Strike in Iowa," *Annals of Iowa* 56 (Fall 1997), 349–78.

4. On the UPWA's 1946 strike objectives, see Horowitz, *"Negro and White, Unite and Fight!"* 167–74. On the 1946 strike in Ottumwa, see Warren, "The Limits of New Deal Social Democracy," 521–22.

5. *Ottumwa Daily Courier*, 15, 19, 31 March; and 1, 2, 5 April 1948.

6. Ibid., 6–10 April 1948; Jim Collins, interview with author, 12 August 1981.

7. Virgil Bankson, interview with Paul Kelso, 1978, Iowa Labor History Oral Project (ILHOP), State Historical Society of Iowa (SHSI), Iowa City, Iowa.

8. *Ottumwa Daily Courier*, 15, 16, 21–23 April 1948.

9. On the Taft-Hartley Act, see Christopher L. Tomlins, *The State and the Unions: Labor Relations, Law, and the Organized Labor Movements in America, 1880–1960* (Cambridge, 1985), 247–316.

10. *Ottumwa Daily Courier*, 27, 28 April, 8 May 1948; Kenneth Ellis and Donald Jones, interview with Paul Kelso, 20 October 1978, ILHOP; Frances Calhoon, Donald Jones, and Virgil Bankson, interviews with Leslie Orear, 14 January 1974, Local P-1 Records, SHSI; and Edward Filliman, UPWA field representative, Weekly Report, 12 February and 16 April 1949, folder 7, box 411, UPWA Records, SHSW.

11. Horowitz, *"Negro and White, Unite and Fight!"* 188–94; and Fehn, "Ruin or Renewal," 372–78. On the rural versus urban component of union members during the strike, see "Addresses of Union Scabs in 1948," folder 2, box 23, Local P-1 Records, SHSI.

12. This observation is based on a workforce profile developed for Morrell workers who were employed at the plant in 1951. Using information included in obituaries in the *Ottumwa Courier* between 1988 and 1991, supplemented by information on these workers provided by the 1951 Polk's Ottumwa City Directory, I developed profiles for 116 deceased Morrell workers who had worked in the plant in 1951. Whereas 31 (27 percent) lived at rural or small-town addresses in that year, the other 85 (73 percent) lived in Ottumwa. Typically, the *Courier*'s obituaries provide consistent and detailed information about workers' ages, marital status, veteran status, and religious affiliations as well as lists of their memberships in various social organizations. In terms of birthplaces, 72 percent of the urban component had been born in either Wapello County or adjacent counties versus 87 percent for the rural component. Regarding marital status, 86 percent of the urban proportion were married, while 81 percent of the rural workers were married. The largest segments of both groups were

members of fundamentalist Protestant sects (54 percent for the urban, 45 percent for the rural), and almost one-half of both groups' males were veterans of World War II (43 percent for the urban, 48 percent for the rural). These small differences contrast with those marking the difference between the two groups on other social memberships: 54 percent of the urban workers belonged to one or more social organizations compared to only 29 percent of the rural workers.

13. *Ottumwa Daily Courier*, 12 and 26 May 1948.

14. The UPWA international union added farmer-labor relations to its program in 1946. Ottumwa's Local 1 was one of the first UPWA unions to form a local committee in 1947. The *Packinghouse Worker* consistently noted the UPWA's farmer-labor political activities after the mid-1940s. See especially *Packinghouse Worker*, 30 March 1945, 4–5; and December 1952, 2. Also see "UPWA Program for Building Toward Farmer-Labor Unity," 9 April 1947, folder 10, box 490, UPWA Records, SHSW. This document offers the union's rationale for initiating the program, reviews its efforts to date, and gives a preliminary assessment of the success of the program. For a sample of the UPWA's evaluation of Local 1's farmer-labor efforts, see "A Roundup of What is Happening in Farmer-Labor Relations," ca. August 1947, folder 11, box 298, UPWA Records, SHSW. The obituary data suggest that a large number of the rural workers who were increasingly employed by Morrell at this time had had some farming experience. Although the available literature on the impact of the growing influx of farmers into Iowa factories in the immediate postwar period is slight, there have been a few studies on the characteristics of Iowa farmers who quit farming in the decade of the 1950s and who found urban employment. See, for example, Jeffrey Allan Robinson, "Perceptions and Experiences of Young Iowa Farm Families who Changed Residence and Occupation" (M.S. thesis, Iowa State University, 1962); and William Marion Edwards, "Occupational Adjustment among Iowa Farm Operators" (M.S. thesis, Iowa State University, 1971). Typically, such "quit" farmers were likely to be tenant farmers. According to Robinson (p. 24), between 1940 and 1959 the number of tenant farmers in Iowa dropped by 40,000.

15. See especially *Morrell Magazine*, December 1948, February 1949, and April 1952; *National Provisioner*, 17 December 1949; *Ottumwa Daily Courier*, 23 February, 1 May 1949, 24, 26 March 1951; the *Bulletin*, 15 April, 2, 16 May, 6, 20 June, 13, 18, 25 July, 15 August, 19 September 1949, folder 7, box 411; and box 441, UPWA Records, SHSW; "Agreement of John Morrell and Co. and Local Union No. 1 and Local Union No. 174, UPWA-CIO, Ottumwa, Iowa, and Topeka, Kansas," Local P-1 Records, SHSI; and *Packinghouse Worker*, 1 October 1948 and 9 September 1949. Edward Filliman's weekly reports to the UPWA international office, including the 1949 reports in folder 7, box 411, and the 1950–51 reports in folder 13, box 415, UPWA Records, SHSW, are also vital to understanding this struggle. For more information on Edward Filliman, see *Morrell Magazine*, December 1948, 1. For a discussion of the national context of wildcat strikes and walkouts during the late 1940s, see George Lipsitz, *Rainbow at Midnight: Labor and Culture in the 1940s* (Urbana, IL, 1994), 229–52.

16. Filliman, *Weekly Reports*, 30 April 1949 and 7 May 1949, folder 7, box 411, UPWA Records, SHSW.

17. The *Bulletin*, 15 April 1949, folder 7, box 411, UPWA Records, SHSW; John Morrell and Co., Executive Department Announcement, 16 April 1949, folder 7, box 411,

UPWA Records, SHSW; newspaper clippings in folder 7, box 441, UPWA Records, SHSW; and the *Bulletin*, 2 May 1949, box 441, UPWA Records, SHSW.

18. *Packinghouse Worker*, 18 February 1944; 16 February 1945; 7 February 1947; Local 1 Officers List, 10 March 1948, folder 2, box 314, UPWA Records, SHSW; *Morrell Magazine*, December 1948; and Proceedings, Tenth Annual Constitutional Convention, Iowa State Industrial Union Council, CIO, 1948, pp. 83–85, Iowa Federation of Labor (IFL), AFL-CIO Records, SHSI.

19. Charles B. Simpson, Local 1 recording secretary, to Lewis J. Clark, UPWA secretary-treasurer, 9 February 1951, folder 2, box 314, UPWA Records; Report of UPWA international on problems in Local 1, signed by Ralph Helstein and Russell Bull, 17 December 1951, Regular Membership Minutes, 1951–52, Local P-1 Records, SHSI; A Joint Statement from Local No. 1, UPWA (CIO) and John Morrell and Co., 1 November 1952, Local P-1 Records, SHSI.

20. Horowitz, *"Negro and White Unite and Fight!"* 220–30; idem, "'This Community of Our Union': Shopfloor Power and Social Unionism in the Postwar UPWA," in Shelton Stromquist and Marvin Bergman, eds., *Unionizing the Jungles: Labor and Community in the Twentieth-Century Meatpacking Industry* (Iowa City, 1997), 96–127; Fehn, "'The Only Hope We Had': United Packinghouse Workers Local 46 and the Struggle for Racial Equality in Waterloo, Iowa, 1948–1960," *Annals of Iowa* 54 (Summer 1995), 185–216; and idem, "Striking Women: Gender, Race and Class in the United Packinghouse Workers of America (UPWA), 1938–1968" (Ph.D. diss., University of Wisconsin–Madison, 1991), chapters 4–5. On the UPWA's antidiscrimination efforts in Chicago, also see Halpern, *Down on the Killing Floor*, 237–45.

21. Report of UPWA international on problems in Local 1, signed by Ralph Helstein and Russell Bull, 17 December 1951, Regular Membership Minutes, 1951–52, Local P-1 Records, SHSI; Kenneth Ellis and Donald Jones, interview with Paul Kelso, ILHOP; "By-Laws for Ottumwa Committee for Civic Progress," 25 October 1948, First Presbyterian Church, folder 7, box 411, UPWA Records, SHSW; *Ottumwa Daily Courier*, 23 February 1949, 27; *Morrell Magazine*, April 1952, 3; and Filliman, Weekly Reports, 10 February 1951 and 7 July 1951, folder 13, box 415, UPWA Records, SHSW. On this facet of Local 1's history, also see Wilson J. Warren, "The Limits of Social Democratic Unionism in Midwestern Meatpacking Communities: Patterns of Internal Strife, 1948–1955," in *Unionizing the Jungles: Labor and Community in the Twentieth Century Meatpacking Industry*, eds. Shelton Stromquist and Marvin Bergman (Iowa City, IA, 1997), 145–47.

22. On the 1952–1953 receivership issue, see "A Joint Statement from Local No. 1, UPWA (CIO) and John Morrell and Co.," 1 November 1952, Local P-1 Records, SHSI; and Regular Membership Meeting minutes, 28 October 1952, 19 November 1952, and 18 February 1953, Local P-1 Records, box 11, SHSI. The receivership appears to have been lifted by March 1953. Jack McCoy, interview with Merle Davis, 18 May 1983, ILHOP, also recounts the 1952 receivership controversy, albeit in a somewhat biased fashion since he was one of the local union leaders opposed to the walkouts and the union's militancy.

23. For a more complete discussion of the internal union conflict in Omaha, St. Joseph, and Topeka following the 1948 strike, see Warren, "The Limits of Social Democratic Unionism in Midwestern Meatpacking Communities," 132–37.

24. Horowitz, *"Negro and White, Unite and Fight!"* 225–27; Halpern, *Down on the Killing Floor*, 242–45; and Fehn, "'The Only Hope We Had,'" 200–201. For details on the demographics of various midwestern packing plants in 1935 and 1950, see Warren, "The Limits of New Deal Social Democracy," appendix B. Herbert Gutman's emphasis on interracialism in "The Negro and the United Mine Workers of America: The Career and Letters of Richard L. Davis and Something of Their Meaning, 1890–1900," in *The Negro and the American Labor Movement*, ed. Julius Jacobson (New York, 1970), and later reprinted in Gutman's classic *Work, Culture, and Society in Industrializing America* (New York, 1977), ignited a flurry of scholarly research that has stressed the limitations of interracial solidarity among workers and within labor unions. Particularly significant in focusing on the ways that whites organized (and identified) themselves in opposition to blacks is Herbert Hill, "Myth-Making as Labor History: Herbert Gutman and the United Mine Workers of America," *International Journal of Politics, Culture and Society* 2 (Winter 1988), 132–200; idem, "Race, Ethnicity and Organized Labor: The Opposition to Affirmative Action," *New Politics* 1 (Winter 1987); idem, "Lichtenstein's Fictions: Meany, Reuther and the 1964 Civil Rights Act," *New Politics* 7 (Summer 1998), 82–107; idem, "Lichtenstein's Fictions Revisited: Race and the New Labor History," *New Politics* 7 (Winter 1999), 148–63; David R. Roediger, *The Wages of Whiteness: Race and the Making of the American Working Class* (London, 1991); and Noel Ignatiev, *How the Irish Became White* (New York, 1995).

25. By "religion," I am referring to the large proportion of fundamentalist Christians among the Ottumwa workforce and the revival atmosphere of much of the 1930s organizing effort. On McCoy, see Regular Membership Meeting minutes, 18 February 1953, box 11, Local P-1 Records, SHSI; the *Bulletin*, 25 January 1954, box 23, Local P-1 Records, SHSI; *Morrell Magazine*, January 1955, 12; and *Packinghouse Worker*, February 1955, 11.

26. Jack McCoy, interview with Merle Davis, 18 May 1983, ILHOP.

27. Local No. 32 Picnic Program, 15 August 1937, UPWA Local P-3 Records, SHSI (includes a list of the first officers of Ottumwa Packinghouse Workers' Organizing Committee (PWOC) Local 32, later UPWA Local 1); and McCoy, interview, ILHOP. Virgil Bankson's sentiments about the preunion era of labor-management relations can be gleaned from his interviews with Paul Kelso, 1978, and Merle Davis, 11 March 1983, ILHOP. Filliman made the reason for his militancy clear in a September 1951 report to the UPWA international office. "You may say [that continued walkouts are] not justified, but I say the men were right. I helped break down this kind of [arbitrary work] assignment and condition years ago. [This] was one of the big deals when we organized our union[.] [T]his is a fighting deal, this old company method of do as your [*sic*] was one of the things that brought on unionism. . . . [We] have to fight to keep from going back to those days again." See folder 13, box 415, UPWA Records, SHSW.

28. Proceedings, Tenth Annual Constitutional Convention, Iowa State Industrial Union Council, CIO, Davenport, Iowa, 6–8 August 1948, pp. 83–85, IFL, AFL-CIO Records, SHSI.

29. Jack McCoy recalled the ostentatious displays of wealth of the Foster family and their "down the nose attitude" toward the people of Ottumwa in his ILHOP interview. Segments of this part of the interview are quoted in Shelton Stromquist, *Solidarity and Survival: An Oral History of Iowa Labor in the Twentieth Century* (Iowa City, IA, 1993),

54–55. On McCallum, see *Morrell Magazine*, January 1954, 3; April 1954, 5; December 1958, 7; and the *Bulletin*, February 1954, box 23, Local P-1 Records, SHSI.

30. On McCallum's financial strategy for Morrell, see *National Provisioner*, 21 August 1954, 25; *Morrell Magazine*, September 1954, 3; July 1955, 6; January 1956, 10; February 1956, 11; June 1956, 3; October 1959, 2; January 1960, 2; May 1960, 2; January 1962, 2; June 1962, 4; January–February 1963, 2; January–February 1964, 3; and May–June 1964, 15.

31. Sources describing the traditional financial strategies of the Big Four packers include Richard J. Arnould, "Changing Patterns of Concentration in American Meat Packing, 1880–1963," *Business History Review* 45 (Spring 1971), 18–34; Jimmy M. Skaggs, *Prime Cut: Livestock Raising and Meatpacking in the United States, 1607–1983* (College Station, TX, 1986); Mary Yeager, *Competition and Regulation: The Development of Oligopoly in the Meat Packing Industry* (Greenwich, CT, 1981); and Warren, "The Limits of New Deal Social Democracy," 41–55, 66–72. IBP awaits its historian, but crucial historical information is available in a series of articles Dale Kasler wrote for the *Des Moines Register*, 18–25 September 1988. Many management employees of Morrell communicated their criticisms of McCallum's financial strategy to me over the years. Lawrence Reedquist, a traffic engineer at Morrell for nearly fifty years, described McCallum's objective of buying old plants instead of constructing new ones as pushing Morrell's fortunes from "bad to worse" during the 1950s and 1960s. Reedquist, interview with author, 11 August 1981 (notes in author's possession).

32. For details about Hansel's career, see *Morrell Magazine*, March 1944, 8; August 1955, 6; October 1956, 8; and September 1962, 3.

33. Harry Braverman's *Labor and Monopoly Capital: The Degradation of Work in the Twentieth Century* (New York, 1974) contains one of the most fully developed treatments of Frederick Taylor's conception of piecework and incentive pay. See also Stromquist, *Solidarity and Survival*, 191–99, for a more complete discussion of the widespread use of incentives and gain time in Iowa factories after World War II.

34. The *Bulletin*, 31 January 1955; 23 March 1955; and 2 May 1955, Local P-1 Records, SHSI. Although not indicative of the internal divisions affecting local union politics, Jack McCoy's election to the state legislature on the Democratic ticket in November 1954 did indicate the powerful local presence exerted by labor in Ottumwa and Wapello County. See *Packinghouse Worker*, February 1955, 11.

35. The *Bulletin*, 9 January 1956; 25 January 1956; and 5 March 1956, Local P-1 Records, SHSI.

36. The *Bulletin*, 24 May 1956, Local P-1 Records, SHSI.

37. Local No. 1 Special Executive Board Meeting, 8 June 1956, box 11, Local P-1 Records, SHSI; the *Bulletin*, 28 January 1957, box 23, Local P-1 Records, SHSI; 3 February 1953 membership meeting, box 11, Local P-1 Records, SHSI; Arthur G. Johnson *Ottumwa Courier* obituary (died 14 January 1991), Ottumwa-Morrell workers obituary file, in author's possession; and Polk's Ottumwa City Directory, 1957. Jack McCoy characterized both Dave Hart and Lester Bishop as leaders of the "new" generation of anti-Filliman local union officials. See McCoy interview, ILHOP.

38. Tom Cohagan *Ottumwa Courier* obituary (died 3 May 1989), Morrell-Ottumwa obituary file, in author's possession; Edward Filliman, UPWA field representative weekly report, 23 June 1951, folder 13, box 415, UPWA Records, SHSW. For further in-

formation about the genesis of the anticommunism of Lewis Clark and his role in the internal politics of the UPWA international, see Horowitz, *"Negro and White Unite and Fight!"* 132, 135, 137, 170–71.

39. The *Bulletin*, 18 February 1957; 6 May 1957, box 11, Local P-1 Records, SHSI.

40. Regular Membership Meeting, 14 May 1957; Special Executive Board Meeting, 16 May 1957; Special Executive Board Meeting, 1 June 1957; and the *Bulletin*, 3 June 1957, box 23, Local P-1 Records, SHSI.

41. Given declining rank-and-file participation in virtually all union activities in the 1950s across the United States, the 23 percent turnout for the vote (652 total ballots cast out of about 2,800 members) on receivership indicates a fairly high level of interest in union affairs at the Ottumwa plant. See Special Membership Meeting minutes, 3 June 1957, box 11, Local P-1 Records, SHSI. For Local 1 membership figures from 1952 to 1960, see folder 7, box 492, UPWA Records, SHSW.

42. The *Bulletin*, 30 September 1957; 14 October 1957; 29 January 1958; 22 December 1958; 30 January 1961; and 19 January 1962, box 23, Local P-1 Records, SHSI. An interesting illustration of the changing concerns of Local 1's membership was the formation of the Iowa Avenue Club in May 1957 for workers interested in stock market investments. See *Morrell Magazine*, March 1960, 3.

43. *Morrell Magazine*, August 1962, 7; and the *Bulletin*, 17 December 1962, box 23, Local P-1 Records, SHSI. My calculations of workers' residences are based on systematic samples of the 1935 McCoy's Ottumwa City Directory, 1957 Polk's Ottumwa City Directory, and 1965 Polk's Ottumwa City Directory. I am defining the east end as corresponding to precincts one and two as described in Ordinance No. 1313 of the 1934 revision of Ottumwa's Municipal Code.

6. Local 1's Unionism and the Transformation of Iowa's Politics, 1939–1970

1. The standard argument, expressed especially by Harlan Hahn, is that Iowa's Democratic transition rested with both its farmers and urban residents (defined as cities with over 10,000 population). Hahn attributes the support for Democratic candidates among urban residents owing mainly to issues of taxation, liquor control, and legislative reapportionment. Neither he nor James Larew, though the latter is more generous in crediting labor's assistance, focus centrally on the contribution of Iowa's growing labor union movement to the Democratic transition. Shelton Stromquist's synthesis of oral histories on Iowa's labor movement suggests this connection, but it is not systematically examined. See, Harlan Hahn, *Urban-Rural Conflict: The Politics of Change* (Beverly Hills, CA, 1971); James C. Larew, *A Party Reborn: The Democrats of Iowa, 1950–1974* (Iowa City, 1980); Shelton Stromquist, *Solidarity and Survival: An Oral History of Iowa Labor in the Twentieth Century* (Iowa City, 1993), 282–94; and Dorothy Schwieder, *Iowa: The Middle Land* (Ames, IA, 1996), 290–91.

2. James L. Sundquist, *Dynamics of the Party System: Alignment and Realignment of Political Parties in the United States*, rev. ed. (Washington, DC, 1983), 256–57; Larew, *A Party Reborn*, 7; State of Iowa, *Official Register*, 1933–1934 (Des Moines, 1933); and State of Iowa, *Official Register*, 1941–1942 (Des Moines, 1942). Regarding the designation of Ottumwa's Ward One, beginning in the 1932 election, Ward One was reconstituted as Precincts One and Two. I have generally retained use of the designation First Ward (or Ward One) for the sake of continuity with earlier chapters. Although

part of the two-stage realignment, Iowa obviously still lagged behind the political revolution wrought by the Democrats in much of the rest of the urban Midwest and Northeast as early as 1920s. See Richard Oestreicher, "Urban Working-Class Political Behavior and Theories of American Electoral Politics, 1870–1940," *Journal of American History* 74 (March 1988), 1257–86.

3. State of Iowa, *Official Registers*, 1933–34 through 1973–74.

4. Among Iowa's industrial cities in 1940, Roosevelt won 58 percent of the vote in Ottumwa, followed by Fort Dodge with 56 percent, Davenport, Mason City, and Sioux City each with 54 percent, Waterloo with 52 percent, Dubuque and Des Moines with 49 percent, Cedar Rapids with 45 percent, and Burlington with 40 percent. See State of Iowa, *Official Register*, 1941–42.

5. Dolliver quoted in Hahn, *Urban-Rural Conflict*, 17. On the cultural streams of Iowa settlers, see Hahn, *Urban-Rural Conflict*, 35–36; Nicole Etcheson, *The Emerging Midwest: Upland Southerners and the Political Culture of the Old Northwest, 1787–1861* (Bloomington, IN, 1996), 2, 109–27; Morton M. Rosenberg, *Iowa on the Eve of the Civil War: A Decade of Frontier Politics* (Norman, OK, 1972), 18–23; John C. Hudson, *Making the Corn Belt: A Geographical History of Middle-Western Agriculture* (Bloomington, IN, 1994); Jon Gjerde, *The Minds of the West: Ethnocultural Evolution in the Rural Middle West, 1830–1917* (Chapel Hill, 1997), 4–5; and Robert R. Dykstra, *Bright Radical Star: Black Freedom and White Supremacy on the Hawkeye Frontier* (Cambridge, MA, 1993), vii. On Iowa's politics in the late nineteenth century, see Schwieder, *Iowa*, 31–32, 72–73, 76–77, 211–29; Larew, *A Party Reborn*, 1–9; Dykstra, *Bright Radical Star*, 58, 63, 108, 120–23, 250–54, 261; and Jeffrey Ostler, *Prairie Populism: The Fate of Agrarian Radicalism in Kansas, Nebraska, and Iowa, 1880–1892* (Lawrence, KS, 1993), 37–53, 138–42. On Wapello County's nineteenth-century demographics and politics, see Dykstra, *Bright Radical Star*, 145; Mildred Throne, "A Population Study of an Iowa County in 1850," *Iowa Journal of History* (October 1959), 314–18; and 1895 Iowa Census Manuscript.

6. Voting data on Ottumwa and Wapello County were obtained from State of Iowa, *Official Registers*, 1890 to 1931–32. The two exceptions to Ward One's slightly higher level of Democratic support compared to the rest of the city in this period occurred in 1916 and 1926. Ward One's voters cast a higher percentage for the Republican gubernatorial candidate, William Harding, in 1916 because of his anti-Prohibition campaign. In 1926, Republican Smith W. Brookhart, a progressive Republican, captured 60 percent of the First Ward's votes compared to just 48 percent for Ottumwa. Brookhart campaigned particularly on behalf of economic relief for Iowa's hard-pressed farmers. This economic focus reflected Brookhart's conscious rejection of the older state political focus on prohibition and ethnocultural issues. It may be that Morrell workers looked to Brookhart, who would remain a Republican but was "a New Dealer before [there was] a New Deal," more because of this economic focus, an area of concern that certainly would appeal to them during and after the New Deal, than its traditional concerns with Prohibition. On the 1916 gubernatorial race in Iowa, see Edward Franklin Cox, *State and National Voting in Federal Elections, 1910–1970* (Hamden, CT, 1972); and John Thomas Schou, "The Decline of the Democratic Party in Iowa, 1916–1920" (M.A. thesis, University of Iowa, 1960), 122, 135–44, 251–79; 302–7. Note that the 1921–22 official register did not provide detailed county-level

voting results. Only state and county totals are available for the 1920 elections. Wapello County and Ottumwa's large return for Democrats in the 1924 and 1930 U.S. Senate races probably was at least in part owing to the fact that Dan Steck was a native Ottumwan. On the 1926 senate race in Iowa, see George William McDaniel, *Smith Wildman Brookhart: Iowa's Renegade Republican* (Ames, IA, 1995), 196–98, 270–73. The New Dealer label for Brookhart's politics is by Claude Pepper and quoted in Mc-Daniel, *Smith Wildman Brookhart*, 273. On third-party support in Ottumwa and Wapello County, see *Ottumwa Daily Democrat*, 12 August 1901; *Ottumwa Morning Democrat*, 6 September 1903; James Weinstein, *The Decline of Socialism in America, 1912–1925* (New Brunswick, NJ, 1984), 44, 96, 116–18; David P. Thelen, *Robert M. LaFollette and the Insurgent Spirit* (Boston, 1976), 190. On the general lack of voter support for populists in Iowa, see Ostler, *Prairie Populism*, esp. 154–74. On socialism in Iowa, see William H. Cumberland, "The Red Flag Comes to Iowa," *Annals of Iowa* 39 (1968), 453–54.

7. State of Iowa, *Official Registers*, 1937–38 through 1973–74; and Cox, *State and National Voting*.

8. *Ottumwa Daily Courier*, 2–5, 8, 12, 18, and 22 September 1941; Regular Meeting of 17 September 1941 of Local 3, UPWA Local P-3 Records, 1939–1942 Minute Book, State Historical Society of Iowa (SHSI), Iowa City; Convention and Year Book, Iowa State Industrial Union Council, CIO, 1951, Iowa Federation of Labor (IFL), AFL-CIO Records, SHSI, Iowa City; Jacob "Jake" Mincks, interview with Iowa Labor History Oral Project (ILHOP), 18 and 27 October 1978, State Historical Society of Iowa (SHSI), Iowa City; and Proceedings, Fifteenth Annual Constitutional Convention, Iowa State Industrial Union Council, CIO, 1953, IFL, SHSI. Cronin addressed the 1953 convention, held in Ottumwa, by thanking union members for the support they gave him in August 1941 when the Iowa-Nebraska States Industrial Union Council was also held in Ottumwa, and the delegates solidly supported him even though he was from the "rebel" Teamsters group. See Proceedings, pp. 113–23. On the schism between the AFL and CIO branches of the Teamsters, see Arthur A. Sloane, *Hoffa* (Cambridge, MA, 1991), 18–31. On Carl Nilson's IUAW roots, see Peter Rachleff, "Organizing 'Wall to Wall': The Independent Union of All Workers, 1933–1937," in *"We Are All Leaders": The Alternative Unionism of the Early 1930s*, ed. Staughton Lynd (Urbana, IL, 1996), 57–58, 65–66.

9. *Ottumwa Daily Courier*, 28 February 1940; 12 March 1940; 24 May 1940; and 6 November 1940.

10. U.S. Bureau of the Census, *Census of Population: 1950*, vol. 1, *Number of Inhabitants* (Washington, DC, 1952); State of Iowa, *Official Registers*, 1933–34 through 1941–42.

11. *Ottumwa Daily Courier*, 7, 11–12, 17, 19 March 1941; 8 April 1944; 5, 9, 22, 24, 25 May 1944; and 21 June 1944.

12. Program, Fourth Annual Constitutional Convention, Iowa-Nebraska States Industrial Union Council, 1941, IFL, SHSI; Program, Fifth Annual Constitutional Convention, Iowa-Nebraska States Industrial Union Council, 1942, IFL, SHSI; Yearbook, Iowa-Nebraska States Industrial Union Council, 1943, IFL, SHSI; *Packinghouse Worker*, 19 June 1942; 20 November 1942; and 25 December 1942; *Ottumwa Courier*, 27 September 1941; Edward R. Fitzpatrick, PWOC field representative, to J.C. Lewis, PWOC national office, 4 June 1941, United Packinghouse Workers of America (UPWA)

Records, folder 3, box 5, State Historical Society of Wisconsin (SHSW), Madison; Local 1 Regular Meeting of 2 July 1941, Minute Book, 1939–42, UPWA Records, Local P-3, SHSI; Local 1 to Sam Sponseller, UPWA District 3 Director, 8 July 1941, UPWA Records, folder 3, box 5, SHSW; and Fitzpatrick and Theodore M. Covey to Lewis J. Clark, PWOC vice president, 26 May 1942, UPWA Records, folder 3, box 5, SHSW. Fitzpatrick and Covey's report to Clark noted that "there is a very close relationship between the Morrell plant in Ottumwa and the Rath plant here [in Waterloo]. There are many Ottumwa workers here and it is thought by many that Morrell has a large financial interest in Rath."

13. The 1944 general election turnout was second only to that for the 1940 general elections. *Ottumwa Daily Courier*, 8 November 1944, 10 March 1945, and 27 March 1945; *Packinghouse Worker*, 30 March 1945; State of Iowa, *Official Register, 1941–1942* (Des Moines, 1941); State of Iowa, *Official Register, 1945–1946* (Des Moines, 1945); the *Bulletin*, 15 November 1943, folder 2, box 314, UPWA Records, SHSW; Proceedings, Eighth Annual Constitutional Convention of Iowa-Nebraska States Industrial Union Council, CIO, 1946, p. 214, IFL, SHSI; and Officer's Report to the Delegates, Resolutions and Reports of Committee's [*sic*], Iowa-Nebraska States Industrial Union Council, Eighth Annual Convention, 1946, IFL, SHSI. J. David Greenstone notes that "[t]he 1944 campaign . . . marked organized labor's emergence as a major national campaign organization." See *Labor in American Politics* (New York, 1969), 51. Nevertheless, Robert Zieger notes that "the PAC effort had fallen far short of the ambitions of CIO leaders" with Democratic margins no higher in many places with heavy PAC efforts than in those without. See Zieger, *The CIO, 1935–1955* (Chapel Hill, 1995), 187. On PAC's formation and 1944 election efforts, also see James Caldwell Foster, *The Union Politic: The CIO Political Action Committee* (Columbia, MO, 1975), 2–45.

14. State of Iowa, *Official Registers*, 1933–34 through 1969–70.

15. *Packinghouse Worker*, 25 June 1943; 12 November 1943; 31 March 1944; 14 April 1944; and 19 January 1945; and Yearbook, Iowa-Nebraska States Industrial Union Council, CIO, 1943, p. 29, IFL, SHSI. Particularly useful for understanding the CIO's creation of worker loyalties to union goals in a larger political and cultural sense by the end of World War II is Elizabeth A. Fones-Wolf, *Selling Free Enterprise: The Business Assault on Labor and Liberalism, 1945–60* (Urbana, IL, 1994).

16. Proceedings, Eighth Annual Constitutional Convention of Iowa-Nebraska States Industrial Union Council, CIO, 1946, pp. 12, 206–7, and 214, IFL, SHSI; Proceedings, Ninth Annual Constitutional Convention, Iowa-Nebraska Industrial Union Council, CIO, 1947, pp. 17–25, 88–135, IFL, SHSI; and Proceedings, Organizational Meeting, Iowa State Industrial Union Council, CIO, 1947, pp. 118–40, IFL, SHSI.

17. Proceedings, Tenth Annual Constitutional Convention, Iowa State Industrial Union Council, CIO, 1948, pp. 76–85, SHSI. On the FE, see Toni Gilpin, "Left by Themselves: History of the United Farmer Equipment and Metal Workers Union, 1938–1955" (Ph.D. diss., Yale University, 1992). On left-wingers and the 1948 presidential campaign, see Robert H. Zieger, *The CIO*, chapter 9.

18. *National Union Farmer*, 1 June 1947.

19. The FE's first farm relations director was Homer Ayres, a former lieutenant governor candidate in South Dakota in 1934 on the Communist-led United Farmers League ticket. See Homer Ayres, Biographical Sketch, Fred W. Stover Progressive

Party Records, box 1, University of Iowa Libraries, Special Collections, Iowa City; *Iowa Union Farmer*, 11 May 1946; *FE News*, 8 May 1946; *The Unionist and Public Forum*, 23 May 1946; and Allan Mathews, "Agarian Radicals: The United Farmers League of South Dakota," *South Dakota History* 3(Fall 1973), 408–21. Lee Simon was the UPWA's first farm relations director. On his appointment, see *Packinghouse Worker*, 18 April 1947. On Fred Stover's labor union views, see Fred W. Stover, interview with Alan K. Lathrop, 12 February 1969, Fred W. Stover Progressive Party Records Special Collections, University of Iowa Libraries, Iowa City; *Iowa Union Farmer*, 30 June 1945; 14 July 1945; and 11 August 1945.

20. On the UPWA's post–World War II social democratic agenda, see especially Wilson J. Warren, "The Limits of Social Democratic Unionism in Midwestern Meatpacking Communities: Patterns of Internal Strife, 1948–1955," in *Unionizing the Jungles: Labor and Community in the Twentieth-Century Meatpacking Industry*, eds. Shelton Stromquist and Marvin Bergman (Iowa City, 1997), 128–58; Roger Horowitz, "'This Community of our Union': Shopfloor Power and Social Unionism in the Postwar UPWA," in *Unionizing the Jungles*, 96–127; Horowitz, *"Negro and White, Unite and Fight!": A Social History of Industrial Unionism in Meatpacking, 1930–1990* (Urbana, 1997), 206–42; and Rick Halpern, *Down on the Killing Floor: Black and White Workers in Chicago's Packinghouses, 1904–54* (Urbana, IL, 1997), 201–45. On the social democratic programs of other CIO unions, see Kevin Boyle, *The UAW and the Heyday of American Liberalism, 1945–1968* (Ithaca, 1995); Gilpin, "Left by Themselves"; and Ronald W. Schatz, *The Electrical Workers: A History of Labor at General Electric and Westinghouse, 1923–60* (Urbana, IL, 1983). Also useful is Steve Rosswurm, ed., *The CIO's Left-Led Unions* (New Brunswick, NJ, 1992). For a perceptive analysis of the limitations of social democracy within the Democratic political order, see David Plotke, *Building a Democratic Political Order: Reshaping American Liberalism in the 1930s and 1940s* (Cambridge, 1996), esp. 174–76, 364–67.

21. *Ottumwa Daily Courier*, 5 April 1947; *Iowa Union Farmer*, 19 April 1947; 17 May 1947; *Packinghouse Worker*, 18 April 1947; *The Unionist and Public Forum*, 28 August 1947; and First Congregationalist Church file, Ottumwa Public Library, Ottumwa.

22. *Iowa Union Farmer*, 20 September 1947; *Ottumwa Daily Courier*, 28 August 1947; 1–2 September 1947; *The Unionist and Public Forum*, 31 July 1947; McCoy's *Ottumwa City Directory*, 1947; and Proceedings, Ninth Annual Constitutional Convention, Iowa-Nebraska Industrial Union Council, CIO, 1947, pp. 262–63, IFL, SHSI. On the FE's efforts, see Wilson J. Warren, "The 'People's Century' in Iowa: Coalition-Building among Farm and Labor Organizations, 1945–1950," *Annals of Iowa* 49 (Summer 1988), 380–82.

23. Proceedings, Eighth Annual Constitutional Convention of Iowa-Nebraska States Industrial Union Council, CIO, 1946, p. 189, IFL, SHSI; Proceedings, Ninth Annual Constitutional Convention, Iowa-Nebraska Industrial Union Council, 1947, pp. 302–9, IFL, SHSI; *FE News*, December 1947; *Iowa Union Farmer*, 17 January 1948; and 16 October 1948; *Des Moines Register*, 7 November 1948; and Ben Henry to Fred Stover, 30 October 1948, box 1, Stover Records. On the struggle over Wallace's candidacy within the UPWA international union, see Horowitz, *"Negro and White, Unite and Fight!"* 198–201. On the Farmers Union and the Wallace campaign, see William C. Pratt, "The Farmers Union and the 1948 Henry Wallace Campaign," *Annals of Iowa*

49 (Summer 1988), 349–70; Bruce Field, "The Price of Dissent: The Iowa Farmers Union and the Early Cold War, 1945–1954," *Annals of Iowa* 55 (Winter 1996), 1–23; and idem, *Harvest of Dissent: The National Farmers Union and the Early Cold War* (Lawrence, KS, 1998).

24. *Packinghouse Worker*, 9 September 1948; 1 October 1948; 7 October 1948; 8 December 1950; *The Unionist and Public Forum*, 14 October 1948; 14 July 1949; and FE *News*, March 1949; Marianne Robinson, interview with author, 28 January 1999 (tape in author's possession).

25. Mincks, ILHOP interviews, Part I and II; Regular Meeting Minutes of 12 October 1948 and 8 November 1948, Minute Book, 1946–49, UAW Local No. 74 Records, State Historical Society of Iowa (SHSI), Iowa City; Proceedings, Thirteenth Annual State Convention of Iowa State Industrial Union Council, CIO, 1951, pp. 175–76, IFL, SHSI; and Jack McCoy, interview with ILHOP, 18 May 1983, part I, SHSI.

26. Proceedings, Organizational Meeting, Iowa State Industrial Union Council, 1947, pp. 94–113, IFL, SHSI; Proceedings, Twelve Annual Iowa State CIO, 1950, pp. 14–17, SHSI; Reports, Thirteenth Annual Convention, Iowa State IUC-CIO, 1951, pp. 19–20; Proceedings, Thirteenth Annual State Convention of Iowa State Industrial Union Council, CIO, 1951, p. 1, IFL, SHSI; and Proceedings, Fourteenth Annual Convention, Iowa State IUC-CIO, 1952, pp. 163–91, IFL, SHSI.

27. Proceedings, Thirteenth Convention, 1951, pp. 2–6, 119–23, 175–76; Proceedings, Fourteenth Convention, 1952, pp. 6–12, 70–76, 149–56. On Local 1's support for Loveland, see Edward Filliman, UPWA field representative, Weekly Report, 4 November 1950, folder 13, box 415, UPWA Records, SHSW. Morrell-Ottumwa workers' efforts on behalf of PAC in 1950 for Loveland's campaign were most similar to those of Rockford, Illinois, Industrial Union Council's efforts as described by Fay Calkins in *The CIO and the Democratic Party* (Chicago, 1952), 86–111. Although unsuccessful, the OIUC was the inside force in Wapello County's Democratic party's support for Loveland in 1950. Robert Zieger's analysis of PAC's ability to more successfully generate large amounts of money for liberal candidates rather than mobilizing union voters and influencing party leaders was true of the Loveland campaign on the state level but not in Ottumwa. See Zieger, *The CIO*, 306–12. On the Brannan Plan, see Barton J. Bernstein and Allen J. Matusow, eds., *The Truman Administration: A Documentary History* (New York, 1966), 135–39; Allen J. Matusow, *Farm Policies and Politics in the Truman Years* (Cambridge, MA, 1967), 196–214; Grant McConnell, *The Decline of Agrarian Democracy* (New York, 1977), 141–43; John L. Stover, *First Majority-Last Minority: The Transformation of Rural Life In America* (De Kalb, IL, 1976), 247–48; and Gilbert L. Fite, *American Farmers: The New Minority* (Bloomington, IN, 1981), 96–98.

28. Proceedings, Thirteenth Annual State CIO Convention, 1951, pp. 247–76; and Proceedings, Fourteenth Annual State CIO Convention, 1952, pp. 163–91.

29. *Morrell Magazine*, December 1948; and February 1949; and *Ottumwa Daily Courier*, 8 June 1948; 12 February 1949; 23 February 1949; and 16 March 1949.

30. On Loveless's background, see *Ottumwa Daily Courier*, 12 February 1949, 13; and 9 May 1989, 6; Larew, *A Party Reborn*, 54–56; Hahn, *Urban-Rural Conflict*, 79; and the *Bulletin* (Local 1's official newspaper), 24 March 1949, UPWA Records, box 441, SHSW.

31. The *Bulletin*, 24 March 1949.

32. The *Bulletin*, 28 March 1949; and *Ottumwa Daily Courier*, 28–29 March 1949.

33. Filliman, Weekly Reports, 20 January 1951; 27 January 1951; 10 February 1951; and 23 June 1951, folder 13, box 415, UPWA Records, SHSW; Charles B. Simpson, Local 1 recording secretary, to Lewis J. Clark, UPWA international secretary-treasurer, 9 February 1951, folder 2, box 314, UPWA Records, SHSW; and Filliman to Russell Bull, UPWA District 3 director, 15 June 1951, folder 13, box 415, UPWA Records, SHSW.

34. Local 1 Union Officers, 8 February 1951, folder 2, box 314, UPWA Records, SHSW; and *Ottumwa Daily Courier*, 14 March 1951; 27 March 1951; 17 October 1953; and 4 November 1953.

35. *Ottumwa Daily Courier*, 29 April 1953; 27 July 1953; 21 October 1953; 31 October 1953; and 4 November 1953; and 21 July 1953 Membership Meeting of Local 1, Minute Book, October 1952–February 1955, Local P-1 Records, SHSI. The decline in workers' personal involvement in local politics dovetails with the findings of researchers during the same period who noted persistent support for labor union and Democratic political agendas by workers yet low levels of personal participation. See, for example, Arthur W. Kornhauser, Harold L. Sheppard, and Albert J. Mayer, *When Labor Votes: A Study of Auto Workers* (New York, 1956), 145; and Angus Campbell, Philip E. Converse, Warren E. Miller, and Donald E. Stokes, *The American Voter* (New York, 1960), 379.

36. McCoy, interview with ILHOP. This portion of McCoy's interview is reproduced in Stromquist, *Solidarity and Survival*, 284.

37. Mincks, interview with ILHOP; and McCoy, interview with ILHOP, part 1. On McCoy's election to state office in 1954, also see *Morrell Magazine*, January 1955, 12; and *Packinghouse Worker*, February 1955.

38. Proceedings, Fifteenth Annual Constitutional Convention, Iowa State IUC, CIO, 1953, pp. 3–5, IFL, SHSI; and David Hart, interview with ILHOP, 12 April 1978, SHSI.

39. Proceedings, Fourteenth Annual Convention, Iowa State IUC-CIO, 1952, p. 8; and Proceedings, Fifteenth Annual Constitutional Convention, Iowa State IUC, CIO, 1953, pp. 2–5, 11, 96–98, 191–200. On Iowa's Republican-IMA alliance as connected to the reapportionment debate, see Hahn, *Urban-Rural Conflict*, 123, 198–209; Larew, *A Party Reborn*, 11–12, 31–34, 63–71, 85–87, 109, 144; and, especially, Charles W. Wiggins, "The Post World War II Legislative Reapportionment Battle in Iowa Politics," in *Patterns and Perspectives in Iowa History*, ed. Dorothy Schwieder (Ames, IA, 1973), 405–30.

40. Reports, Sixteenth Annual State IUC-CIO Convention, 1954, p. 11, IFL, SHSI; and Proceedings, Seventeenth Annual Constitutional Convention, Iowa CIO IUC, 1955, pp. 11, 25–32.

41. Stromquist, *Solidarity and Survival*, 264–71; Program, Eighteenth Annual Convention, Iowa State Industrial Union Council, 1956, pp. 10–24, IFL, SHSI; Mincks, interview with ILHOP; OIUC Minutes, 1955–56, UPWA Local P-1 Records, SHSI; and Proceedings, Tenth Annual Convention, IFL, AFL-CIO, 1965, p. 24, IFL, SHSI.

42. Proceedings, First Merged Convention, Iowa Federation of Labor (IFL), AFL-CIO, 1956, pp. 1–3, IFL, SHSI; Proceedings, Second Annual Convention, IFL, AFL-CIO, 1957, p. 4, IFL, SHSI; George S. May, "The Political Campaign," *The Palimpsest* 36 (July 1955), 250; Larew, *A Party Reborn*, 51–52; and Hart, interview with ILHOP.

43. On the NFO's early history, see Fite, *American Farmers*, 158–64; Schwieder, *Iowa*, 286–87; and especially chapter 4, "The National Farmers' Organization and Collective Bargaining in Agriculture," in Jon Lauck, "American Agriculture and the Problem of Monopoly: The Political Economy of Grain Belt Farming, 1953–1980" (Ph.D. diss., University of Iowa, 1997).

44. Proceedings, Second Annual Convention, IFL, 1957, pp. 41–44. On the BHLC's farmer-labor organizing efforts, see Paul Larsen, interview with ILHOP, Cedar Falls, Iowa, 15 July 1981; Merle Thompson, interview with ILHOP, Waterloo, 14 July 1981; and John Cooney, interview with ILHOP, 16 July 1981.

45. Cooney, interview with ILHOP; and Larson, interview with ILHOP.

46. Larew, *A Party Reborn*, 53–58.

47. State of Iowa, *Official Registers*, 1945–46 to 1973–74; Larew, *A Party Reborn*, 58–63; Hahn, *Urban-Rural Conflict*, 74–85; and Sundquist, *Dynamics of the Party System*, 257, 262. Mincks, interview with ILHOP. Until 1964, representation in the Iowa House was by county. Beginning in 1964, some counties' representation was consolidated and several urban counties received more representation. This process continued through the 1970s. For the state senate, redistricting was also ongoing after 1964. Wapello County's rate of support for Democrats was quite comparable to that for counties outside Iowa that were much more urban and industrialized. From 1944 to 1952, Wapello County returned a rate of support for Democratic presidential candidates that was comparable to that returned by the ten strongest CIO counties in the United States: 57, 58, and 47 percent for Wapello County compared to an average of 59, 56, and 53 percent for the ten counties. This is even more impressive when one considers that with 29 percent of its population defined as rural in 1950, Wapello County had a higher percentage of rural residents than all but one of the ten strongest CIO counties in the country. The ten strongest CIO counties, as identified by Foster in *The Union Politic*, were Lake and St. Joseph in Indiana; Genessee and Wayne in Michigan; Lucas, Stark, and Summit in Ohio; and Allegheny, Northhampton, and Westmoreland in Pennsylvania. See Foster, The *Union Politic*, appendix 1952A, 219.

48. Proceedings, Second Annual Convention, IFL, AFL-CIO, 1957, pp. 23–27, IFL, SHSI; *Ottumwa Courier*, 9 May 1989, 6; and Larew, *A Party Reborn*, 59–60, 65–67.

49. Hahn, *Urban-Rural Conflict*, 82–84; Larew, *A Party Reborn*, 68–69; and Proceedings, Fourth Annual Convention, IFL, AFL-CIO, 1959, p. 69, IFL, SHSI.

50. Larew, *A Party Reborn*, 73–87; Harold E. Hughes with Dick Schneider, *The Man from Ida Grove: A Senator's Personal Story* (Lincoln, VA, 1979), 75–89, 107, 122–24; Hahn, *Urban-Rural Conflict*, 123, 198–210; Wiggins, "The Post World War II Legislative Reapportionment Battle in Iowa Politics"; and State of Iowa, *Official Register*, 1965–66, 416.

51. In 1948, only 25 of the Iowa's 108 representatives in the House were Democrats. This fell to 12 in 1950 and just 3 in 1952. In 1954, however, there were 17, followed by 30 in 1956, 49 in 1958, 29 in 1960, and 17 in 1962. After a majority following the 1964 elections in the Iowa Senate, Democrats held a majority again in 1966 before tailing off but remaining competitive between 1968 and 1972. State of Iowa, *Official Registers*, 1945–46 to 1973–74; Proceedings, Seventh Annual Convention, IFL, AFL-CIO, 1962, pp. 4–5, 9, IFL, SHSI; Proceedings, Eighth Annual Convention, IFL, AFL-CIO, 1963,

pp. 17–20, IFL, SHSI; Proceedings, Ninth Annual Convention, IFL, AFL-CIO, 1964, p. 1, IFL, SHSI; and Proceedings, Tenth Annual Convention, IFL, AFL-CIO, 1965, pp. 6–7, IFL, SHSI.

52. Proceedings, Eleventh Annual Convention, IFL, AFL-CIO, 1966, pp. 13–19, IFL, SHSI; Proceedings, Thirteenth Annual Convention, IFL, AFL-CIO, 1968, pp. 10–11, IFL, SHSI; Larew, *A Party Reborn*, 127–76; and Stromquist, *Solidarity and Survival*, 283–94.

53. Larson, interview with ILHOP; and Cooney, interview with ILHOP. See also Stromquist, *Solidarity and Survival*, 285.

54. On UPWA Local 46's antidiscrimination and civil rights efforts, see Bruce Fehn, "'The Only Hope We Had': United Packinghouse Workers Local 46 and the Struggle for Racial Equality in Waterloo, Iowa, 1948–1960," *Annals of Iowa* 54 (Summer 1995), 200–213. On the BHLC's civil rights initiatives, see Cooney, interview, ILHOP.

7. Fallout from the "Grudge Operation"

1. On the decline of labor's political influence in modern America, see Karen Orren, "Union Politics and Postwar Liberalism in the United States," *Studies in American Political Development* 1 (1986), 215–52; Michael Goldfield, *The Decline of Organized Labor in the U.S.* (Chicago, 1987); Kim Moody, *An Injury to All: The Decline of American Unionism* (New York, 1988); and Melvyn Dubofsky, *The State and Labor in Modern America* (Chapel Hill, 1994).

2. Clarence Orman, interview with author, 1982 Morrell Survey, collection in author's possession. Orman's impassioned response was only slightly more emphatic and elaborate than the other thirty-six negative responses I received to the question about the impact of the plant's closing. More typical was an anonymous respondent who answered the question with one word: "*Bad*."

3. On the impact of deindustrialization on midwestern communities, see Charles Craypo and Bruce Nissen, eds., *Grand Designs: The Impact of Corporate Strategies on Workers, Unions, and Communities* (Ithaca, NY, 1993).

4. Richard Dougherty, *In Quest of Quality: Hormel's First 75 Years* (Austin, MN, 1966), 65–66.

5. On the combination of technology and gain time used by Morrell to shut down many departments, see Ethel Jerred, interview with Merle Davis, 5 October 1981, Iowa Labor History Oral Project (ILHOP), State Historical Society of Iowa (SHSI), Iowa City. Between 1952 and 1957, Local 1's total membership ranged between 2,700 and 2,950. It then fell to 2,400 in 1958 before recovering a bit to just over 2,500 in 1960. See folder 7, box 497, United Packinghouse Workers of America (UPWA) Records, State Historical Society of Wisconsin (SHSW), Madison. I interviewed Paul Bissell on 10 January 1983 (notes in my possession). The *Bulletin* describes job losses owing to technological and time study changes in its issues of 11 March 1963; 25 March 1963; and 30 March 1964, box 23, Local P-1 Records, SHSI.

6. For more general analyses of the impact of technological innovations in the meatpacking industry on women's employment and concerns, see Bruce Fehn, "Striking Women: Gender, Race and Class in the United Packinghouse Workers of America (UPWA), 1938–1968" (Ph.D. diss., University of Wisconsin–Madison, 1991), chapter 6;

and idem, "'Chickens Come Home to Roost': Industrial Reorganization, Seniority, and Gender Conflict in the United Packinghouse Workers of America, 1956–1966," *Labor History* 34 (Spring–Summer 1993), 324–41. Between 1961 and 1963, another 12,300 jobs were eliminated nationwide in meatpacking. See, Fehn, "'Chickens Come Home to Roost,'" 333.

7. For comparative statistics on the percentages of men and women workers in midwestern meatpacking, see Wilson J. Warren, "The Limits of New Deal Social Democracy: Working-Class Structural Pluralism in Midwestern Meatpacking, 1900–1955" (Ph.D. diss., University of Pittsburgh, 1992), appendix B. Dennis A. Deslippe in "'We Had an Awful Time with Our Women': Iowa's United Packinghouse Workers of America, 1945–75," *Journal of Women's History* 5 (Spring 1993), 13–14, notes that before passage of Title VII of the Civil Rights Act women in UPWA District 3 made up just 13 percent of the membership as opposed to 21 percent throughout the entire union. Moreover, Ottumwa was even more thoroughly a bastion of male packing workers than many other midwestern plants. In 1950, for instance, the Rath plant in Waterloo employed 23 percent female workers and Armour in Mason City employed 26 percent. The Ottumwa percentages of women workers at Morrell come from Polk's *Ottumwa City Directories* for 1935, 1951, and 1957. My information on Mary Shoemaker comes from her *Ottumwa Courier* obituary of 18 February 1991. For the sexism issue, see Jesse Merrill, interview with Merle Davis, 16 September 1981, ILHOP; and Virgil Bankson, ILHOP interview, quoted in Shelton Stromquist, *Solidarity and Survival: An Oral History of Iowa Labor in the Twentieth Century* (Iowa City, 1993), 231. For further context on the women's struggles at the Ottumwa plant, see Fehn, "'Chickens Come Home to Roost,'" 335–39; and idem, "Striking Women," 276–87.

8. Fehn, "'Chickens Come Home to Roost,'" 334, 337–39; Deslippe, "'We Had an Awful Time with Our Women,'" 17–21; Jerred, interview; and David J. Dutton to President, Local No. 1, UPWA-CIO, 18 April 1966, folder 8, box 25, Local P-1 Records, SHSI.

9. *Morrell Magazine*, September 1962, 3; and Jerred, ILHOP interview.

10. Deslippe, "'We Had an Awful Time with Our Women,'" 20–22.

11. Ibid., 22–23; the *Bulletin*, 17 September 1961; and 21 September 1964, box 23, Local P-1 Records, SHSI; and Merrill, interview with Davis, ILHOP. Comments about the constant threat of a closing by the early 1960s are a constant refrain in most of the interviews I have conducted with Morrell workers as well as in the Morrell Survey questions I distributed among Morrell retirees at their annual plant closing reunion in 1982. Stromquist's *Solidarity and Survival*, 224–33, provides additional discussion of the women's battle at the Ottumwa plant.

12. For a perceptive discussion of the "merger mania" in meatpacking at the end of the 1960s, see Harold B. Meyers, "For the Old Meatpackers, Things are Tough All Over," *Fortune* (February 1969), 90, 134. Bennett Harrison and Barry Bluestone's *The Great U-Turn: Corporate Restructuring and the Polarizing of America* (New York, 1988), chapter 3, is a good source on the 1960s restructuring mania. Eli Black and United Brand—AMK's new name after its purchase of United Fruit—quickly fell on hard times not long after 1968. In 1975, Black committed suicide by leaping from his New York City skyscraper office, apparently because of the impending scandal over his $1.25 million payment to a Honduras head of state's Swiss bank account in exchange

for a seventy-five-cents-a-box banana export tax reduction. Two weeks after news of the scandal was released, the Honduras government toppled and United Brand's stock fell to an all-time low. See *Everybody's Business: An Irreverent Guide to Corporate America* (San Francisco, 1980), 78–79.

13. Meyers, "For the Old Meatpackers, Things are Tough All Over," 90, 134.

14. The *Bulletin*, 24 February 1970; 23 November 1970; 30 November 1970; 8 February 1971; 9 April 1971, box 11, Local P-1 Records, SHSI; Jack Moses, interview with author, 12 September 1982 (notes in author's possession); and Merrill, ILHOP interview.

15. Paul to Gorman, 24 April 1973; Merrill and Trimble to Gorman, 6 May 1973; Gorman to Merrill and Trimble, 11 May 1973, box 11, Local P-1 Records, SHSI.

16. Reedquist, interview with author; Moses, interview with author; and Mickey Lauria and Peter S. Fisher, *Plant Closings in Iowa: Causes, Consequences, and Legislative Options* (Iowa City: Institute of Urban and Regional Research, University of Iowa, 1983), 52. Chapter 5, pp. 41–64, of Lauria and Fisher's study deals specifically with the meatpacking industry. Among the 1982 Morrell surveys I collected, Elizabeth J. "Sue" Smith gave credence to the Sioux Falls "theory" by noting how she had been told that Morrell closed the wrong plant.

17. *Gold's Newsletter* (Greater Ottumwa Labor Development Corporation), ca. March 1972, box 11, Local P-1 Records, SHSI; Gene Redmon, Chuck Mueller, and Gene Daniels, "A Lost Dream: Worker Control at Rath Packing," *Labor Research Review*, 5–23; and John Portz, "An 'Offset' Response: Waterloo, Iowa, and the Rath Packing Company," in *The Politics of Plant Closings* (Lawrence, KS, 1990), 54–84.

18. On the historic Big Five's dominance of meatpacking, see Richard J. Arnould, "Changing Patterns of Concentration in American Meat Packing, 1880–1963," *Business History Review* 45 (Spring 1971), 18–34; Robert Mitchell Aduddell, "The Meat Packing Industry and the Consent Decree, 1920–1956" (Ph.D. diss., Northwestern University, 1971); and Richard Charles McGinity, "Technological Change and Agribusiness Structure: The Beef System" (D.B.A. diss., Harvard University, 1980). On the modern Big Three's dominance of meatpacking, see Dale Kasler, "IBP Keeps Tight Grip on Market," *Des Moines Register*, 24 September 1988; Michael J. Broadway, "From City to Countryside: Recent Changes in the Structure and Location of the Meat- and Fish-Processing Industries," in *Any Way You Cut It: Meat Processing and Small-Town America*, ed. Donald D. Stull, Michael J. Broadway, and David Griffith (Lawrence, KS, 1995), 17–40; Steve Bjerklie, "On the Horns of a Dilemma: The U.S. Meat and Poultry Industry," in *Any Way You Cut It*, 41–60; Jimmy M. Skaggs, *Prime Cut: Livestock Raising and Meatpacking in the United States, 1607–1983* (College Station, TX, 1986), 190–96; Daniel Nelson, *Farm and Factory: Workers in the Midwest, 1880–1990* (Bloomington, IN, 1995), 188–89; Carol Andreas, *Meatpackers and Beef Barons: Company Town in a Global Economy* (Niwot, CO, 1994); and Deborah Fink, *Cutting Into the Meatpacking Line: Workers and Change in the Rural Midwest* (Chapel Hill, 1998). Fink's book is especially good in providing an insider's perspective on the dislocations caused by IBP in the small town of Perry, Iowa, since the late 1980s. Also good in that respect is Mark A. Grey, "Turning the Pork Industry Upside Down: Storm Lake's Hygrade Work Force and the Impact of the 1981 Plant Closure," *Annals of Iowa* 54 (Summer 1995), 244–59; and idem, "Storm Lake, Iowa, and the Meatpacking Revolution:

Historical and Ethnographic Perspectives on a Community in Transition," in *Unionizing the Jungles: Labor and Community in the Twentieth-Century Meatpacking Industry*, ed. Shelton Stromquist and Marvin Bergman (Iowa City, IA, 1997), 242–61. For a broad overview of beef packing changes, see Jeremy Rifkin, *Beyond Beef: The Rise and Fall of the Cattle Culture* (New York, 1992), 113–50; Michael J. Broadway and Terry Ward, "Recent Changes in the Structure and Location of the U.S. Meatpacking Industry," *Geography* 75 (January 1990), 76–79; and Skaggs, *Prime Cut*. Jon K. Lauck's "Competition in the Grain Belt Meatpacking Sector after World War II," *Annals of Iowa* 57 (Spring 1998), 135–59, raises intriguing questions about the relative degree of competition within the newly reconstituted Big Three oligarchy. On the tremendous incidence of injury in modern meatpacking, see Donald D. Stull and Michael J. Broadway, "Killing Them Softly: Work in Meatpacking Plants and What It Does to Workers," *Any Way You Cut It*, 61–83.

19. On IBP's labor relations policies, see Dale Kasler's series on IBP in the *Des Moines Register*, especially 21 September 1988; Skaggs, *Prime Cut*, 192–93, 204–5; and Charles Craypo, "Strike and Relocation in Meatpacking," in *Grand Designs*, 185–208. For an overview on the decline of effective unionism in modern meatpacking, see Roger Horowitz, *"Negro and White, Unite and Fight!": A Social History of Industrial Unionism in Meatpacking, 1930–90* (Urbana, IL, 1997), 245–79.

20. Lauria and Fisher, *Plant Closings in Iowa*, 41; John C. (Jack) Moses, interview with author, 1982 Morrell Survey, collection in author's possession; *Ottumwa Courier*, 13 July 1973. Jimmy Skaggs's *Prime Cut*, 187, notes that the number of meatpacking establishments in the United States peaked at 6,188 in 1967 before declining to 4,534 in 1977.

21. *Ottumwa Courier*, 16 July 1973; 23 August 1990; and 29 January 1991.

22. *Work Force, Employment and Unemployment, Iowa: Statewide and Areas, 1971–1972* (Iowa Employment Security Commission, July 1973), 111; *Statistical Profile of Iowa, 1995* (Mt. Pleasant, IA: Public Interest Institute), 62; *Ottumwa Courier*, 29 January 1988; 22 November 1989; 16 February 1990; 14 March 1990; and 26 July 1991; and *Des Moines Register*, 6 September 1987; "Communities in Schools," Basic Fact Sheet, February 1996, Ottumwa Community Schools; "The McCarroll Message," Dropout Rate, 13 March 1997, Ottumwa Community Schools; and "The McCarroll Message," Dropout Rate, 4 December 1997. My thanks to Sue Meadows and Pat Warren for the information on Ottumwa's students.

23. *Ottumwa Courier*, 24 February 1987.

24. Dan Varner, interview with author, 7 August 1996 (tape in author's possession).

25. Varner, interview; *Ottumwa Courier*, 24 February 1987.

26. Ibid.

27. Ibid.

28. Skaggs, *Prime Cut*, 203–4; Hardy Green, *On Strike at Hormel: The Struggle for a Democratic Labor Movement* (Philadelphia, 1990), 45; and Peter Rachleff, *Hard-Pressed in the Heartland: The Hormel Strike and the Future of the Labor Movement* (Boston, 1993), 52.

29. Varner, interview.

30. *Ottumwa Courier*, 24 February 1987; Dave Hage and Paul Kaluda, *No Retreat, No Surrender: Labor's War at Hormel* (New York, 1989), 82–83, 271; Green, *On Strike at Hormel*, 51–57; Rachleff, *Hard-Pressed in the Heartland*, 52; and Varner, interview.

31. Hage and Klauda, *No Retreat, No Surrender*, 156–57; Green, *On Strike at Hormel*, 62–69, 77–83, 93–95; Nelson, *Farm and Factory*, 199; Horowitz, *"Negro and White, Unite and Fight!"* 268–75; and Varner, interview.

32. *Ottumwa Courier*, 27 January 1987; and 24 February 1987; Hage and Klauda, *No Retreat, No Surrender*, 271–73, 291, 302–3, 325–26; Green, *On Strike at Hormel*, 146–52; and Michael T. Fahey, *Packing It In! The Hormel Strike, 1985–1986* (St. Paul, 1988), 223–24.

33. *Ottumwa Courier*, 27 January 1987; 24 February 1987; 30 January 1988; 5 March 1988; 29 March 1988; and 24 November 1988; Hage and Klauda, *No Retreat, No Surrender*, 335; Green, *On Strike at Hormel*, 166–71, 193–94; and Rachleff, *Hard-Pressed in the Heartland*, 67.

34. *Ottumwa Courier*, 24 February 1987; Green, *On Strike at Hormel*, 215–81; Nelson, *Farm and Factory*, 199; and Varner, interview.

35. *Ottumwa Courier*, 24 February 1987.

36. Varner, interview; and *Ottumwa Courier*, 27 January 1987; 24 February 1987; 25 February 1987; and 27 February 1987. One of the more organized efforts to sanitize Ottumwa's strong labor image was a workshop conducted by the Greater Ottumwa Area Labor Management Council in early 1988. See *Ottumwa Courier*, 28 January 1988. On the efforts to create economic growth and jobs in Iowa in the 1980s and 1990s regardless of workers' needs, see Fink, *Cutting Into the Meatpacking Line*, 180–83. Also useful for additional context on the experiences of midwestern communities with corporations is Charles Craypo and Bruce Nissen, "The Impact of Corporate Strategies," in *Grand Designs*, 224–50.

37. *Ottumwa Courier*, 1–3 September 1987; 21 September 1987. The economic incentives plied on Excel provide an excellent example of the type of progrowth strategies pursued by city and state officials in Iowa as described by Fink in *Cutting Into the Meatpacking Line*.

38. *Des Moines Register*, 6 September 1987; *Ottumwa Courier*, 30 October 1987; 19 November 1987; 3 March 1988; and 4 October 1988; Rachleff, *Hard-Pressed in the Heartland*, 124; and Fink, *Cutting Into the Meatpacking Line*, 64.

39. *Ottumwa Courier*, 10 September 1991; and 17, 22–26 October 1991.

40. Varner, interview; *Ottumwa Courier*, December 1989; 5 January 1990; 10 April 1990; 14 August 1990; and 3 July 1996; and *Des Moines Register*, 20 March 1988.

41. Carol Hammersley, interview with author, 17 May 1997 (tape in author's possession).

42. *Ottumwa Courier*, 15 and 21 April 1998; *Des Moines Register*, 12 April 1998; Grey, "Turning the Pork Packing Industry Upside Down"; and Fink, *Cutting Into the Meatpacking Line*. IBP's most recent recruiting tactic, which packers like Excel will undoubtedly mimic, is to recruit dislocated Bosnians from Utica, New York, and Chicago to its plant in Waterloo. As of April 1998, IBP had recruited 3,000 to 4,000 people to their porkpacking plant there.

43. On the racial and ethnic history of Iowa, see Fink, *Cutting Into the Meatpacking Line*, chapter 4. On the impact of immigrant workers on meatpacking communities in the rural Midwest in the 1980s and 1990s, see especially Stull, Broadway, and Griffith, eds., *Any Way You Cut It*, particularly the essays by Lourdes Gouveia and Donald D. Stull, "Dances with Cows: Beefpacking's Impact on Garden City, Kansas, and Lexing-

ton, Nebraska," 85–107; Mark A. Grey, "Pork, Poultry, and Newcomers in Storm Lake, Iowa," 109–27; and Robert A. Hackenberg and Gary Kukulka, "Industries, Immigrants, and Illness in the New Midwest," 187–211. Also see Grey, "Turning the Pork Industry Upside Down"; and idem, "Storm Lake, Iowa, and the Meatpacking Revolution."

44. *Ottumwa Courier*, 3 September 1990; 26 September 1990; 14 November 1990; 18 April 1991; 26 April 1991; 4 May 1991; and 17 July 1996. See also Molly Myers Naumann and Brian Schultes, *An Intensive Level Architectural and Historical Survey of the John Morrell and Company Meat Packing Plant, Ottumwa, Iowa* (City of Ottumwa, April 1991), 59–61, 101, and 115–17.

45. *Ottumwa Courier*, 27 January 1995; 1 February 1995; 10 February 1995; and 4 March 1995.

46. *Ottumwa Courier*, 1 February 1995; 16 February 1995; and 31 May 1995.

47. *Ottumwa Courier*, 25 February 1995; 31 March 1995; and 31 May 1995.

48. *Des Moines Register*, 8 October 1995.

8. The Legacy of Militant Unionism

1. Among the many books reflecting on workers' powerlessness in contemporary America owing to deindustrialization are Jeanne Prial Gordus, Paul Jarley, and Louis A. Ferman, *Plant Closings and Economic Dislocation* (Kalamazoo, MI, 1981); John C. Raines, Lenora E. Berson, and David McI. Gracie, eds., *Community and Capital in Conflict: Plant Closings and Job Loss* (Philadelphia, 1982); Barry Bluestone and Bennett Harrison, *The Deindustrialization of America: Plant Closings, Community Abandonment, and the Dismantling of Basic Industry* (New York, 1982); John Portz, *The Politics of Plant Closings* (Lawrence, KS, 1990); Charles Craypo and Bruce Nissen, eds., *Grand Designs: The Impact of Corporate Strategies on Workers, Unions, and Communities* (Ithaca, NY, 1993); and Dale A. Hathaway, *Can Workers Have a Voice?: The Politics of Deindustrialization in Pittsburgh* (University Park, PA, 1993).

2. In his essay "Successful Labor-Community Coalition Building," Bruce Nissen offers three conditions where coalitions of labor unions and communities might successfully exercise power against corporations: local conditions must be such that corporations will not seek other courses of action, corporations must be amenable to the influence of labor and community groups, and unions and communities must bridge their own differences and work together for their common good. See *Grand Designs*, 222–23.

3. Dale Hathaway asserts the importance of workers' participation in corporate decisions in the context of community "morality," but it seems difficult to attribute morality to communities unless there is a genuine sense of commonality among people. See Hathaway, *Can Workers Have a Voice?* chapter 6. Deborah Fink's *Cutting Into the Meatpacking Line: Workers and Change in the Rural Midwest* (Chapel Hill, 1998) effectively conveys the lack of real community among meatpacking workers in Iowa today.

4. On the balance and tension between structure and agency in workers' meatpacking union history, see Shelton Stromquist and Marvin Bergman, "Introduction: Unionizing the Jungles, Past and Present," in *Unionizing the Jungles: Labor and Community in the Twentieth-Century Meatpacking Industry*, ed. Stromquist and Bergman (Iowa City, 1997), 1–15.

5. On the 1969 IBP strike, see Roger Horowitz, *"Negro and White, Unite and Fight!"*: *A Social History of Industrial Unionism in Meatpacking, 1930–90* (Urbana, IL, 1997), 260–63; and Charles Craypo, "Strike and Relocation in Meatpacking," in *Grand Designs*, 188–93.

6. For similar pleas for ethnic and racial harmony among contemporary midwestern meatpacking workers, see Horowitz, *"Negro and White Unite and Fight!"* 281–86; and Fink, *Cutting Into the Meatpacking Line*, 191–201.

7. On the decline of organized labor's influence in the Democratic party, see, for instance, Thomas Byrne Edsall, *The New Politics of Inequality* (New York, 1984); Mike Davis, *Prisoners of the American Dream* (New York, 1986); Steve Fraser and Gary Gerstle, eds., *The Rise and Fall of the New Deal Order, 1930–1980* (Princeton, 1989); and Ronald Radosh, *Divided They Fell: The Demise of the Democratic Party, 1964–1996* (New York, 1996). For an incisive analysis of labor unions' decline in the United States, see Michael Goldfield, *The Decline of Organized Labor in the United States* (Chicago, 1987). A very clear argument for the necessity of labor-community alliances can be found in Bruce Nissen, "Successful Labor-Community Coalition Building," in *Grand Designs*, 209–23. Also see Charles B. Craver, *Can Unions Survive?: The Rejuvenation of the American Labor Movement* (New York, 1993).

INDEX